GERARD MANLEY HOPKINS AND THE VICTORIAN TEMPER

Gerard Manley Hopkins was an unusual combination of Victorian aesthetician and Jesuit priest, and critics have tended to ascribe his complex poetry to one or the other of these sides to his nature. In this book, Professor Sulloway is concerned to demonstrate that Hopkins's poetry unmistakably reflects his vision of himself as both priest and Victorian poet.

The author studies Hopkins's poetry in the context of Victorian England. She shows that as much as the writings of his contemporaries, Carlyle, Ruskin, Mill, Newman, or Tennyson, Hopkins's poetry expresses the moral and psychological analysis of the self in society that typifies the Victorian temper. She concludes that his poems may be records of his Jesuit mission, and of his private joys and private burdens, but they are more than that. They are records of the joys and burdens of Victorian England.

This stimulating study will interest those concerned both with Victorian literature and with the prevailing character of the age.

This study of Hopkins and the Victorian temper, prepared under the Graduate Faculties of Columbia University, was selected by a committee of those Faculties to receive one of the Clarke F. Ansley awards given annually by Columbia University Press.

Gerard Manley Hopkins
and the Victorian Temper.

Alison G. Sulloway

Cedar Crest College,
Allentown, Pennsylvania

Routledge & Kegan Paul
London

First published 1972
by Routledge & Kegan Paul Ltd
Broadway House, 68–74 Carter Lane,
London EC4V 5EL
Printed in Great Britain by
C. Tinling & Co Ltd, Prescot and London
© A. G. Sulloway 1972
No part of this book may be reproduced in
any form without permission from the
publisher, except for the quotation of brief
passages in criticism

ISBN 0 7100 7354 2

To Murat Nemet-Nejat

Contents

Preface and Acknowledgments   ix

References and Abbreviations   xiii

Introduction   1

1 'The Sense of Gentle Fellowship' and 'The Spy in the
   Wilderness': the Years at Oxford   9

2 'Heaven's Sweet Gift': Hopkins, Ruskin, and the
   Plenitude of God   64

3 'New Nazareths in Us': the Making of a Victorian
   Gentleman   115

4 'The Horror and the Havoc and the Glory of it': *The
   Wreck of the Deutschland* and the Calamitarian Mood   158

   Appendix A   Chronology for Oxford and the Tractarian
   Wars, with a Chronology for Hopkins   196

   Appendix B   Brief History of the Tractarian Wars   200

   Notes   203

   Selected Bibliography   230

   Index   241

Preface and Acknowledgments

A book that has taken eight years to complete required the professional assistance and the charitable support of many people. My gratitude to the Ansley Committee of Columbia University and to the Columbia University Press is naturally without stint, yet there are debts antedating these by many years. Before and during the writing of this book I was trained under professors who surveyed their students' work objectively, and whose instruction was always meticulous and often inspired. I had access to some of the most ample libraries and the most experienced librarians in the country, and I have had fellowships that provided me with the precious gift of time at moments when without them I could not have gone on.

My first fellowship came from the American Association of University Women in 1963. I was a winner of the Lizette Fischer Fellowship from my department, and later I was a Columbia University President's Fellow. My latest indebtedness of this kind is to Cedar Crest College. The moment I received the news about publication, my Chairman, Professor James Gottshall, and the Academic Dean, Henry Pommer, burrowed in some discretionary pockets, so that I could afford to visit libraries and begin revisions; and again and again the Business Office here has granted me stipends for typing and travel. In the summer of 1969 I was the fortunate winner of one of the new Cedar Crest fellowships from the President and Trustees' Fund for Faculty Research, and I have the honour to be one of the first faculty members to have completed a book with the assistance of this fund.

My debts to libraries and to librarians are as large as those to stipend and fellowships committees; my largest is naturally to the Butler Library and its staff at Columbia University. I have worked happily at the New York Public Library, the Union and General Theological Libraries, the Widener at Harvard, the Linderman at Lehigh, and the libraries of the Universities of North Carolina at Chapel Hill and of Wisconsin at Madison. I want to thank particularly the library staffs at Cedar Crest and at Beloit College, who demonstrated how patience, concern, and ingenuity will solve many problems often thought insoluble at small liberal arts libraries. When such Reference Librarians as Sara Whildin of the Cressman Library at Cedar Crest take one's bibliographical problems to heart, university libraries seem much closer than they actually are.

My debt to my dissertation committee, chaired by Professor Marshall Suther, is immeasurable. The criticism of each man was precise and voluminous, and it differed surprisingly little from one man to the other. Yet there was a healthy diversity in emphasis. Professor John D. Rosenberg has an impeccable sense of style and tone, and a distaste for clutter that I found bracing. Professor Carl Woodring brought his awesome talent for logistics to my aid. He could see trees and woods both near and far; he would hint tactfully but firmly, for instance, where I was going in the first chapter and where I therefore ought to be going in subsequent chapters, although I could not see that I was going anywhere at all. I worked almost exclusively with Professor Suther during the last three years, and under his sustained tutelage and his own firm sense of clarity, logic, and progression, I was able to wring whatever order there is out of the chaos there was. I go on benefiting daily from the skill of these three men as writing clinicians, and I like to think that my students do as well.

I have been assisted by two other Victorian giants, one of whom knowingly helped me, and one who has never heard of this book. Early on, Professor Wendell Stacy Johnson, of Hunter College, looked over crucial places in the second chapter, and gave me excellent advice. And just as Hopkins had his silent don in John Ruskin, who never knew of Hopkins's existence, I had mine in Professor Walter Houghton of Wellesley College. Time and again I raided the bibliography of Professor Houghton's *The Victorian Frame of Mind,* and what is equally important, Houghton taught me how amorphous, yet how traceable intellectual and moral ideas are, how they change shape and outline almost like amoebae under a microscope, even while maintaining distinct borders. After a year in Professor William Nelson's seminar in the English Renaissance at Columbia, I was even more ready than I would have been for Houghton's refusal to deal easily and cheaply with intellectual history. Both these scholars seek large and small patterns in the literary history under their scrutiny, but they refuse to invent what was not there.

I must say something about the generosity of my department at Cedar Crest. Busy as the members of my department are, they have respected my work, they have often teased me out of doubts, and they have supported my need to be free of committee assignments. David Meredith, now of Kent State, read the Introduction, and made some important suggestions that improved not only the introductory material, but the book as a whole.

I wish to thank Peter Janson-Smith, Ltd, literary agents for the Society of Jesus, and Oxford University Press, joint copyright holders of Hopkins's prose and poetry, for their kind permission to quote copiously.

Because my typist, Marilyn Henry, of Madison, Wisconsin, was editor as well as typist, I must thank her again here, although she said she was only doing her job. Mrs Stephen Fistner, of Bethlehem, Pa., tackled the last revisions with great skill and patience. And I was equally lucky in finding David Steinhart, a fellow Victorian, at Lehigh University. Mr Steinhart was a most meticulous editor and proof-reader; he was another professional of conscience and talent whom I had the good fortune to meet and upon whom I leaned unashamedly.

I want to offer my most profound thanks to the readers and editors and Routledge & Kegan Paul Ltd, for their willingness to help me get so large a book ready for publication. I wish especially to thank my editor, Priscilla Metcalf, for her excellent editorial eye. Her comments were ample and scrupulous, and I accepted all her suggestions without hesitation.

Finally, my most profound debt to any one person is to my friend, Murat Nemet-Nejat, now of the Dwight School in New York, and once a fellow graduate student. He brought to the problems of this book his rich knowledge of English poetry. As a poet himself, he knows Hopkins well, and with his flair for language and syntax, his critical gifts, and his patience, he supplied the continuous support and frank advice over the last eight years that every writer needs.

References and Abbreviations

All abbreviations are followed by page numbers and usually appear in parentheses after the quoted text.

CD   for *The Correspondence of Gerard Manley Hopkins and Richard Watson Dixon,* ed. Claude Colleer Abbott, Oxford University Press (London, 1955).

FL   for *Further Letters of Gerard Manley Hopkins,* ed. Claude Colleer Abbott, 2nd ed., Oxford University Press (London, 1956).

JP   for *Journals and Papers of Gerard Manley Hopkins,* ed. Humphry House and Graham Storey, Oxford University Press (London, 1959).

LB   for *The Letters of Gerard Manley Hopkins to Robert Bridges,* ed. Claude Colleer Abbott, Oxford University Press (London, 1955).

S   for *Sermons and Devotional Writings of Gerard Manley Hopkins,* ed. Christopher Devlin, S.J., Oxford University Press (London, 1959).

All references to Hopkins's poems are drawn from the fourth edition: *The Poems of Gerard Manley Hopkins,* ed. W. H. Gardner and N. H. MacKenzie, 4th ed., Oxford University Press (London, 1967). References to poems are by number only.

All references to Ruskin's works are drawn from the Cook and Wedderburn edition: *The Works of John Ruskin,* 39 vols, eds E. T. Cook and Alexander Wedderburn, Library Edition, George Allen (London, 1903–12). I refer to Ruskin's works by volume (large Roman numerals) and page number only.

Hopkins wrote under a great deal of tension at all times; his prose is frequently erratic in its spelling and punctuation. For that reason I prefer to dispense with the ugly (*sic*) where problematical spelling and punctuation occur in Hopkins's letters, journals, and sermons, since its inclusion would lead to some unattractive clutter.

Introduction

Gerard Manley Hopkins has not always been considered a conspicuous example of the Victorian temper. But that temper itself is an elusive mood, shifting all the way from unqualified optimism to the blackest distress, and its prismatic quality may be one of its most distinguishing features. In some quarters it appeared in almost buoyant guises: men thought of themselves as bearers of a new science, a new renaissance hellenism, or an invigorated hebraism. In other quarters men feared that the breakdown in faith and in the remnants of the ancient feudal order presaged the end of England as a civilized power.

Under these conditions many of the most sophisticated Victorians who interest us today found themselves attempting to reconcile polaric attitudes so that they might look out upon their new world without falsifying it and at the same time achieve some sort of moral poise. Inevitably these Victorian humanists, struggling to discern what Matthew Arnold called the spirit of the whole, were victims of the same mood swings that characterized the age itself. And it is this shifting spirit, now exuberant, now tentatively hopeful, or at least reconciliatory, now gloomy, if not actually apocalyptic, that places Hopkins so firmly in the centre of the Victorian tradition. He suffered the classic religious traumas for which the age was famous. In his case he resolved his religious crisis by submission to Rome. As an undergraduate Hopkins had soaked himself in Ruskin's works; Ruskin had reassured his disciples that nature's bounty was an earnest of God's concern, and Hopkins gratefully rejoiced in that bounty. Ruskin had warned his disciples that the foul towns, the ravaged countryside, and the starving citizenry were all symbols of England's moral decay, and Hopkins's own warnings on the condition of England paraphrase

Ruskin's where they do not paraphrase Carlyle's. Ruskin, Carlyle, Thomas Arnold, and innumerable other Victorians had preached that to work is to pray, and that only a working Christian had the right to call himself a gentleman; almost a third of Hopkins's mature poems deliver the same sermon. He was as ambivalent about art, nature, and the aesthetic life as many of his contemporaries, and he shared with the gloomier Victorian prophets a sense of impending doom, so that art seemed frivolous at times, if not actually immoral, and nature no longer a comfort.

But we are bound to ask ourselves very precisely how this prismatic Victorian mood differs from the transitional mood of earlier centuries. It did differ sharply in certain ways, and we ought to let a few literate Victorians tell us how. That they do so in chorus, from the eighteen-thirties onward, suggests something about the mood itself. For these Victorians saw themselves as creatures of a particular self-consciousness quite new in Christendom. They were peculiarly and often painfully aware of the self and its tentative place in a society undergoing radical changes. Sometimes they analysed the self and all its properties and its settings with cool detachment. At other times they behaved as though they were trapped alone in a room full of mirrors on all sides, so that no matter how long and how honourably they tried, they could not rid themselves of the vision of their fragmented selves. In 'Characteristics' Carlyle warned that the modern psyche, now 'too conscious of many things', might well have destroyed forever 'that first state of Freedom and paradisiac Unconscious' he considered man's birthright.[1] A quarter of a century later, in his preface to the poems of 1853, Matthew Arnold informed his readers that 'the dialogue of the mind with itself has commenced' and along with this dialogue had come 'doubts', 'discouragement', and the loss of 'calm', 'cheerful', 'disinterested objectivity'.

The battle of the self took many forms.[2] Most Victorians agreed with Tennyson, Carlyle, Ruskin, and George Eliot that the self could not find serenity in a chaotic age until it had merged with something larger than itself. But the very code of social usefulness had its stern critics; armed with the warnings of Matthew Arnold and Clough, many men turned the Biblical paradox around, claiming that a Christian cannot lose his life if he had observed no life worthy of losing, and that the fragmented self must first find its splintered shards before it could heal itself and be useful to society. In one curious poem of Arnold's, called 'Self Dependence', the modern soul 'weary' of itself 'and sick of asking' not only what it is, but what it 'ought to be', discovers that it will be unable to shed its misery until it has resolved to be itself and to be sufficient to itself, moving in its orbit with no more fuss than the stars in the firmament.

Hopkins was as ambivalent about the rights and the duties of the self as any other Victorian. He had dedicated himself with joyous abandon to his Maker. Yet not only was he profoundly aware that artists cannot function without valid and realized selves, and that England needed artists, but by the eighteen-eighties he had tortured himself into an admission that it was not at all easy for any human being to get rid of the self's imperious clamour: 'God's most deep decree', he warned himself, 'Bitter would have me taste: my taste was me'; and he yearned to shed the 'Selfyeast of spirit a dull dough sours'. He described the damned as suffering 'like this and their scourge to be . . . their sweating selves; but worse' (Poem 67). In another late poem he described a soul in anguish on 'a rack/Where, selfwrung, selfstrung, sheathe-and-shelterless, thóughts agáinst thoughts ín groans grínd' (Poem 61). But in another late poem Hopkins seemed to be arguing that for sheer survival he must cherish and protect his selfhood more, or at least live 'hereafter kind,/Charitable' to his 'sad self' (Poem 69).

The nineteenth-century self-consciousness had its counterpart in an intensely acute examination of the society behind the self. Men thus became ever more conscious in ever larger groups of the way their neighbours were being defrauded. When Hopkins wrote to Bridges in defence of the rioting poor that 'it is a dreadful thing for the greatest and most necessary part of a very rich nation to live a hard life without dignity, knowledge, comfort, delight, or hopes in the midst of plenty' (*LB*, 27–8, 1871), a plenty they themselves produce, he might almost have been quoting Carlyle. And when he acknowledged to his old schoolmaster, Canon Dixon, 'My Liverpool and Glasgow experience laid upon my mind a conviction, a truly crushing conviction, of the misery of town life to the poor, and . . . of the misery of the poor in general, of the degradation even of our race, of the hollowness of the century's civilization (*CD*, 97, 1881)', he was saying what Ruskin, Dickens, Elizabeth Barrett Browning, and a host of popular Victorian writers had said in earlier decades. It has always been a Christian truism that man is his brother's keeper, but this 'truly crushing conviction of the misery of the poor in general' had never before so haunted the conscience of so many Englishmen.

John Stuart Mill was one of the first social critics to describe the Englishman's new sense of himself and of his chaotic society. 'A change', he said, 'has taken place in the human mind; a change which, being effected by insensible gradations, and without noise, had already proceeded far before it was generally perceived.' He thought the nineteenth century would 'be known to posterity as the era of one of the greatest revolutions of which history has preserved the remembrance', not only a revolution 'in the human mind' but 'in the whole constitution of human society'. True, as Mill remarked, every age is an age of transition, but this age was profoundly conscious of transition, and its very consciousness altered the nature of the transition itself:[3]

> The 'spirit of the age' is in some measure a novel expression. I do not believe that it is to be met with in any work exceeding fifty years in antiquity. The idea of comparing one's own age with former ages, or with our notion of those which are yet to come, had occurred to philosophers; but it never before was itself the dominant idea of any age.

The nineteenth-century Englishman's preoccupation with the quality of his society can best be suggested by the titles of essays written early in the century. A man could turn from Carlyle's 'Characteristics' to his 'Signs of the Times', from John Stuart Mill's 'The Spirit of the Age' to his 'Civilization: Signs of the Times', from Macaulay's 'Southey's Colloquies on Society' to his 'State and Prospects of the Country', or from Croker's 'Stages of the Revolution' to Thompson's 'Labor Rewarded' and Maginn's 'The Desperate System: Poverty, Crime, and Emigration'.[4]

Hopkins was very much aware that he was a latter-day commentator upon an extraordinary age. His letters and journals are full of pungent comments about the great Victorians, and, as decade after decade he took the measure of many of the public figures who interested him, his prose offers us fascinating sketches of poets and painters, Royal Commissioners and parliamentarians, educators, Prime Ministers, and princes of the Church, most of them going about their business without any awareness of his existence.

Many of Hopkins's complaints about his fellow poets centred upon what he considered their archaic language and their thoroughly outmoded treatment of outmoded subjects. But it was largely their style, the symbol of spiritual laziness, that engaged his criticism. 'A perfect style must be of its age' (*CD*, 99, 1881), he confided to Dixon, and by a perfect style, fit to mirror such a tumultuous age, Hopkins meant something fresh and startling, no matter how much it borrowed from the past, a style able to encompass a poet's feelings and his beliefs, and much of the heterogeneous stuff of his own times. To be sure, Hopkins

4

also asserted over and over the right of the artist to a highly personal style, capable of doing justice to the assertive self; and critics and literary historians have given him his due here, as he would have wished them to do. They have analysed his sprung rhythm, his word coinings, and his alliterative techniques. They have recognized as well the role of the past in his rich prosody, from the classical, medieval, and metaphysical strains to the pastoral lyricism of the Romantic poets. But as yet Hopkins's critics have only partially taken him at his word, and there have been very few to suggest that his manner as well as his matter is more often than not a reflection of self-conscious Victorian England. He fashioned his style according to his own critical canons—no man more so; and his poetry contains the stamp of Victorian England as well as of England's past. Highly idiosyncratic as it is, it transcends private idiosyncrasy to speak of Victorian concerns.

Hopkins would have thought it entirely fitting that he is now celebrated as one of the most remarkable poets 'in Christ's Company' (*CD*, 3, 1878). The evidence of his love affair with God is unmistakably audible throughout his poetry. But like many Victorians he was afflicted with a tortured chauvinism, as though troubled England was an extension of himself, and his love affair with 'the land that bred' him and his painful exile from 'her homes and fields that folded and fed' him (Poem 156) provided a timbre to his poetry as audible as the voice of the self in search of its Maker. When Hopkins mourned for England, he mourned for contemporary England:

> England, whose honour O all my heart woos, wife
> To my creating thought. . . . (Poem 66, 1885?)

And his marching song 'What Shall I Do For the Land That Bred Me', for which he even provided a tune, sounds more like a poet laureate's product for some special occasion than the usual elliptic rhetoric we associate with Hopkins.

The unconscious supposition that Hopkins was mostly excluded from the drama of the Victorian age has been quite natural, and until he had been presented to us for his own sake, it was even advisable. Hopkins's work was not published until the twentieth century and therefore contemporary poets instinctively claim him as a splendid colleague of immediate pertinence to themselves. He has thus been lifted out of his age as his own contemporaries have not. There has been no prior call for the particular act of historical imagination that would perceive Hopkins, first and foremost, walking and talking among other Victorians, as we think of Shakespeare in Renaissance London,

Matthew Arnold in Victorian Oxford, or as Hopkins quite obviously saw himself. And then Hopkins's gnarled and tense prosodic style, usually so different on the surface from the more spacious and rhetorical prosody of his post-Romantic contemporaries, has blurred the Victorian voice behind the radical prosodist.

Perhaps Hopkins's conversion and his 'unEnglish' vocation as a Jesuit priest have also deflected our attention from the fact that he was born in the 'hungry forties' and died on the eve of the 'yellow nineties', and that even as a Jesuit in exile, he took his past with him as all men do. But as twentieth-century scholars now admit, conversions, even conversions to Catholicism, were as common in Victorian England as conversions to agnosticism or to some latitudinarian faith. Each conversion was the response of a specific man at a specific time in his country's history, and it represents a way of dealing not only with crises of the self but crises in the society. And Hopkins's poems and prose are as full of these public crises as the works of Carlyle, Tennyson, Ruskin, Newman, or either of the Arnolds. His work reflects the anguish of religious strife, abuse of labour, the scandal of privileged cruelty, the horrors of rampant industrialism pouring its scum and smoke all over England, the search for personal and national prescriptions, and above all, the anatomy of mental suffering. 'My sap is sealed,/ My root is dry' (Poem 127), Hopkins lamented time and again. Like all serious Victorians he experienced the sensation of being crushed at times by private conflicts and public outrages. His fear for England—

> My people and born own nation,
> Fast foundering own generation (Poem 41, 1878)

—was a common fear, that she was wasting her spiritual patrimony. His desire for her was common also, that by adhering to the origins of her greatness, whether those origins were seen to have been in Periclean Athens or in a stable in Bethlehem, she might arrest the rot in her soil and in the hearts of her citizens.

Hopkins's poems are not all expressions of Victorian anxiety. We should remind ourselves that the sensuous imagery in which he delighted was nothing new in Victorian poetry and that it was the Victorian poet's business to teach his readers by comforting them, cheering them, and even by exciting them, as well as by warning them of selfish narcissism or of national peril. And so there are many exquisite little glimpses of the 'sweet especial rural scene' (Poem 43) as yet unspoiled by industrial blight. There are poems of people at work and people at play, and of people growing up, marrying, and dying. Hopkins may have prayed for England as a Catholic and as a Jesuit priest, but he prayed for her also as an Englishman; and the steady Victorian ground-tone of these poetic prayers can always be heard beneath their exotic rhythms. I believe he would have been shocked to know that he is not yet as readily admitted into the company of the Victorians as he is in 'Christ's Company', where he also belongs. For his poems may be records of his Jesuit mission, and of his private joys and private burdens, but they are more than that. They are records of the joys and burdens of Victorian England.

'The Sense of Gentle Fellowship' and 'The Spy in the Wilderness': the Years at Oxford

On 18 April 1863 a gentle pious young man from Hampstead went up to Oxford to be matriculated. Gerard Manley Hopkins had come up from Highgate, a small unfashionable grammar school, where he had been a scholar for the better part of nine years. After enduring a series of attacks by his headmaster, popularly known as 'blustering Dyne' (*FL*, 395–6, *JP*, 289), Hopkins had managed, quite without support from anyone at Highgate, to win a coveted scholarship to Balliol College. Thankful to escape a demoralized headmaster, Hopkins found the intellectual maturity of Balliol wonderfully bracing, and he was proud of the brilliant achievements of her scholars. But as a devout Tractarian[1] he must have been quite suspicious of Balliol's liberal tone and its influence upon young men of wavering faith.*

At the time of Hopkins's matriculation, Balliol was the most intellectually vigorous of the Oxford colleges, and under the leadership of

* Obviously, the history of the Tractarian wars at Oxford and elsewhere, which I have undertaken in this chapter, is a selective one. It ignores a small replica of the Oxford movement at Cambridge, and it does not discuss many important events and some important figures—even at Oxford—before, during, and after Hopkins's residence there. But the title of this book, *Gerard Manley Hopkins and the Victorian Temper*, indicates the reason for my selectivity. The purpose of the book is to discover how certain events, certain figures, and certain intellectual currents in Victorian England shaped Hopkins, and therefore his poetry. Figures, events and currents that he totally ignored in his letters and journals, or that in no way emerge through his poetry, do not belong in this book, however fascinating they are, or wherever else they belong in Victorian history.

A book, even a long book, which attempts to describe the influence of a complex time upon a complex man, will itself be selective. Again, my rule was to allow Hopkins to guide me. I think, from what little he says about the Pre-Raphaelites, and from his poetry itself, that their stamp upon him has been somewhat exaggerated, whereas I believe that the effect upon his poetry of the Tractarian wars, Ruskinian aestheticism, the Victorian concept of a gentleman, and the nineteenth-century apocalyptic mood, has not been sufficiently considered.

Benjamin Jowett, the translator of Plato's dialogues, it had become one of the most important war camps of the liberal religious party. For to a surprising extent it was the Fellows at Balliol, or Balliol graduates, or men openly sympathetic to Balliol and to Jowett's long struggle to escape censorship, who mounted the final successful campaign against all prescribed orthodoxy, and particularly against the neo-Catholic Tractarians at Oxford. And if, in its first decade, during the eighteen-thirties and -forties, the Tractarian movement contained 'all the features of a great tragic drama',[2] the collapse of Tractarian power at Oxford in the eighteen-sixties prepared the movement's Thermopylae.

G. M. Young has commented that 'somewhere about 1860 a rift opens up in the English intelligence'.[3] And Geoffrey Faber adds:

> There was certainly no lack of movement in the air of the eighteen-sixties. Perhaps no other decade of the nineteenth century so well exhibits the kaleidoscopic character of that secular *renaissance* which we inadequately label as the Victorian age.

According to innumerable Victorian commentators and modern historians alike, nobody was more responsible for that 'rift . . . in the English intelligence' than Jowett. Faber goes so far as to say:

> Fully to understand the nature of the ascendancy, which Jowett came to exercise, would be to understand not only Jowett himself, and his Oxford environment, but the greater part of nineteenth-century England.

It is difficult to believe that Faber has exaggerated 'the nature of the ascendancy, which Jowett came to exercise'.[4] The Tractarian movement, from its inception at Oxford in 1833, five years before Jowett was made a Fellow at Balliol, had split the Anglican Church apart. Thereafter in that decade, when the three formidable Oxford Tractarians, Newman, Pusey, and Keble, were making war against infidelity of thought and deed, the sympathies of the nation were as divided as the national Church. And now once again, in the eighteen-sixties, during the last phase of the Tractarian wars at Oxford, Broad Church Anglicans and their lay adherents, a loose confederation of men sympathetic to science and to rigorous analysis of Biblical texts, were engaged in defensive counter-attacks against prescribed ortho-doxy of any sort. And again, as in the 'thirties and 'forties, the Press exploded, and all of England's eyes, including the Queen's, were fastened upon the Tractarians and the Broad Churchmen, the two most bitterly contending parties within the national Church; and nobody caused more public commotion than the two most prominent agents of the contending parties within the Oxford Colleges, the implacable Tractarian, Dr Edward Bouverie Pusey of Christ Church, and the indomitable Broad Churchman, Jowett of Balliol.

In 1870, the first year of Jowett's Mastership of Balliol College, Richard Nettleship, who had been an undergraduate friend of Hopkins, made some acute comments about the Broad Church temper at Balliol, as Jowett had quietly been helping to fashion it for almost three decades:[5]

> And there is this special interest about Balliol, that while I believe it teaches its men a more really Christian spirit than any other college, yet owing to the very small clerical element in it now and the unorthodoxy of its fellows, it has got a sort of cloudy rumour of infidelity about it, as indeed Oxford generally has in great measure.

But in 1870, it was three years since Hopkins had taken his degree, and the Tractarian wars had been all but over at Oxford for five; whereas when Hopkins came into residence at Balliol, the Jowett party there was unable to command a majority, and Hopkins himself wrote his mother that there was a sturdy 'High Church section at Balliol among the students' (*FL*, 76, 1863). By 1865, the year that Hopkins started confessing to Dr Pusey, his Tractarian mentor, and the year before his conversion to Roman Catholicism, the Balliol Fellows sympathetic to Jowett had gained a majority position there, and they were able to make their weight felt throughout the university.[6]

With respect to his own temperament and his Tractarian sympathies, Hopkins might have been spared considerable conflict of loyalties if he had won a scholarship to Christ Church rather than to Balliol; but in any case he would probably have been converted to Roman Catholicism. His attempts to explain this conversion to his father make very topical—and very dreadful—reading, and the sentence ending, 'the Tractarian ground I have seen broken to pieces under my feet' (*FL*, 92, 1866), suggests how closely he had been following the Tractarian wars at Oxford and elsewhere, during the past three years of his residence, and how profoundly he had previously considered his religious future to be bound up with a successful outcome of the last Tractarian attack upon heresy.

Obviously, even in 1863, Balliol was not a college in which a newly matriculated Tractarian could feel altogether at home. To a large extent for reasons of belief, and to some extent as a protective device on behalf of men like Jowett, whose careers were always in jeopardy, Broad Churchmen all over England had enlisted in the counter-Tractarian movement that G. M. Young describes as a 'battle . . . being fought not for the destruction of old beliefs or the affirmation of new hypotheses, but for the social recognition of the right to follow the argument wherever it goes'. In the early eighteen-sixties, Jowett, the don who most ardently followed this Socratic concept, 'was one of the most exciting men alive, and it was difficult not to talk about him', or, it would seem, 'to fall quite under the spell'. To the Tractarians, Jowett's 'spell' seemed like the work of the devil, and indeed, his Socratic techniques were considered heretical to all orthodox and conservative priests, while to the liberals of his own party he was looked upon as a martyr to censorship. His name and fame were house-hold legends, and one enterprising young lady, forbidden to 'keep his essays on the Pauline Epistles', for fear that her faith might be con-taminated, slyly defied her elders and 'had made extracts, which she circulated among her friends'.[7]

Jowett's sin, where the orthodox priests were concerned, was that he apparently saw nothing incompatible between his role as an Anglican priest and his publicly avowed doubts about the divinity of Christ and the historicity of the Bible. And it was a fact that in Victorian Oxford, to keep a Fellowship, Jowett had to be a priest, and to be a priest he was supposed to subscribe in detail to every one of the Thirty-nine Articles.

In 1860, among scientists and Broad Churchmen, at least, there were moments of hope and gaiety, and even of the comic relief so dear to cartoonists;[8] but for the most part, the events in the 'sixties leading up to the destruction of the Tractarian power at Oxford, and thus to Hopkins's conversion to Roman Catholicism, took place with the grave, yet swift processional pace of tragic drama. Hopkins was still a schoolboy at Highgate in 1859, when Mill published *On Liberty* and Darwin published his *Origin of Species*. But although Hopkins was only fifteen years old, and apparently unconscious of national upheaval, he was nonetheless expressing it; he won a school prize for his first poem, 'The Escorial', a poem that was highly Catholic in both subject and treatment. A year later, in 1860, Hopkins had three more unpleasant years ahead of him at Highgate; in that year, so G. M. Young informs us, the Broad Churchmen must have been full of innocent rejoicing, for the 'grand assault' upon orthodoxy 'had begun; the air was as thick with contending banners as the streets of a country town on polling day'.[9]

The year of the 'grand assault' upon orthodoxy must indeed have appeared to Tractarians and their sympathizers as a diabolic attack. In February 1860, one layman and six priests—Jowett among them—published *Essays and Reviews*, a collection of seven essays on theological subjects that attempted to blend the old Anglican spirit of piety with the rigorous spirit of the new sciences and of German Biblical scholarship. That summer the notorious Huxley–Wilberforce debate on Darwin's theories took place in Oxford; the British Association played hosts to the contenders, and the debate ended, so the Huxley forces insisted, with the polemical disgrace of Samuel Wilberforce, the Tractarian Bishop of Oxford.

If 1860 was in truth the year of 'the grand assault' upon prescribed orthodoxy, the years between 1861 and 1865 must have seemed to Broad Churchmen as though the Spanish Inquisition had descended upon Anglican Christendom. In October 1861 Bishop John Colenso of Natal published his *Commentary on the Epistles to the Romans*. His fellow Bishop, Gray of Cape Town, was outraged by the heretical matter he found in Colenso's commentary, and so were orthodox priests in England. Gray then began the sort of pre-trial skirmishing that was to characterize the 'Puseyite' management of the *Essays and Reviews* case.[10] In December, the Rev. Henry Bristow, the editor of *Essays and Reviews*, and the Rev. Rowland Williams, a contributor, were summoned before the Court of Arches in the see of Canterbury, to face charges of heresy. But before the trial took place, the Tractarian priests, with Dr Pusey very much in evidence among them, engaged in a good deal of private and not so private manoeuvres; and by the time the two parish priests came to face their trial, all seven of the contributors to *Essays and Reviews* had been nationally stigmatized as 'Septem Contra Christum'. The trial ended in the penalty of a year's suspension for both priests and the penalty was appealed.

And then, between 1862 and 1863, the irrepressible Colenso published the first three volumes of his seven-volume work on the dubious historicity of the Pentateuch and the Book of Joshua. Colenso seems to have brought to the task of Biblical criticism all the literal innocence of the Zulus whom he was presumably instructing in Christianity, but Colenso was a mathematician as well as a bishop, and scripture could not square with his intellectual equations.

Still at Highgate in 1862, Hopkins appeared as yet to take no interest in the ecclesiastical dogfights going on all around him. His second prize poem, 'A Vision of the Mermaids', is a highly sensuous poem for so pious a young man, but just as Colenso found elements in his nature that did not take easily to dogma, there were elements in Hopkins's nature that did not. It is perhaps symbolic that his first two schoolboy poems each express the two most divergent elements in his character, the visionary prophet whose prophecies rest upon firm dogmatic foundations, and the visionary aesthete, whose descriptions of God's world issue from the evidence of his own eyes. In the letter to his father explaining the grounds of his conversion, Hopkins said that Catholic dogma—or Anglican dogma, for that matter—'is a gross superstition unless guaranteed by infallibility' (*FL*, 92, 1866). In 'A Vision of the Mermaids', he contented himself with Keatsian word pictures, and he was clearly not conscious of the conflict between the peremptory evidence of dogma and the pleasing evidence of the eyes. His conversion, and the grim intellectual and moral struggle that went on before it, solved this conflict to a considerable extent. Hopkins simply reaffirmed an ancient hierarchy of values: the things of the visible world are not as important as the things of the eternal world.

But for Broad Churchmen of Colenso's stamp, or Jowett's, the problem was not as easily solved. For the struggle going on in England, as on the Continent, was the struggle between two kinds of truths, revealed truth, and observable truth. 'What can I believe?' men were asking themselves, or rather, 'How can I reconcile *this* belief with *that* belief?' If one were troubled by scripture and its historicity at all, there seemed to be three solutions. Either one said to one's self: 'What shall I believe in order to be saved?' which argued belief in the first place, belief in a God who damns or saves eternally; or, one said, as the Broad Churchmen did: 'I do not literally believe in this God of scripture, since scripture has been found to lie, but it is a symbolic lie, so I shall believe what I find attractive in it.' Or one said as Huxley did, and Mill did: 'The God of scripture does not conform to what I know of the world, and therefore I cannot admit that such a God exists at all.'

Like all men trying to mediate between two irreconcilable positions, Jowett and Colenso were horribly vulnerable. The Tractarians at home could no more allow Jowett's infractions against the revealed truth of scripture to go unpunished than they could allow Colenso's. In February 1863, three months before Hopkins's matriculation, Jowett was summoned before the Vice-Chancellor of Oxford for his contribution to *Essays and Reviews*. Although he was not specifically tried for this offence, his own brand of Socratic pedagogy was particularly odious to the Tractarian priests because it drew forth the questions from the students themselves, and often left them to supply their own answers. Before Jowett's advent, Greek philosophy at Oxford had begun with Aristotle, in the medieval fashion; but Jowett was possessed by the idea that no man ought to consider himself a classicist if he had not read Plato. His lectures on the Platonic dialogues and his use of the Socratic techniques in his discussion on Christianity were as refreshing to the liberal dons as they were frightening to the conservative priests of all persuasions. And the Tractarian priests, particularly, sensed that Jowett was using Plato to carry on his quarrel with Christian dogma, and especially with those Tractarians who saw themselves as the guardians of Christian orthodoxy. Jowett's name had long been an anathema upon their lips, and they did the best they could to counteract his influence in the lecture halls by their thunderous sermons against the sin of speculative thought.

Jowett's case, whose legal title was 'Pusey and Others v. Jowett',[11] had clearly originated from the Tractarian headquarters at Christ Church. Jowett refused to appear, and his counsellors succeeded in getting the charges dismissed. For the next three months, the Puseyite forces brooded over their next move against Jowett; Jowett himself evidently feared more blows in the dark, for after the trial he said to one of his counsellors: 'You don't know Pusey; he has the tenacity of a bulldog.'[12] By May 1863 Jowett was temporarily out of his misery, for the Puseyite forces wrote the court that they contemplated no further action.[13]

Hopkins's early comments about Jowett during this anxious period of waiting were not highly complimentary. He appears to have been the victim of some of Jowett's famously ungracious silences, and no doubt he felt he deserved revenge:

> Jowett is my tutor; when you can get him to talk he is amusing, but when the opposite, it is terribly embar(r)assing. Ilbert thinks that Fearon's story about him which is well known here, if not true, 'embodies a great truth'.

We shall never know what 'Fearon's story' was; but Hopkins was clearly indulging in the pleasure of gossip, while at the same time denying that he was gossiping. Either Hopkins did not yet realize that his tutor was racked with anxiety, or he was too young and too self-centred to care. For the Puseyites to have been successful, and for Jowett to have been forced out of Balliol would have been a kind of death, an exile of the spirit that Hopkins was not yet familiar with. In any case, perhaps to make amends for a moment's irreverence, Hopkins went on to describe to his mother how he was the recipient of Jowett's equally famous kindness, at a moment, whether Hopkins was aware of it or not, when Jowett himself knew that to render such kindnesses might shortly be put out of his power altogether (*FL*, 73; 22 April 1863).

As the year 1863 came to a close, events in the last important phase of the Tractarian wars at Oxford began to occur almost month by month. In November, Bishop Gray of Cape Town tried Colenso *in absentia*, for Colenso, like Jowett, refused to acknowledge the authority of a hierarchical equal. By December, Gray had deposed Colenso, and Colenso's case was on its way to the Privy Council, which sat upon the case for over a year. In England the appeal of Wilson and Williams for their contributions to *Essays and Reviews* was still to be heard, and the month of February saw the judgments against these men overturned, while at Oxford, the scandalous affair of Jowett's salary now took a bizarre turn. Ever since Jowett had been appointed to the Regius Chair of Greek in 1854, his salary of forty pounds a year, which was disbursed by Christ Church, that is to say, by the Puseyites, was kept at a figure one-tenth that of other—and less heretically tainted—chairs. For almost a decade there had been public and private attempts to rectify this sordid condition, some of them by Pusey himself, who wanted to do justice to Jowett without appearing to countenance heresy. The scandal of the underpaid chair was debated in March 1864, while cheering and hissing undergraduates followed events from the gallery. Pusey's proposal to re-endow Jowett's chair out of university funds rather than Christ Church funds was voted down, and it was voted down again in October.

Between March and October, the Tractarians returned their attentions to *Essays and Reviews*. Once before, the book as a whole had been condemned for probable heresy before the Lower Synodical House, so that the most vulnerable of its writers could be tried for heresy in person. Now, balked of legal redress against the person of any of its authors, the Tractarians once again brought the seven essays before the Upper and Lower Houses, and this time both Houses condemned the book for its heretical views. In July, 'The Oxford Declaration', signed by over eleven thousand priests, was submitted to the Archbishop of Canterbury for his signature; it affirmed the truth of eternal reward for the faithful and of eternal punishment for mortal sin.

By now, Hopkins found the moral tensions at Oxford almost unendurable. While living at Balliol, he must have anxiously watched the growing numbers of Fellows and tutors who came to Balliol to support Jowett's cause, or who cheered on Balliol's hero from other colleges. Balliol's chapel was no place for Hopkins to worship, and so for his religious duties he took himself over to Christ Church. But here, too, anxiety must have reigned, for he was among Tractarian priests whose melancholy task it now was to preside over the Oxford movement's last stages.

The conflict of allegiance was all the more painful for Hopkins in that Jowett demanded as much exclusive loyalty to himself, to his college, and to his speculative brand of Christianity as the Tractarian priests at Christ Church tried to preserve for themselves and for the movement they espoused. By definition a Balliol man was proud of his college and anxious to do splendidly, more that he might add lustre to her name than that he might add lustre to his own. To perform splendidly under Jowett's tutelage—and apparently Hopkins did—meant to engage in Jowett's version of the Socratic techniques, a procedure that was dangerous to the faith Hopkins held even as a Tractarian.

Hopkins's poetry for 1864 clearly indicates the distress he was beginning to feel about the Church of England. If his poems are autobiographical, he now thought of himself as 'One of the Spies Left in the Wilderness' (Poem 5, 1864), and his poem 'New Readings' (Poem 7, 1864), with its allusion to the parable of the sower, suggests that he had already begun to wonder whether both Tractarians and Broad Churchmen were not throwing their seed upon rocks and thorns.

1865 opened like every other year in this protracted struggle, as though matters would end once again in a deadlock. The Privy Council had not yet delivered judgment in the Colenso case, and the affair of the Regius Chair of Greek had not been settled; the scandal of Jowett's salary was so widespread that even the Archbishop of Canterbury threatened to take a hand in the proceedings himself, with the assistance of the Archbishop of York, if it were not brought to a close before Parliament met.[14]

In January, *The Times* received a statement from a legal historian, offering incontrovertible proof that Christ Church alone was responsible for the salary attached to Jowett's chair. In February Christ Church replied, through the agency of its lawyers, that although historically the funds for the Regius Chair of Greek had been given them to disburse to that professor, Christ Church was not legally obligated to do so. Nonetheless, Christ Church now consented to raise Jowett's salary from forty pounds a year to five hundred. For the first time Jowett was about to receive a salary commensurate not only with the work he accomplished every year, but with the salaries of other Regius chairs at Oxford.

A month later the Privy Council upheld Bishop Colenso's findings that the Bishop of Cape Town had no authority to depose him or to make any judgment upon him at all, and Colenso left for Natal. But when he returned to South Africa in triumph, he was greeted by an order of excommunication; if the Crown would not move against heretics, Bishop Gray seemed to say, he at least, was prepared to do so. Again Colenso refused Gray's authority over him, and so affairs went on in this undignified fashion until Gray's death in 1883, for Gray had appointed an alternate bishop, and there were in fact two congregations, one loyal to Gray, and one loyal to Colenso.

Hopkins was well aware of the Colenso scandal. In a paragraph full of topical allusions to Tractarian affairs, he wrote to E. H. Coleridge, an undergraduate friend: 'Why does not Colenso's trial go on? I always become so ignorant of Church matters in the Vac.' (*FL*, 18 January 1865). An undated and enigmatic comment in his journal for the autumn of 1865: 'Note that if I ever should leave the Church of England the fact of Provost Fortescue . . . is to be got over', indicates that he was still torn with anxiety about his decision. On 6 November there is a cryptic note: 'On this day by God's grace I resolved to give up all beauty until I had His leave for it', which is almost immediately followed by the unambiguous entry: 'I confessed to Dr. Pusey, Dec. 16, 1865' (*JP*, 71).

Hopkins's poems during this year and 1866 are increasingly descriptive of a man in a severe state of anxiety. Newman's *Apologia pro Vita Sua* had been popular reading at Oxford since its publication in 1864; Hopkins's poem 'The Half-way House' (1865) refers to Newman's statement that 'there are but two alternatives, the way to Rome and the way to Atheism: Anglicanism is the halfway house on the one side, and Liberalism is the halfway house on the other.'[15]

In June 1866, Hopkins and his closest friend, William Addis, went to visit Dom Paul Wilfrid Raynal at Belmont, a Benedictine monastery in Hereford. Addis dates Hopkins's conversion to Roman Catholicism, as well as his own, to this visit, although he believed that Hopkins had never talked to a Roman Catholic priest before.[16] Addis seemed to be implying that the prolonged Tractarian siege against heresy, and its pitiful results, were as much as anything else the agents of Hopkins's conversion, as well as his own. All too often young members of the Oxford movement had seen Tractarian priests attempt to demolish heresy; all too often they had seen their priests defeated, in public debate and in the ecclesiastical courts, and the heretical priests left at large, with ever increasing power to preach and minister to ever more numerous doubting undergraduates. And yet, although by now Hopkins must have felt that Anglican Christendom, as he had known it and trusted it, was as ephemeral as the gleaming towers of Camelot, he still appeared to hesitate. Even as late as Lent 1866, he was still saying 'not yet, not yet', and the Lenten poem 'Nondum' carries as a subtitle the verse from Isaiah xlv.15: 'Verily Thou art a God that hidest Thyself.'

God appeared to have gone into hiding, not only from him, but from all men not under the banner of Rome, for by now there was nothing to choose between the defeated Tractarians at Oxford and the triumphant Broad Churchmen clustered around Jowett. Even as a first-year man at Balliol, Hopkins had wished to make his life a glad submission to some established authority. Religious to the point of painful scrupulosity, yet vulnerable in his affection for old friends in the enemy camp, he had become an agitated seismograph for the fortunes and disasters in both Anglican camps. His letter to his mother the day before Newman received him into the Roman Catholic Church is full of anguish. Early in the letter Hopkins complained: 'My father seems to think that I am off my head.' He ended this letter with the admission that every angry or pleading message from home broke him down 'afresh', and his closing sentences must have brought as little comfort to his family as they did to him: 'In this way I have no relief. You might think that I suffer too' (FL, 100, 1866).

Certainly the strains Hopkins had undergone would have been demoralizing even for a man much less sensitive and much less concerned about the problems of liberty and authority than he. But Hopkins's strains were personal as well as theological, for he must have felt as though he were being crushed to death between two killers, Pusey and Jowett, each of whom eyed him as fiercely for signs of disloyalty as they eyed one another for signs of fatal weakness. For Pusey, who had constituted himself the Jeremiah of the Oxford movement, was not content with delivering spine-chilling sermons and issuing legal summons and statements of his feelings to the nation at large. From Christ Church, he and Henry Parry Liddon, also Hopkins's confessor and one of the most humane of the Tractarian priests, went out among the colleges and the debating societies at Oxford, as though these student watering-places were the byways of Galilee, gathering in the pious Tractarian undergraduates, or those who loved the Church of England but were afflicted with the palsy of religious doubt. These two priests, one possessed of a raging hatred of secularity in all its forms, the other, moved by a profound pity for Christian souls in doubt, comforted the troubled young men with seminars on religious questions of the day. Gradually Pusey, through his awesome sermons on everlasting punishment, and Liddon, through infinite patience, were able to introduce many of the distraught undergraduates to the ancient rites of confession, contrition, and penance. These two men formed a sort of Metaphysical Society of the eighteen-sixties; the 'club' consisted of a mixed lot of men, but its aims were clearer than those of the Metaphysical Society of the 'seventies. It was formed to preserve the dogmas of Christianity by challenging all contemporary scientific assumptions and all recent Biblical scholarship, and, by disposing of anything that looked like presumption, to strengthen the hearts of doubters with counter-scientific arguments. During their evangelical tea-parties, Pusey and Liddon also tried to infuse the members of this young Tractarian club with some of the primitive Christian passion, so long held in suspicion by the matter-of-fact Protestant Englishman.[17]

All during Hopkins's residence at Balliol, the ghosts of the western world's two archetypal martyrs stalked through Oxford, spreading among the students with any historical imagination poignant memories of the last days of Christ—or Socrates—upon earth. Jowett's favourite students, seeing him on trial for corrupting the young at Oxford, and remembering his daring lectures on Plato's dialogues, must have compared themselves to Crito as he talked with Socrates, while the beloved master, chained to the wall with a leg-iron, awaited execution in the Athenian prison. Even Jowett's acquittal and the final restitution in the matter of his salary did nothing to diminish the horror he and his party felt over the conduct of the Tractarian priests. As far as Jowett was concerned, intellectual integrity had been strangled in England. Henceforth he abandoned all public speculation on Christianity, and sensing the affinity between his predicament and that of Socrates, he embarked in earnest upon the monumental translation of Plato's dialogues. Jowett's voluminous introduction to the complete dialogues are full of passages describing the diseases in the political and social life of Athens, the strangling of all fair public debate, and the tragic abuses of power by leaders of the old, aristocratic party. His translation of the *Phaedo*, unfaithful to the Greek as it is commonly held to be, is a masterpiece of clear and moving prose, and his treatment of Socrates' final moments in prison, as the master tried to comfort his grieving disciples, has an urgency and a simple passion missing in most contemporary, and reportedly more accurate, translations.

On the other hand, men like Pusey and Liddon of Christ Church felt the presence of the martyred Christ ever among them in the last days of the Oxford movement. Both men were racked with worry over the fate of the Church of England in the modern world, caught as she was between a new militant Roman Catholic movement in England and the insistent claims, hitherto largely denied, of pragmatism and Biblical criticism from abroad. Both priests had been passed over for preferment on several occasions because of the strictness of their denominational opinions. These two men appeared to their students and penitents as the apostles, in academic gowns, of the crucified Christ and martyrs for the faith once again threatened by a materialism as heartless and as sterile as anything to be found in imperial Rome.

When Hopkins had first arrived at Balliol after the miseries of Highgate and the vindictiveness of Dr Dyne's treatment, he had hoped for several years free of stress while he was deciding upon a profession, years in which to savour what he called 'the sense of gentle fellowship' (Poem 107, 1864-5), the famous Oxonian atmosphere of lyric affections and pensive beauty that Matthew Arnold was shortly to celebrate in his preface to the first series of *Essays in Criticism,* and that Hopkins himself used as a setting for two undergraduate poems.[18] He had come up from Highgate with a passionate yearning for new and trustworthy friends and for the ideal of friendship that he described in his undergraduate poem, 'Fragments of *Richard'*. In fact, Hopkins was searching for the sort of intense male friendship that Oxford, and Victorian Oxford in particular, fostered as pedagogical weapons in forming and chastening the young.[19]

'The sense of gentle fellowship' and its counterpart—missionary zeal—were part of the *genius loci* and recognized as such by dons and students alike.[20] It was here that a boy made the important friends of his life, if he had not, like Arnold and Clough, already done so at his public school. Here he took the last deliberate steps toward choosing a career and assuming adult responsibility, and in the final steps the friend often played a conspicuous role. In choosing a career a boy was bound to involve himself in contemporary issues, and Hopkins was not the only young Oxonian with a sharp conscience who found these issues frightening. During a stroll arm in arm with a friend and confidant, or at some tutor's fireside, an apprehensive student felt free to discuss the latest skirmishes between Tractarians and liberals or the latest fashions in art and literature. In such reassuring surroundings the Christian conflicts that were distressing most responsible souls in England could be thrashed out, conflicts between faith and science, faith and dogma—or faith and no dogma—or one of the oldest of

Christendom's dogmatic difficulties and one of the sorest points for religious Victorians, the conflict between faith and works.

It was here at Victorian Oxford that generations of young men went about the serious business of making moral artifacts of their lives, consciously shaping their talents to the needs of the Church or the body politic, experiencing, perhaps for the first time as young adults, the difficult balance between beauty and morality that seems almost a *leitmotif* for the responsible Victorian artist. And here again, for an Oxonian undergraduate 'strung by duty' and 'strained to beauty' (Poem 41, 1878), as Hopkins later summed up a common Victorian dilemma, the friends of a scholar's youth played their part, each man carefully scrutinizing the other's potential capacities and his weaknesses as a matter of affectionate obligation. The letters these young men exchanged are filled with agitated or gentle admonitions, as they argue, scold, advise, and chasten, each trying to fit the other for the role of openhearted philanthropist, charismatic priest, prophetic poet, or philosopher statesman.[21]

In their moral assumptions about the nature of friendship and its duties, Oxford and Cambridge symbolized two distinct attitudes battling for supremacy in the Victorian war of ideas. Oxford stood for the idealistic and the didactic impulses in the hearts of the educated Victorians, whereas Cambridge stressed the scientific and the empirical outlook upon men and affairs. Cambridge scholars loved their university, but they were not, as a body of men, consumed with a desire to protect her, reform her, or to preach to one and all of her scholar citizens. Despite the occasional appearance of Tractarian splinter groups at Cambridge during the decades of the Oxford movement, Cambridge dons did not encourage intense missionary friendships between scholars, nor did they engage in national debates with anything like Oxonian zeal or in anything like Oxonian numbers.

Oxford's cult of heroic friendship sprang quite naturally from correlative assumptions about the role of a university; Oxford men had turned their university into a training ground for lay pedagogues and curates—of diverse persuasions, to be sure—to the soul of troubled England. The brooding affection that the serious-minded Oxonians felt for each other was intensified by their passion for Oxford herself and for whatever spiritual commonwealth they had chosen to stand and defend there. The crisis of faith that each man experienced was compounded by a similar crisis involving his friends, his university, his country, and frequently his Church.

In an atmosphere of tense private friendships and explosive public issues a polemical spirit was bound to flourish, and men who played as yet no professional role were driven to exhort each other as they were daily being exhorted by priests and tutors of the warring parties. Time and again the anxiety of these Oxford dons and students for each other and for the moral survival of their university would rise in waves and pour beyond the confines of Oxford to encompass all of England. In their zeal to gather recruits to whichever party they espoused, the Oxonians treated England at large as a pupil whose soul was imperilled by ignorance. They preached to their friends, to their colleagues, and to their families outside the Oxford community, that they might place before as many Englishmen as possible, in high places and in low, the magnitude of the issue being decided at Oxford. Tracts, sermons, and explanatory letters to anxious parents poured out of Oxford during these decades; and now and then men in public places tried their hand at didactic novels, or used the professorial platform to comment on England as she was or England as she ought to be.

One has only to think of such figures as Cardinals Manning and Newman, or the Arnolds, Ruskin, Pusey, Liddon, Jowett, or Arthur Penrhyn Stanley, Dean of Westminster, to sense, even now, something of Victorian Oxford's distinctive mark upon her sons. These men were all polemicists of one sort or another, each in search of some prescription that would minister to the sick soul of industrial England, just as they worried about the corrupt corners in the heart of stricken Oxford or in the hearts of their dearest friends. And one of the fiercest lovers and protectors of Oxford, one of the most earnest, the most driven by anxiety for the spiritual survival of his friends, the most dedicated to England and all her woes—in short, one of the most Oxonian—was Gerard Manley Hopkins, the Tractarian poet turned Jesuit, whose poems, when they do not celebrate God's bounties, look out upon unregenerate man and offer urgent clerical advice for his salvation.

The University of Cambridge, on the other hand, had kept herself largely free of the religious volcanoes that had blasted Oxford since the eighteen-thirties. The typical Cantabrigian who took his religion and his civic duties gracefully, and who looked upon his friends as delightful companions rather than as legitimate targets for his missionary urges, tended to be scornful of the fierce proselytizing that went on at Oxford. Noel Annan, Leslie Stephen's biographer, has described the model Cambridge don's 'conception of a teacher's duty',[22]

which is not only to stimulate his pupils but to inspire them with a passion for enquiry and a determination to discern the true from the false, the profound from the shallow, and to love friends for their own sake and for no other reason.

The Oxonian moral intensity appeared not only faintly nauseating to Cambridge minds, but actually dangerous. The Cantabrigians, highly suspicious of the overheated atmosphere they found at Oxford, preferred 'to keep the soul in its place for fear it may breed fads and enthusiasms'. The Cambridge scholars, returning from visits to Oxford, comforted themselves 'by saying that prophets are half humbug and produce disciples who will be wholly humbug'. The Cambridge rationalists feared any studies that were not 'precise' and failed to 'yield tangible results'. They feared equally Oxford's insistence upon attaching ideas to men:[23]

> To criticise a man's ideas dispassionately is next to impossible if he inspires a Movement. The Cambridge don who, like Stephen, was prepared to give up his time to young men would be their friend, within certain limits their guide, but never the philosopher. In Cambridge ideas were hammered into principles to be judged empirically. The Oxford craving for prophets in Stephen's view weakened the already tenuous hold which Oxford retained on impartial philosophic enquiry.

To Stephen, as to Annan, his biographer, the Victorian climate at Oxford was morbid not only intellectually but personally. All too often the passionate friendships so common at Oxford were being used by tutors in a manner Stephen considered unjust to the defenceless consciences of the young.[24] As Annan commented,[25] boys scarcely out of the schoolroom were being driven to take sides in the Tractarian wars, as each party struggled for fresh recruits:

> By the mystery, charm and hypnotism of their personalities, the Oxford prophets cast a spell over the young, fascinating, enthralling, tearing the heart out of their disciples. Rugbeians venerated Dr. Arnold, Newman inspired passionate loyalty, Balliol men were devoted to Jowett, because these teachers were regarded as great souls at work in the world.

The legendary hypnotic powers of Oxford and her prophets worked their spells in plenty upon Hopkins. Victorian men valued charm and sweetness in each other in any case, as fully as they admired moral earnestness, and they responded to affection openly and with a complete

24

naturalness that may seem hard to believe in a more self-conscious age. At Victorian Oxford a man found the charm and sweetness of his friends doubly precious, and all the more poignant because in partisan Oxford, friendships were so fragile. Oxford men did, in fact, love their friends 'for their own sake' as well as for other reasons, but the silent code of Tractarian Oxford demanded that no matter how deeply attached two men might have become, they must separate as swiftly as they could bring themselves to do, if conflicting religious opinions arose between them. 'You will take orders and have to think me all wrong: you won't be able to help it: the world will make you', said Thomas Hill Green to Henry Scott Holland, an undergraduate friend of Hopkins. For this was a time when the most minuscule differences in religious matters 'were taken gravely as a tragedy, which are now taken lightly, as a comedy'. The anxieties attendant upon conversion or unconversion were almost invariably 'aggravated . . . by separation from old friends', as Green remarked about Hopkins's reception into the Society of Jesus. The impermanence of 'the sense of gentle fellow-ship' (Poem 107) was a symptom of troubled times, and almost any two friends might find themselves faced with the 'terrible calamity' of mutual accusations and a broken or collapsing friendship.[26]

These separations were all the more painful in that they were often assumed to be not only for life but for eternity. Alexander Baillie, who wrote Hopkins's mother after his death: 'All my intellectual growth, and a very large proportion of the happiness of those Oxford days, I owe to his companionship', also admitted that he had given up more than the faith of his childhood when he became 'a kind of Aetheist'; to his infinite sorrow, he forfeited the hope of being able 'somewhere, somehow, to meet Gerard Hopkins again' after death (*FL*, 449, 1889).

Some men, and Hopkins was among them, clung all the more fiercely to men whose religious opinions they thought quite safe, and now and then they found charm in odd places. Even Edward Pusey, embittered as he was by a succession of family catastrophes and innumerable losses of colleagues and students to Roman Catholicism, had his troop of loyal disciples, and he used the harsh power of his religious passions and his 'anxious yearning over souls'[27] to incite these young men to his sacramental ends in a way that was fully as effective with Hopkins, for a time, as Liddon's sweeter and more patient ways. For the rest of the famous Oxonian prophets, the Arnolds, Jowett, Liddon, Newman in his day, and Gerard Manley Hopkins in his day, personal charm and personal ardour were all inseparable tools in their varied missionary purposes. Contemporary comments on all these men stress their 'sweetness' and the utter delight that large numbers of men experienced in their society. That they were capable of 'enthralling' or 'fascinating' other men was considered a mark of God's providence working in them for the salvation of other men, or at least one sign of virtue. Leslie Stephen, who gave Jowett poor marks for integrity and for intellectual stamina, nonetheless remarked on Jowett's charm, on the fact that 'the core of the man's nature was sweet, sound and masculine'. Stephen was fully aware that Jowett's sweetness and charm was one of the most important sources of his didactic influence over Oxford undergraduates. And Matthew Arnold, Stephen said, 'had that obvious sweetness of nature, which it is impossible not to recognize and not to love'.[28] Canon Liddon, whom Hopkins came to love without reserve, was remembered by his contemporaries as 'sweet, grave, thoughtful, complete'.[29] Liddon was the owner of a magnificent voice and his charm in and out of the pulpit was as famous as Newman's, though Liddon's didactic style was gentler and more personal than Newman's.

This heady atmosphere of crises, martyrdom, and above all, of pervasive charm does not seem to have been lost, even upon Hopkins's mature poetry. Josephine Miles has remarked that Hopkins's favourite adjectives were 'sweet', 'lovely', and 'dear', and that these epithets, 'especially in their context', were employed to create an aura of 'aesthetic feeling and affectionate response. They serve to make abstracts more sensible and concretes more personal.' Professor Miles suggests that the adjectives '*Sweet, dear* and *lovely* do not bear a strict Hopkins' label. They sound quite like the 19th Century and perhaps, except for *lovely*, like the sixteenth.' Whatever debt Hopkins's language owes to Keats and to the Ruskin of *Modern Painters*, as Professor Miles says, his 'violence of imagery' and the sense of 'multitudinousness' that it imparts obviously does express his 'intense piety' and his 'rushing to meet life';[30] in fact it expresses the very Oxonian impetuosity that the typical nineteenth-century Cambridge man feared as a peril to intellectual honesty and that Hopkins, most fortunately for us, preserved in his poetry in one way or another, until he died.

A number of Hopkins's poems and many of his letters bear further witness to his Tractarian past at Oxford. They contain innumerable analyses of morally attractive natures, for in such people Hopkins espied glimpses of the hidden Christ and reassuring evidences that Christ's purposes, for which He accepted crucifixion, were going forward in the world. And the accounts of moral crises in so much of Hopkins's poetry—the little vignettes of almost helpless humans held at bay by the forces of evil and protected only feebly by the thin strand of Christ's love—correspond exactly to the atmosphere of imminent catastrophe that he endured all during his residence at Oxford.

Apparently Hopkins made very much the same impression on his friends and contemporaries as the more famous Oxonian prophets made upon theirs. After his death Hopkins was described as

> so lovable—so singularly gifted—&, in his saintliness, so apart from & different to, all others. Only that [*sic*] his beautifully gentle and generous nature made him one with his friends; & led us to love & to value him—feeling that our lives were better, & the world richer, because of him (*JP*, 301, 1889).

Sometimes one is left with the impression that Hopkins's Christ, especially in the sermons,[31] is a supernatural college don, handsome to look at before the crucifixion, and afterward, more to be loved and cherished in His apparent downfall than ever before. For Hopkins the priest, Christ possessed just that combination of morally braced vigour, courage in the face of danger, tenderness for humanity in moral peril, and sweet attractiveness that Hopkins the Anglican student had first found in his friends and tutors of various parties.

Leslie Stephen, the rational analyst of Cambridge, was not the only Victorian observer to comment on Oxford's climate of moral intensity. An occasional Oxford man, perhaps more objective or less perfervid than the rest, could sense its inherent dangers. These young men were separated almost entirely from the society of women; they were often taught by fiercely partisan, celibate tutors, for whom diverse causes and the perennial procession of students took the place of family affections. It is no wonder that they often found themselves over-whelmed by an atmosphere of panic. Nor is it any wonder that they turned to each other for comfort with such outpourings of affection that their relationships often contained some of the passions usually directed toward heterosexual love. And the greater the anxiety they felt in polemical Oxford, the more passionately they would turn to one another, and the more passionately they turned to one another, the more anxiety they would feel. Hopkins's friend, Henry Scott Holland, admitted with refreshing candour the temporary homosexual tinge to some of the Oxford friendships. As Holland took a retrospective glance at some of his undergraduate friendships, he traced the pattern that these friendships frequently followed.[32] First comes the 'delighted discovery of sympathy with another', the period when 'delicious sympathies may cross, and recross from one to another', when the spirit of each man 'is brimming with good measure: and it longs to give itself in fullness, running over, that with the same measure that it metes, it may receive it back into its bosom'. The period of 'delighted discovery' is followed by sourness, a time when one is only conscious of

> the fever, the fretfulness, the angry irritation, the dreariness of the inevitable failure. Something of the awful barrenness of lust comes over it, in that it is struggling to slake the thirst for the higher with the waters of the lower.

It seemed clear to Holland that these friendships were a temporary substitute for something else:

> We fall back exhausted: disappointed: barren: we feel as if friendship broke down under us, and we had no outlet but despair. But only because we are struggling to get out of friendship what is not there—more than can be there.

Yet the very frankness of Holland's admissions, and the open endearments with which all the young men saluted each other from time to time in their letters, prompts the suggestion that these friendships were bred not only of panic, of missionary excitation and of the exalted cult of masculine love, but also, quite simply of the innocent and ardent admirations that typify delayed adolescence.

Holland was not the only Oxford man to consider Oxonian friendships painful as well as delightful. Many of Hopkins's undergraduate letters suggest fervid or aborted friendships and he may well have been troubled by the tenor of some of them, for he recommended an article on 'The Ethics of Friendship' to Baillie. The anonymous author, evidently a connoisseur on the subject, describes various kinds of friendships. There is a type 'which is formed at school or college in very early life among the young of either sex'. It 'resembles love rather than friendship, and is distinguished by a fervid enthusiasm, a tormenting jealousy, great sensitiveness, and utter absence of all calculation, distrust, or even prudence'. These friendships are followed in later life by more restrained models that foster 'great development in individuality and a fearlessness in asserting it'. The more mature concept of friendship is not a two-by-two affair; it includes 'a few choice people', a 'charmed circle', where 'there is an atmosphere of sympathy at once personal, vivid, and profound, well calculated to have a stimulating or almost intoxicating effect on the powers of those who breathe its perfume'.[33]

The telltale phrases that describe the maturing phase of friendships, 'few choice people', 'charmed circle', the two evocative adjectives, 'stimulating' and 'intoxicating', and the perfumed 'atmosphere of sympathy at once personal, vivid and profound', makes one suspect that the anonymous writer had once been an Oxford man who clung to his friends as men under fire huddle together for comfort, finding unexpected charms and heroic virtues in unlikely people. The common affections of an ordinary, placid existence may well pale beside the psychology of the trenches; and one is continually struck by the metaphors of heterosexual love and of trench warfare so prevalent in both contemporary and modern accounts of Tractarian Oxford.

At the moment of Hopkins's matriculation he had the whole world of Oxford to pick his friends from, nor was he as yet estranged from any of them by religious conflicts. Undoubtedly his new friends, like everybody else's, were 'sweet, sound and masculine'. And to Hopkins, as to all devoted Oxonians, Oxford herself was sweet, whatever else she might be in this troubled decade, and according to the Victorian custom, he gave Oxford the same unabashed adulation that he expended upon his friends. Hopkins described her as the unobtrusive civilizer of men who

> put taught graces on his country lip,
> And brought the sense of gentle fellowship,
> That many centres found in many hearts,

while she provided him with new vistas of 'the humanities and the round of arts', always to the persistent accompaniment of 'the much music of our Oxford bells'. Hopkins finished these 'Fragments of *Richard*' in July 1865, while he was compiling his case against the Church of England; this may account for the elegiac note:

> A spiritual grace
> Which Wordsworth would have dwelt on, about the place
> Led Richard with a sweet undoing pain
> To trace some traceless loss of thought again.

Despite his growing fears of Tractarian impotence, Hopkins found it almost impossible to free himself from Oxford's spell. Only a few months before he wrote these lines, he had made a note in his journal reminding himself to read 'Arnold's *Essays*' (*JP*, 56, 1865). These were undoubtedly the first series of *Essays in Criticism* published that year. Hopkins's evocation of Oxford's 'spiritual grace' that was capable of piercing a man with 'sweet undoing pain' (Poem 107) is reminiscent of Arnold's even more rhapsodic cry: 'Beautiful city! so venerable, so lovely', and of his adoring tributes to the 'ineffable charm' of 'this queen of romance', who captures all hearts, 'steeped in sentiment as she lies, spreading her gardens to the moonlight, and whispering from her towers the last enchantment of the Middle Age'. But by 1865 Hopkins could no longer have agreed with Matthew Arnold that Oxford was a 'serene' or 'adorable dreamer' with an incurably romantic heart, whose greatest gift to industrial England was her capacity to keep herself 'so unravished by the fierce intellectual life of our century'.[34] Both these Balliol men saw Oxford through a mist of memories; both saw her in keeping with their present spiritual needs. Arnold's celebration of Oxford was based upon a premise he needed to believe—that Oxford changed only slowly, if at all—whereas Hopkins, in some ways far clearer-sighted than Arnold in this respect, feared that for his purposes she had already been fatally corrupted by the winds of change.

By May 1866, five months before his reception into the Catholic Church, Hopkins observed in his journal that things at Oxford looked 'sad' and 'difficult' for him indeed. But his interest in intellectual affairs did not wane, and the presence of an eminent Balliol graduate, Matthew Arnold, as Professor of Poetry, was obviously comforting to him, for another journal entry two weeks later announced that 'Matthew Arnold lectured on the Celtic element in English poetry' (*JP*, 137, 1866). Despite Hopkins's harrowing state of mind, Matthew Arnold could hardly have had a more receptive listener at his last lecture of the season than the young poet and amateur philologist in the audience, who was later to spend a third of his life among Celts and was to set himself to learn Welsh, not primarily, as he wryly admitted, *ad maioram Dei gloriam*. While he was up at Oxford Hopkins gobbled up everything by Arnold that he could get his hands on. To the end of his life he respected the sanity and the perspicacity of Arnold's criticism, even going so far as to call Arnold a 'rare genius and a great critic', while admitting that in some things the critic was 'very wrong' (*LB*, 172, 1883).

Arnold had a good deal to say in the last University Lecture of this series about the various 'modes of handling nature'. He identified four of them: the faithful, which was adequate, the Celtic and the Greek, which were admirable, and the conventional, which was unacceptable. 'In the faithful way of handling nature, the eye is on the object, and that is all you can say.' Arnold insisted that the eye must be on the object and that it must report accurately what it sees, but he was equally insistent that objectivity of this sort is not enough by itself. Artists must shape what they report with as much skill as the aptitude with which they report what they see. And so he went on to praise the Celtic way of handling nature, that is, the 'magical way', in which 'the eye is on the object, but charm and magic are added'. Arnold's praise of the Celtic way was almost as exalted as his praise of the Greek way, in which 'the eye is on the object, but lightness and brightness are added'. The Greek and Celtic modes of handling nature won Arnold's respect because both modes demanded that the artist be simultaneously accurate and illuminative. But there was one way of handling nature that Arnold condemned utterly, along with most Victorian writers on aesthetics, and that was 'the conventional way'; here the artist is as blind as one of the Academy painters upon whom Ruskin heaped so much scorn, because, as Arnold said, his 'eye is not on the object' at all.[35] The conventional artist insults nature twice over, first by distorting her and then by refusing her the benefit of his artistic alchemy.

Arnold's aesthetic theories represent a Victorian commonplace about reproducing nature that goes far beyond emotion recollected in tranquillity. In this climate of objectivity and emotion combined, Ruskin could demand both accurate and exhilarated copying of the book of nature, and Rossetti could feel it incumbent upon himself to report, even as he lay in the grass, grieving, that 'the woodspurge has a cup of three'—not a cup of two blossoms, or four, or five, but three. Hopkins's aesthetic concepts embodied in his terms 'inscape'—the whole object as it is in all its wholeness and in each of its specific parts—and 'instress'—the onlooker's emotional response to that object—would have been as acceptable to earlier Victorian aestheticians as theirs were to him.

Walter Houghton has suggested that the educated Victorians admired aesthetic enthusiasms almost as much as they admired 'earnestness'.[36] And what was welcomed in the observers of art was demanded of the artist. Thus, Ruskin's and Hopkins's moral imperatives—delight in the transcribing artist's heart and accuracy in his mind—or Matthew Arnold's insistence upon seeing the object as in itself it really is, but with felicitous additions, and Hopkins's 'inscape' and 'instress', all appear as versions of a post-Romantic sensibility, a process that begins almost in scientific empiricism and ends in piety, or at least in moral elevation. It must have been crucial for Hopkins's purposes that Ruskin and Arnold both stressed the importance of the artist first as a camera eye and then as a transforming alchemist, a remaker of beauty in his own right.

In Arnold's last lecture of the Celtic series, he seemed as concerned with the problem of how to see ideas accurately and richly as he was with the problem of how to see objects accurately and richly, and his discussion progresses quite naturally from objects to ideas—from specific poems and kinds of poetry, to the moral uses of culture. For the whole lecture is really a call to all disinterested yet enthusiastic souls to declare themselves ready for 'angelic revenges upon the Philistines', who invariably sinned against objectivity, if not enthusiasm, or enthusiasm, if not richness and complexity of vision. Arnold was not a Balliol man for nothing, and he was possessed of a missionary urge to soften the ordinary Englishman's 'hard unintelligence, which is just now our bane'. This mulish unintelligence could never be 'conquered by storm', but it might slowly be 'suppled and reduced by culture, by a growth in the variety, fullness and sweetness of our spiritual life'.[37] Arnold knew full well 'how unpopular a task one is undertaking when one tries to pull out a few more stops in that powerful, but at present somewhat narrow-tone organ, the modern Englishman',[38] and in his final lecture on Celtic poetry he deplored the 'narrow Philistinism which has long had things its own way in England'. He went on to list mournfully the virtues England had 'sacrificed to Philistinism': 'culture, and insight, and dignity, and acceptance and weight among the nations, and hold on events that deeply concern us, and control of the future', and he added ironically that Philistinism could not even supply the 'fool's paradise' it had promised the average Philistine.[39]

Arnold is insisting that qualities normally thought incompatible are not incompatible at all, but are actually incomplete without each other. Under no circumstances can dogmas of any sort justify spiritual ugliness, nor can culture justify spiritual flabbiness, and this urbane blending of morality and civility must have been as important for Hopkins to hear praised as its natural corollary, the blending of objectivity with enthusiasm.

As Arnold's lectures come down to us in the form of slightly revised essays, they sound full of wisdom and decorum, but later in life Hopkins mixed praise and censure for Arnold's sometime capacity to be serious:

Besides he seems a very earnest man and distinctly seeing the difference between jest and earnest and a master of both. . . . But then very unhappily he jokes at the wrong things, as I see by a very profane passage quoted from his new book: however that passage though profane is not blasphemous, for we are obliged to think of God by human thoughts and his account of them is substantially true.

Hopkins's mature estimate of Matthew Arnold obviously contains an unconscious memory of 'Merry Matt', the witty professor who had come up to embattled Oxford with the express intention of stirring up laughter. In this letter to an old undergraduate friend, Hopkins, usually so deferential to those with higher rank than his own, spoke of reading 'Mat Arnold's poems, the Empedocles volume', as though his Oxonian friend would be in on the 'Merry Matt' joke (*FL*, 58, 1873). As Walter Pater's biographer recounted the atmosphere Arnold created, the discourses offered by the urbane Professor of Poetry were not just the usual mummifying preachments that passed for lectures; 'owing largely to his "jibes" at the "Philistines",' the report soon got around that these lectures were actually funny. Full of 'impudence' and 'invincible insouciance', they 'attracted wide attention', and Arnold suddenly found himself quite the thing at Oxford. John Addington Symonds, a contemporary of Pater, remembered Arnold 'swaggering around with just that touch of arrogance that nobody minded in him'.[40]

There was at least one scholar at Oxford who minded. Max Müller, the eminent German philologist and emigrant to Oxford, was quite perturbed by Arnold's 'French persiflage', and he accused Arnold of playing a 'dangerous game'. Arnold, Müller complained, cared far more that his audiences dared to laugh than he did for 'their serious opposition or their convinced assent'. Such lack of decorum was not, in Müller's opinion, the proper conduct for a national hero who was already 'among the living worthies of England'.[41]

The Teutonic Müller was too new to England and Oxford to see what Arnold was up to. 'French persiflage' in skilful hands undermines the complacent solemnity of tenth-rate imaginations or the rigidity of evangelical consciences, and it does so without open rebellion. So may 'lightness and brightness' or 'charm and magic'. Müller was right for the wrong reasons: if Arnold had wished to perpetuate the unlovely strain of grimness at Oxford, which of course he did not, he would indeed have been playing a 'dangerous game'. In suggesting to his audience by example that the intellect and the moral sense may play as well as plod, Arnold was undermining the atmosphere, not entirely devoid of Philistinism, that Tractarians and liberals alike counted on to do half their work for them.

Leslie Stephen saw what Hopkins saw and what Müller could not see, that Arnold's 'singular fulness of perception', his pungent flashes of sarcasm, even 'certain little defects, when he seems to be rather forcing himself to be humorous, and becomes liable to an accusation of flippancy', were all tools to his final purpose, to deliver 'truths as undeniable as they are unpleasant, and yet with such urbanity' that the listener was compelled to some rudimentary acceptance of Arnold's premises.[42] Arnold had set himself to be the gadfly of a self-satisfied race. There its younger generation sat before him, scarcely out of the schoolroom. To change men's minds and to disrupt their smooth habits of the past was a Balliol mission, as well as a Christ Church mission. Pusey, Liddon, and Newman before them, had known how to reduce their congregations to tears of contrition or to fits of trembling. 'Merry Matt', no doubt irritated by the mantle of 'living English worthy' that Oxford tried to drape upon him, chose to substitute laughter for tears and terror as an instrument for swaying the souls of undergraduates. That he could have won the allegiance of Hopkins, a critic so radically different in purpose and in temperament, is a compliment to the effectiveness of Arnold's techniques. And it is pleasant to think that the poet and critic who graced the Chair of Poetry offered the harassed undergraduates a rare opportunity to break into laughter; it is even pleasanter to think that the serious poet and priest in the making, who sat in the audience, may have permitted himself to laugh with the rest.

Yet to Hopkins, whose conscience was a delicate instrument, always quivering for material by which to measure itself, these lectures and essays must have been something of an ordeal, exhilarating, soothing, and troubling by turns. And Arnold was by no means the only disturbing mentor Hopkins had to deal with. Even at this late date, he was still as smitten as everyone else at Balliol with Jowett, 'the captivator of ardent and intelligent youth'.[43] In his pseudonymous satire of Balliol and Oxford,[44] Martin Geldart recorded the degree of Hopkins's captivity to Jowett's charm:

> Even my ritualistic friend Gerontius Manley acknowledged what he called the 'purity' of our hero—what had he been a Catholic, he would have called his 'saintliness'—as something which struck him more in Professor Jewell than in almost any other.

Hopkins may well have admired the energy that Jowett was able to sustain during the years of his ordeal. And particularly after the shock of his trial, Jowett turned the Victorian energy and earnestness toward intellectual matters; his was now a 'muscular' intellectuality, as Leslie Stephen once suggested:

> At the age of seventy he laid down as a scheme for eight years of work; one year upon Plato, two upon Moral Philosophy, two upon a life of Christ, one upon Sermons and two upon a History of Early Greek Philosophy. We admire the sanguine spirit of the man; we feel his illusions to be pathetic. . . .

The spirit is all the more sanguine when one considers that these schemes of work were to be for the benefit of his students only, or so Jowett often told himself. For although he felt very little urge to publish after his trial, especially upon matters touching Christianity and the life of Christ, there was nothing to prevent him from offering his students the fruits of his various investigations, on Athens or on Jerusalem, and for his students, particularly perhaps if they were Balliol men, Jowett would go to unimaginable lengths. In fact, Jowett always had a 'little difficulty distinguishing between the interests of Balliol and the interests of the universe'. To support the interests of the universe, he had spent the best part of his life 'prodding and rousing'[45] his students to feats of excellence that now and then may have been beyond their natural talents or their stamina. More than ever during the years of Hopkins's residence at Balliol, Jowett turned to his students, driving them with ever fiercer determination, to compete with each other and with other colleges for the greater glory of Balliol.[46]

Jowett is reported to have said that he 'had never met a more promising pupil' than Gerard Manley Hopkins.[47] Between this dogged tutor, who insisted upon weekly reviews of each student's work,[48] and the equally dogged young Tractarian, there must have occurred the unspoken collision of two formidable consciences. Each man was bent upon personal perfection. Each man saw humanity as a collection of precious souls committed to his care. And each, in his time, found himself doomed to a standard of work far short, in both quality and quantity, of what he had hoped to accomplish.

Many an attitude that was congenial to Hopkins the Jesuit he first encountered in Victorian Balliol. Oddly enough, in 1866, the year Newman received Hopkins into the Roman Catholic Church, Jowett remarked to a friend:[49]

> I should like to make all my old pupils ambitious, if I could, of living like men and doing silently a real work. I think this sort of idealism

increases upon me as I get older. But I should be more disposed to allow for difference of individual character.

Jowett himself reminds one of Hopkins's Alphonsus Rodriguez, 'Laybrother of the Society of Jesus', who humbly 'watched the door', during those 'years and years by of world without event'. Jowett guarded the door of Balliol, while he watched his ex-students, flashing 'honour off exploit', and crowding 'career with conquest' (Poem 73, 1888),[50] in the public world of men and events beyond Oxford. Even before he became Master of Balliol, Jowett examined the college from cellar to attic, to be sure that it was functioning properly. There was no problem too menial, no detail too trivial to merit his attention. He is highly reminiscent of Hopkins's almost invisible humble ploughman in 'The Windhover', who adores brilliance, although for Christ's sake he is committed to lowly tasks in God's vineyard. Jowett also turned again and again from the prestige of his office to make 'plough down sillion shine' (Poem 36, 1877). He looked into Balliol's kitchen arrangements, the buttery problems, the purchase of a new organ for the chapel, the personal difficulties of poor or foreign students and, above all, the completion of intellectual reform at Balliol and throughout the university.[51] As Hopkins the priest was later to equate any sort of honest work with worship, Jowett equated any service to Balliol with service to God. Toward the end of his life he was still meditating upon the ways and means of perfection, asking himself whether it was possible 'to live altogether for others and for the highest, not for gain or honour', or even for the satisfaction of personal needs.[52]

Of course, the concept that to labour is to pray is a peculiarly Victorian one, as it is a Christian one; but the Victorian age did see a Christian revival, of which the Tractarian wars were but a small part. And in any case, the missionary note was as typical of intellectually sophisticated Balliol men as it was of Christ Church men, and it is equally typical of the Society of Jesus. The disposition to sacrifice personal comfort, even personal health, for idealistic ends was as clear in Jowett and other Balliol men as it was in Hopkins. Jowett's Balliol disciple, Thomas Hill Green, and Matthew Arnold, sacrificing their talents to the exhausting role of school inspector, did so not only in response to financial need, but also to appease the familiar Balliol itch to diffuse one brand or another of salvation throughout the land. Hopkins's desire to inoculate the world with Christ is reminiscent of Jowett's desire, announced in joke and undertaken in earnest, to 'inoculate the world with Balliol'.[53]

It is doubtful that Hopkins, for all his brilliant achievements under Jowett's attention, ever became one of Jowett's greatest favourites, or that he himself ever fully trusted this man of 'goodness and genius' combined.[54] The viciousness of the Tractarian wars had maimed both men, but each man rehabilitated himself by totally different means. Jowett went his way practising the silent 'wisdom of the serpent and being all things to all men'.[55] The more Jowett's faith in the literal historicity of the Bible waned and the more he came to doubt the divinity of Christ, the more desperately he clung to Balliol, and no one can say what private casuistries he was forced to practise in order to do so. Whatever the price, Jowett paid it, so that he might teach the young what he thought they needed in the modern world. This was obviously not Hopkins's way; he had to choose between religious integrity and his belief in Oxford and the Anglican Church. His decision was unambiguous, but in his own way he paid as significant a price as Jowett had paid, in order that he might extricate himself from the ravages of conflict and fit himself to deal with the disorders in England.

No young man who was known to be 'full of fun' was going to spend his entire time at Oxford in a state of spiritual tension. Despite his disillusioning experiences at Highgate, Hopkins left his grammar school with a reputation for light-heartedness. It may be difficult for readers of his late sonnets to think of him as a wit, 'rippling over with jokes, and chaff, facile with pencil and pen, with rhyming jibe or cartoon', but so a Highgate friend remembered him (*FL*, 395, 1890). In such a mood, at least on the surface, he went up to Oxford, and its delights called him as they had called generations of men before and after him. Like his friend Henry Scott Holland, 'he bought the usual things, attended the usual lectures, went to hear Pusey and Liddon, and so forth'.[56] Hopkins's letters to his mother in his early months at Balliol were lyric with happiness. From four of his six windows he had 'the best view in Balliol' and his staircase boasted 'the best scout in the college, Henry'. On the staircase below him lived Courtenay Peregrine Ilbert, already a third-year man, and naturally, therefore, 'the cleverest man in Balliol, that is in the University, or in the University, that is in Balliol, whichever you like' (*FL*, 69, 70–1). This handsome scholar, who had taken two of the most coveted scholarship prizes, and was, according to Hopkins, 'an admirable Crichton', flattered the shy young fresher by introducing him to one of the most favoured of Oxford's pastimes, the two-by-two constitutional. Ironically, it was Ilbert who became a Fellow of Balliol in 1864, achieved voting status in 1865, and, being of the Jowett party, broke with his single vote the minority position with which the liberals had hitherto had to be content (*JP*, 347).[57]

At the moment no thought of estrangement could have been in either of the young men's minds. Hopkins was 'only too much honoured' to accept the older scholar's invitation, and they enjoyed a 'pleasant walk to some heights that overlook Oxford and past . . . Bagley Wood'. Then followed the usual intoxicating round of break-fast parties, wine parties, and boating twosomes, as the young men tested each other in groups and in pairs, with an eye to the more serious friendships they craved. Hopkins and a new friend, each in his own canoe, discovered its motion to be 'luxuriously delicious', one might even say 'Elysian', in fact, altogether 'Paradisaical'. Hopkins concluded that he must have experienced 'the summit of human happiness'.

Naturally he joined the Union, as any self-respecting Balliol man was bound to do, and he may very well have been in the audience when his closest friend, William Addis, a Tractarian, and like himself an eventual Roman Catholic convert, debated the Tractarian position.[58] The Union's historian informs us[59] that in

> the second half of the decade the debates had a strong religious tinge. . . . The subjects that drew best . . . were such topics as 'The Establishment of Monasticism in the Church of England', on which I remember an eloquent speech by Addis of Balliol, then a High Churchman.

At the Union theology was theoretically debarred in those years, 'as leading not only to purposeless but to disruptive strife'; but this fooled nobody, and soon 'means were found to overstep any incon-venient barrier, so that before long religious problems, under the guise of ecclesiastic politics, were treated as freely as other themes'.[60]

The relations between Church and State were the staple diet of the debates in the eighteen-sixties, but there were other important issues for the orators to settle once and for all in the uncompromising fashion of the young. What, for example, was the proper relationship between art and morals? art and reality? art and literature? What of the Pre-Raphaelites? were they moral? were they sensual? or moral despite sensuality or because of it?[61]

For anyone who knew the Union and its reputation between the two world wars, its reputation for catholicity in Hopkins's decade comes as a surprise. In the nineteen-thirties especially it was a haven for left-wing debaters and for earnest supporters of the labour movement. During Hopkins's time it was the 'centre for men of varied gifts and tastes' and in those days 'everybody belonged to it and more than one Rowing blue was president'.[62]

Although Hopkins never mentioned any of the debates there, he was rather proud of his Union affiliation, at least during his first year. He used it as his mailing address at first, but his nonchalance in the matter could hardly have fooled his mother: 'Yesterday I subscribed to the Union, whence I shall generally send my letters, as more convenient than any other place.' Just in case his mother was not yet suitably impressed, Hopkins felt impelled to point out to 'Dearest Mama' in a later letter: 'I have not much time but I must write a few lines. (The handwriting will show you I am using Union pens.)' (*FL*, 68–9, 75, 1863.)

Hopkins's interest in the Union gradually died away, probably under Liddon's influence. It is surprising that Liddon, ardent Christ Church Tractarian that he was, did not see the possibilities of the Union for furthering his own views. But he was a gentle person, uncontentious except where his faith and his Church were under direct attack, and he may have preferred to do his work from the pulpit and over the tea cups, rather than amid the hurly-burly of a Union debate. At all events, Liddon attended only one debate in his long career at Oxford, and his remark upon that occasion was succinct: 'Disgusted!'[63]

For students not in a contentious mood, or for one who had lost interest in college debates, there were other matters, such as the proper sartorial appearance, which to a Balliol man were of cosmic importance. Despite their moral intensity, and the firsts and double firsts that continued to pour out of Balliol, these young men took their academic honours lightly, and they considered themselves men of the world, at least of the Oxford world, which, as Hopkins might have said, was very much the same thing. Several varieties of costume were correct for Balliol men. For the boating set, blazers and flannels and a straw boater were *de rigueur*. One's boater was the more impressive if one had earned the right to wind the college colours around it as a hat-band. But for non-oarsmen like Hopkins, homburgs were also fashionable. One could wear one's hair flowing almost to the shoulders, or swept aesthetically back in neat wings, in the style Hopkins favoured. Patriarchal beards were permitted, and if one grew a moustache, it could be proud and luxurious, calling clear attention to itself, or like Hopkins's moustache, a mere Pre-Raphaelite brush-stroke of a thing, discreet and natty. One's walking stick could be a casual piece of wood, suitable for trotting along the tow-paths while following the fortunes of the college boat at bump races, or an elegant affair with a gold or silver knob, like the one Hopkins affected.[64]

Balliol did not turn out rowing blues in the 'sixties in the same numbers that she produced firsts and double firsts in the schools. Her historian, admittedly a biased reporter, records that Balliol is not an athletic college, 'not', he remarks with a touch of appealing snobbery, 'to be judged by the same standard as those of Colleges where larger sacrifices are made to athletic prestige'.[65] Balliol scholars, true to their didactic mission, preferred to send men up as presidents of the Union than as oars to eights, if a choice had to be made. Hopkins could not have chosen two more contentious colleges than Christ Church and Balliol, the one in which to worship and go to confession, and the other in which to study; for these two colleges between them supplied half of all the presidents of the Union in the eighteen-sixties, and this pattern prevailed throughout most of the nineteenth century.

But Balliol men by no means ignored the performances of their crews. With or without proper training, the Balliol oarsmen were expected to struggle for perfection, on the river as everywhere else, simply because they were Balliol men. Even as late as 1866, Hopkins found time to mourn the dismal failure of the Balliol boat in a bump race (*JP*, 136), and Jowett, the 'irrepressible Mentor'[66] to all things Balliol, used to trot along the tow-path, shouting encouragement to the Balliol crews, and the 'adventures of the eight were watched by him with hardly less anxiety than the class list of the schools'.[67]

For a first-year man who delighted in everything Oxford had to offer him, there were other pastimes to soothe the mind and distract it from the strenuous world of contests between scholars in the schools, debates in the Union, or eights on the river. With a becoming air of masculine *insouciance*, Hopkins wrote to Alexander Baillie—not, we notice, his mother—that after an examination, a friend named Hardy 'became light-headed, light-hearted, light-heeled. He, Brown and I proceeded to booze at the Mitre, and I forgot to pay my share, but I believe Hardy meant to feast us, in his delight' (*FL*, 200, 1863). And for the delight of the eye and rest for the brain, there was always the architecture of Oxford and its environs. That same year Hopkins described a walk with Addis to see the church of Littlemore, where Newman had preached his 'last sermon before the exodus'. Hopkins, already a devout disciple of Ruskin, admired the rich stained-glass windows, the 'exquisite' altar and reredos, and the fine proportions of everything there, 'the decorations being on a small scale, but most elaborate and perfect'. He ended this letter to his mother with a most charming paean to everything Oxonian:

> I can not go on describing all Oxford, its inhabitants and its neighbourhood, but to be short, everything is delightful, I have met with much attention and am perfectly comfortable. Balliol is the friendliest and snuggest of Colleges, our inner quad is delicious and has a grove of fine trees and lawns where bowls are the order of the evening. Sunk below the level of the quad, from which it is separated by a pretty stone parapet, is the Fellows' garden, kept very trim, and abutting on it our graceful chapel, which cost only one fourth as much as Exeter, and did *not,* as that did, run us into debt. We have no choir, organ, or music, but then the chapel is beautiful and two of our windows contain the finest old glass in Oxford.

In Hopkins's next letter to his mother, written to discuss plans for his first reading party in the long vacation, he remarked prophetically that he was 'almost too happy', and he begged her not to consider it a sign of disloyalty. But 'in fact there are so many companions of my own age and so much liberty to see and do so much, that it ought not to make you think it unkind' (*FL*, 74, 78–9, 1863).

With his acute sensitivity and his discriminating tastes, Hopkins would have been delighted with Oxford's views in any event. But his pleasure in everything there was doubled because even as a schoolboy he had already begun 'to see and do so much' as a disciple of Ruskin, another Oxonian. As early as 1863 Hopkins's journals contain the derivative clues of a young disciple who saw the whole world through the eyes of a new master. Hopkins's Oxonian sketches and drawings of church windows, arches, traceries, or of water, vegetation, earth, and sky, could almost have been done with tracing paper over some of Ruskin's models. And Hopkins's word paintings of natural and man-made objects reveal how much—and how soon—he had adopted Ruskin's particular brand of impassioned objectivity. Hopkins's eye was clearly upon each object he drew, but, as Matthew Arnold might have said, vitality and movement were added.

Ruskin's mark upon Hopkins may well have been as incalculable as Oxford's was and as that of the Society of Jesus was later to be. Throughout his life Hopkins filled his journals with comments on Ruskin's aesthetic laws, artless pronouncements on the superiority of Gothic architecture above all others, 'as Ruskin says' (*JP*, 13, 1863),[68] and admonitions to himself and others to follow Ruskin's advice. With the exuberance of a young intellectual, Hopkins once proposed to read

'Beresford Hope's English Cathedral, E. B. Dennison's book on church-restoring or something of the kind', Matthew Arnold's *Essays,* and *Modern Painters,* among a dozen other titles (*JP,* 56, 1865). And no matter how sternly Hopkins might judge Ruskin and Ruskin's fuzzy dogma, he paid Ruskin the finest compliment one artist can pay another, paraphrasing again and again this man whom he considered the most important critic of the century, offering brief little sketches of Ruskinian arguments in both his prose and his poetry, and occasionally quoting Ruskin verbatim without acknowledgment and perhaps without awareness.[69]

Ruskin played the part of silent don to Hopkins all the more persuasively perhaps, because he was the product of an earlier Oxford, and not therefore tainted in Hopkins's eyes with the religious controversies of the eighteen-sixties. Since Ruskin's teachings were not part of the Oxonian *armamentaria* that Hopkins felt himself obliged to abandon once he became a Jesuit, he may have clung all the more firmly to Ruskin's theocentric aestheticism.

Ruskin himself remembered Oxford without any particular love, and he claimed that he learned almost nothing there. He never looked back at Oxford with the nostalgic sense of loss that afflicted Matthew Arnold and generations of graduates before and after him. But Ruskin's contempt was unusual, whereas Hopkins's frank adoration of the *genius loci,* the 'pleasaunce', the 'park', and the 'charms' of all the 'towers musical', the 'quiet-walled grove' (Poem 12, 1865) so reminiscent of Matthew Arnold's dreaming spires and soft ghosts of lost causes, would be considered quite the proper emotion. Since the turn of the century romantic love of Oxford had become an intense cult, nonetheless genuine and personal because it was fashionable,[70] and the idea of leaving Oxford was as painful to converts like Newman and Hopkins as it was to half-heretics like Jowett. Years later, even after Hopkins returned to Oxford as a missionary priest, he was forced to admit: 'Not to love my University would be to undo the very buttons of my being.' This admission must have been all the more painful because it was wrung from him upon his return to an Oxford he found 'alien', 'chilling and deeply to be distrusted', a place where he 'cd. not feel at home' (*FL,* 244–5, 1880).

As the chill of Oxford began to gather around Hopkins in his last undergraduate years, he was able to turn to one exotic friend who deliberately kept himself aloof from the hell that Oxford had become for all the combatants in the Tractarian wars. Hopkins's earliest mention of Walter Pater occurred in his journals with the entry of 2

May 1866: 'Coaching with W. H. Pater this term. Walked with him on Monday evening last, April 30' (*JP*, 133).

Only a few years older than the students he coached, Pater was a newly elected Fellow of Brasenose College, a casual tutor, determined, like Matthew Arnold, to avoid in conduct and tutorial precepts the ponderous earnestness of Oxford. Pater at that time was a good deal of a poseur, possibly to distract attention from his ugliness and his rebellion against Christianity. Pater, in contrast to his stunningly handsome brother William, had a 'singularly unprepossessing appearance' and, to make matters worse, 'a slightly misformed back', a congenital defect that ran in the family; 'and the Paters, who were rather proud of it than not, called it prettily, "the Pater Poke" '.[71] As an older man Pater must have become far more attractive than he was in Hopkins's day. Will Rothenstein's pencil sketch of him in 1894 shows an amusing face, both pensive and whimsical.[72] But as a young man Pater was considered so ugly that he was known as the 'Caliban of letters'.[73]

Pater and Hopkins must have made an extremely odd pair, the one casual about his tutorial duties to the point of laxness, the other as conscientious about his studies as any morally braced Balliol man could possibly have been; the one so grotesquely ugly that his friends once had a private meeting to discuss which one of them would tactfully beg him to grow a moustache,[74] the other fascinated all his life with the faces and forms of handsome men. There were other considerations more important than either of these that ought to have been a barrier to trust between the two men. Pater had been a 'tremendous Ritualist' as a schoolboy, but the year before his matriculation at Queen's College he had experienced a lightning 'unconversion' whose suddenness had left him shaken.[75] He then began to proselytize as earnestly on behalf of his new non-religion as Hopkins was to do on behalf of the doctrine of the Real Presence.[76] More than one close friend, fearing for his own faith, refused to see Pater again. And even for those of unshaken faith, Pater's flights into and out of devotions to various men and their various causes must have been dizzying to follow, for by 1864 he had been by turns a devotee of 'Keble, Kingsley, Maurice, A. P. Stanley, Heine, Voltaire, Goethe',[77] and toward the end of his life he professed a strong admiration for St Ignatius Loyola.[78] One would have expected Hopkins to have been repelled by such flightiness, but he merely commented tersely: 'Pater talking two hours against Xtianity' and he continued to harbour a strong affection for his heretic tutor (*JP*, 138, 1866).

When Hopkins first started to study with Pater in 1866, the recluse of Brasenose was busy erecting a shell around himself, deliberately isolating himself from old friends, while he formed for himself a 'placid, white marmoreal, monastic, subtle equable, nebulous soul'[79] that could never again be betrayed by the transient loyalties at Oxford and the unstable vagaries of Victorian faith. In one of the religiously determined shifts that occurred in Tractarian Oxford with the regularity of a game of musical chairs, Pater had had to leave Queen's, his own college, in order to accept one of the few non-priestly fellowships available to him throughout Oxford. He was then forced into Brasenose, a college totally uncongenial to him in its tastes and its history.

Pater survived from a human point of view at sporting Brasenose mostly because he was intent upon his own pursuits and was not ambitious for his scholars. Unlike most Oxford tutors during these decades, he went his way and allowed his scholars to go theirs. He thought of an undergraduate as a 'child of nature' whom he hated to see robbed 'of all his grace' by severe study or unnecessary curbs upon the exuberance of youth. To emphasize his kinship with his young charges he gave charming dinners in his room for them,[80] where gauche undergraduates might find themselves in the company of the great of Oxford and the world beyond.

It is not hard to see why Pater might have been starved for a responsive pupil like Hopkins, who could generate his own intellectual eagerness, and why Pater might have adopted the delicate young Tractarian, like himself a bit of an eccentric, and therefore among the beefy types somewhat beyond the pale. And it is equally easy to imagine how Hopkins could have been attracted to a don who combined 'dainty ways' and a love of beauty with 'ascetic simplicity'. Pater, it seemed, despite his vague reputation for self-indulgence, 'never took afternoon tea' and 'never smoked', and his private meals 'were plain to austerity'.[81]

When the usual Tractarian breach occurred between the two men, it was of Pater's making, not Hopkins's. Just before Hopkins's conversion, Pater had asked Hopkins to spend part of the long vacation with him (*FL*, 38). After the conversion became public, causing a good deal of consternation in the common-rooms, Pater's letter definitely extending the invitation never arrived; and a good deal of hurt and disappointment was summed up in Hopkins's terse comment to a friend: 'Pater has now written' (*FL*, 40, 1867). Soon the breach appeared to have been healed (*JP*, 167, 1868), and after Hopkins's return to Oxford as a Catholic priest, Pater was one of the few Oxonians whom he could bear to see, and much to his own delight and comfort, he saw Pater often.[82]

In the year 1864 Pater circulated among his friends an ephemeral little essay called 'Diaphaneité', which celebrated a man of 'clear, crystal nature', part saint, part philosopher-artist, who lived a life of 'colourless, unclassified purity',[83] deliberately, yet passively 'discontented with society as it is'. Such a soul would be the happy possessor of 'a moral sexlessness, a kind of impotence, an ineffectual wholeness of nature, yet with a divine beauty and significance of its own'.[84] While not aspiring to the deliberate and harsher 'struggle of the *Imitatio Christi*', the crystal man shuns even more the spirit of the *imitatio mundi*, the spirit 'which regards life as a game of chance'.[85] The crystal-souled man observes all colours, passions, clashes, forms, events, but he does not imitate them in his own behaviour; he simply observes and transmits them passively. He possesses the energy neither of the common man nor of the poet, philosopher, or saint, all of whom contend far more directly than he with the common man's assumptions. His soul and his life are 'evanescent shade', too muted in colour to attract attention, but constantly on the alert to see life in others and to interpret it for others. Pater's crystal-souled man does not challenge the committed man; rather he exists 'to fill up the blanks between contrasted types of character', like a soothing interstice between clashing temperaments and philosophies.

Pater's 'crystal soul', who lives far away from 'the noise of axe or hammer', is a clear dismissal of the loud crusades at Oxford. As quietly, yet as obstinately as 'Merry Matt's' impudent *insouciance*, Pater's bland aesthetic emulsion functioned as a protective covering, a theory devised in part to cope with a series of traumatic emergencies. Pater's theory absorbed the best from all the contending worlds and it sanctioned the love and study of nature that appealed so strongly to those Victorians who would be morally healthy as well as morally braced. Pater was trying to construct a belief that was synthetic and reconciliatory rather than divisive. The 'crystal soul' was to practise a 'truthfulness of temper', a receptivity that permits its possessor to see without distorting inaccuracies the intimate, 'life-giving ... affinities' between the 'established order of things', the 'nobler elements in that order', and the 'soul's own elements'.[86]

Here in nebulous form is another forerunner of Hopkins's circular theory of religious art, which also postulates 'life-giving links' between the soul, the 'established order of things', and the 'nobler elements in that order'. What Pater called the 'established order of things' Hopkins called 'inscape'—the exact laws of natural things, their looks and their conduct. What Pater called 'the nobler elements in that order', Hopkins frankly called divine, or the principle of 'instress'. Hopkins used the term 'instress' to mean many things, but its composite meaning encompasses God's plan for the world as it is revealed in the looks and the conduct of natural things—as opposed merely to those things themselves; and instress also signifies man's response to the divine plan as he praises it and makes copies of it in his art. In Hopkins's and Pater's theories, as in Ruskin's and Arnold's, there is an intimate 'life-giving link' between the object or the idea to be observed and the recording sensibilities of the beholder. Despite their obvious religious dissimilarities, all four men are concerned about the crucial moment between observation and transmission, and they all insist that no dishonest Philistinism of any sort should get in the way of the recording and transmitting process.[87] As the crystal soul reveals more and more of its aims, it becomes clearer how much of the animus must have had its origin in Tractarian Oxford:[88]

> There is a violence, an impossibility about men who have ideas, which makes one suspect that they could never be the type of any widespread life. Society could not be conformed to their image but by an unlovely straining from its true order.

The rancour against Oxford becomes even plainer in Pater's jibes against the contentious milieu in which he had received his training and his desire to escape to some scene 'without the noise of axe or hammer'. 'Not the saint only', Pater remarks, but 'the artist also, and the speculative thinker, confused, jarred, disintegrated in the world, as sometimes they inevitably are, aspire for this simplicity to the last'.[89] Pater's slightly malicious argument is that this simplicity is quite beyond them all.

Pater's man with the diaphanous soul has much in common with other Victorian models of young men who are lost of the world through easeful death or through deliberate withdrawal. Arnold's scholar-gypsy and his Thyrsis are both mercifully quit of a sick world, racked with the restless fever of contention. Tennyson's poetry often sketched the dilemmas of stunned minds, 'Second-Rate Sensitive' or otherwise, trying feebly to mediate between conflicting social demands. The death of young Arthur Hallam, Tennyson's closest undergraduate friend, undoubtedly intensified the desire for escape from the futile 'noise of tongues and deeds' and the 'dust of systems and of creeds'.[90] But a strong response to public tensions was apparent in Tennyson even before Hallam's death made him long to rid himself of the insufferable 'noise of life'[91] in contumacious England.

Hopkins's undergraduate poetry also offers several models of tired young men. His 'Alchemist in the City' is afflicted with an 'incapable and cumbrous shame'; he can no longer deal with men—he is now more 'powerless than the blind or lame', and he desires only 'the wilderness/ Or weeded landslips of the shore'. He fancies a suitable retirement from a breathless race he can no longer run, and muses upon a 'houseless shore' and a 'free', 'kind' wasteland, where he will be surrounded by bones of the dead, bare rocks, and 'silence and a gulf of air' (Poem 15, 1865). In another undergraduate poem called 'Heaven-Haven', and subtitled 'A nun takes the veil', the ache for escape is in strong contrast to the pain of combat:

> I have desired to go
> > Where springs not fail
> To fields where flies no sharp and sided hail
> > And a few lilies blow.

> And I have asked to be
> > Where no storms come,
> Where the green swell is in the havens dumb,
> > And out of the swing of the sea.   (Poem 9, 1864)

The emotions evoked here are fully as much those of a man exhausted by prolonged emotional strain as the active response of a woman called to a religious vocation. Another curious poem of Hopkins's undergraduate days only makes sense if we assume that Hopkins was trying to create his own version of a 'crystal soul', a diaphanous person that could hold at bay the irascible luminaries at Oxford. In one poem Hopkins likens himself to a feminine 'slip of comet' whom an onlooker might observe hiding 'in some corner' and 'bridging the slender difference of two stars'. Hopkins's two stars, like Pater's violent revolutionary men, are 'suddenly engender'd/By heady elements'. In this enigmatic poem there is a brief allusion to Gideon, the Israelite, whose people were being ground to destruction between two warring tribes. Hopkins's 'slip of comet' first 'sucks the light as full as Gideon's fleece'; next 'she falls off',

> And then goes out into the cavernous dark.
> So I go out: my little sweet is done:
> I have drawn heat from this contagious sun:
> To not ungentle death now forth I run. (Poem 103, 1864)

In these works of Tennyson and the three Oxonians, Arnold, Pater, and Hopkins, the archetypal court-country quarrel, with its undertone of pastoral longing, has acquired a more sombre mood than one usually finds in earlier centuries. In these Victorian examples, the pastoral mode is far from the delightful Renaissance convention that may or may not mask personal bitterness. The bitterness is plain and there is usually no vigorous pleasure in the scenes to which the escaping souls remove themselves. In Pater's essay the pastoral note is more inferential than actual, but all these literary figures long to leave the Victorian equivalent of 'the court' forever, or at least to stay there above the battle, cocooned in deliberate impotence. The conventional shepherd's pipe, the symbol of pastoral felicity, is absent, or when it sounds, it has taken on much of the weariness or the harshness of the Victorian scene at Oxford and elsewhere.

If Hopkins's early pastoral poetry followed older nineteenth-century models, and if he often expressed feelings of impotent frustration under the mask of justified withdrawal, he copied his post-Romantic models fully as often in linking beauty and the beholder in an aesthetic chain. His undergraduate love poem 'To Oxford' (Poem 12, 1865) is in part a study of the way the eye of the beholder could first report architectural objects just as they are and then reshape them according to its own private satisfactions, as Matthew Arnold and Pater had both suggested the artist ought to do. One playful stanza even gives the onlooker leave to make imaginative changes in the architecture of a college chapel, so that its horizontal lines, which now displease him, will shape themselves into 'bows', that is into Gothic arches. The poet onlooker accomplishes the alchemic process by what he calls 'falsifying' or 'visual compulsions', a wilful redecorating of the chapel before him, so that its lines may now conform in his imagination to his new-found admiration for Gothic architecture. Here Hopkins seems to be anti-cipating by almost a decade what Pater was later to demand of all artists and lovers of art. In the 'Conclusion' to *The Renaissance* Pater insisted that the artist's impressions of objects are even more important than the objects he loves, whereas Arnold merely suggested they were equally important. Hopkins also seems to be saying here 'What is this engaging chapel to me?', as though he were trying on, first Arnold's aesthetic theories, then going a step further and adopting for the moment, something like Pater's imperiously self-derived aestheticism.

Hopkins's poem 'To Oxford' was written the week after Easter in 1865, during one of those spiritual crises that were the almost inevitable lot of the religious combatants at Oxford during the Tractarian wars.

48

For Hopkins this crisis proved to be one of the most severe trials he was ever to undergo.[92]

Even after the onset of the spiritual crisis, Hopkins's love of Oxford did not wane. If anything it became deeper and more tender, as though he were unconsciously seeing Oxford as the scene of past delight and present anxiety, and as though he sensed the imminence of far greater anxiety to come. The undertone in Hopkins's love poem to Oxford is distinctly elegiac, and yet it was written ostensibly as a conventional *jeu d'esprit*; and despite the tinge of melancholy, Hopkins made attractive use of the sonnet convention. Oxford herself is the lovely lady whom all men of gentle hearts are bound to love:

> New-dated from the terms that reappear,
> More sweet-familiar grows my love to thee,
> And still thou bind'st me to fresh fealty
> With long-superfluous ties, for nothing here
> Nor elsewhere can thy sweetness unendear.

The third, fourth, and fifth lines contain a flash of insight into events to come, as though the poet were attempting to ward off loss by vehement protestation. The lines express the assurances of a man whose devotion is at its peak and who fears that once it wanes it can never be recaptured. The first stanza parades the usual catalogue of the lady's charms, in this case, her musical towers, her groves, and her parks, and it offers the usual modest acknowledgment that the lady Oxford will undoubtedly 'other suitors move':

> And all like me may boast, impeached not,
> Their special-general title to thy love.

Stanza II refers to the restoration that had been going on at Oxford from the end of the eighteen-fifties and was in full swing at this time.[93] Hopkins had found the Balliol chapel 'beautiful' when he first came up to Oxford (*FL*, 74). With his new respect for Gothic architecture, his tastes in the 'beautiful' had changed. If the chapel in stanza II is the Balliol chapel, Hopkins would now have come to despise Butterfield, the restorer of 1857, who had decorated the chapel walls with horizontal bands of pink stone, alternating them with bands of dark stones. The chapel became known as 'Butterfield's pink obscenity',[94] and it looks as though Hopkins concurred in the judgment:

> Thus, I come underneath this chapel-side,
> So that the mason's levels, courses, all

The vigorous horizontals, each way fall
In bows above my head, as falsified
By visual compulsion, till I hide
The steep-up roof at last behind the small
Eclipsing parapet; yet above the wall
The sumptuous ridge-crest leave to poise and ride.

Stanza II represents one of the earliest direct examples of Hopkins's rejection of the sordid present for the more satisfactory past, the modern for the medieval. It must have struck him that the architectural restoration going on at Oxford would be as futile as the spiritual restoration represented by the Tractarian revival of the 'sixties.

In its sober way Hopkins's poem to Oxford is a repetition of his anxious cry to his mother two years earlier: 'I am almost too happy' (*FL*, 79, 1863). The poet who wrote 'To Oxford' is already a more mature man than the excited fresher who had made himself breathless between classes rushing up and down the stairs leading to his tower room at Balliol (*FL*, 69, 1863), and who boasted to his mother of his social success with the proud remark: 'At the present rate it appears likely I shall know all Oxford in six weeks. I have not breakfasted in my room for 10 days I think' (*FL*, 75, 1863).

If Hopkins's passion for Oxford was quieter now in the spring of 1865, there was good reason for it. During the winter he had met Robert Bridges's friend, Digby Dolben, an appealing young Tractarian from Eton, who was hoping to matriculate at Balliol the following year. Once Dolben left Oxford after failing his entrance examinations, Hopkins never saw him again, but as Bridges commented, Hopkins 'must have been a good deal with him, for Gerard conceived a high admiration for him, and always spoke of him afterwards with great affection'.[95] Dolben and Hopkins exchanged poems,[96] but there was apparently something in Hopkins that Dolben feared, for the affection seemed to come mostly from Hopkins. By spring, after Dolben had left Oxford, Hopkins was driven to enlist Bridges's support in a sad, sly little way: 'Give my love ... to Dolben. I have written letters to the latter without end without a whiff of answer' (*LB*, 1, 1865?). Hopkins's letter to Bridges was probably written during the long vacation, but it was not until November of the same year that the breach between Hopkins and Dolben, however it came about, was healed in some manner.

All the evidence points to some Tractarian shock to 'the sense of gentle fellowship' that their common religious crisis must have precipitated.[97] Of the two men, Hopkins was the better poet even as an undergraduate. His temperament, for all his tendency toward emotionalism, was far sturdier than Dolben's, and his conversion was not tainted with such adolescent hysteria as he and Dr Newman both suspected Dolben's to be.[98] But in other respects the two young Tractarian poets were uncannily alike. To read descriptions of both of them, then to read Robert Bridges's preface to his collections of Dolben's poems, and above all, to read the poems themselves, is to feel that one is confronting the mind and heart of Gerard Manley Hopkins in another man's skin. Fifteen years after Hopkins had left Highgate, Canon Dixon, who had been teaching there when Hopkins was a student, described his memories of his pupil:

> I think that I remember you in the Highgate School. At least I remember a pale young boy, very light and active, with a very meditative & intellectual face, whose name, if I am not vastly mistaken, was yours. If I am not deceived by memory, that boy got a prize for English poetry. (CD, 4, 1878)

Canon Dixon was not 'vastly mistaken' nor 'deceived by memory', and his retrospective portrait of Hopkins could have been substituted for Bridges's retrospective portrait of Digby Dolben. For Dolben was also 'pale, and of delicate appearance', Bridges's preface informs us; his 'face was thoughtful and his features intellectual'. Dolben had no more natural capacity for games than Hopkins, and with his frailty, he 'was a boy who evidently needed both protection and sympathy'. With his hesitating speech, gentle voice and 'fine dark melancholy eyes', he 'seemed a different species, among the little ruffians a saint, among sportive animals a distressful spirit'.[99]

For Hopkins, the similarity of physique, talents, temperament, and religious aims must have been at first a delight and then a haunting, even shocking experience, as though he had encountered his own double. Both young men had the ardent capacity for discipleship that Victorian Oxford and Victorian Balliol welcomed in its students when it was spontaneously present, and fostered artificially when it was not. Both men worshipped the crucified Christ;[100] and Dolben was already considering conversion to Catholicism and the celibate life. Both men were capable of idealistic affections for their fellow students. Each man knew that the life he contemplated demanded sacrifices beyond his present capacity. Dolben faced the problem more directly than Hopkins; he was then closer to the way of the cross and he was more openly affectionate:[101]

> No, Love! Love! Love! Thou knowest that I cannot,
> I cannot live without Thee. Yet this way—
> Is there no other road to Calvary
> Than the one way of sorrows?

Dolben concluded that there was no other road, that 'happy people are apt to forget something about the prince of this world and perhaps find it out too late'.[102]

Three months after Dolben left Oxford, Hopkins wrote a cryptic sonnet (Poem 13). For all the ambiguity as to its genesis, it was the most personal of his poems so far, and in its own way, one of the most painful poems ever to come from him. Its first four lines—

> Where art thou friend, whom I shall never see,
> Conceiving whom I must conceive amiss?
> Or sunder'd from my sight in the age that is
> Or far-off promise of a time to be—

read like a dirge to all the death-dances of temporal love at Oxford, and it foreshadows the privation of the last sonnets. In those poems the lost friend is Christ, but in this sonnet, the lost friend—

> Thou who canst best accept the certainty
> That thou hadst borne proportion in my bliss—

is clearly an earthly one, and the sonnet expresses fear that 'the sound/ Of God's dear pleadings have as yet not moved' the friend, despite his many 'virtues'.

On the surface this sonnet may look less painridden than the late sonnets of 1885–9. But the very obscurity of its meaning, the lack of coherence between the rather wild parenthetical dashes, and the reiterative cries of one of the original last lines, which reads: 'No, no, no, but for Christ who knew and loved thee' (*JP*, 60), all suggest a poem wrung from him to express some private grief beyond containment.

After Dolben's departure in the winter of 1865, Hopkins's poems deal almost exclusively with themes of loss, leave-takings, weeping, renunciations, disgust with the world and the flesh, fear of the devil, and cries to God for some 'authentic cadence' (Poem 19). He is now haunted by feelings of 'incapable and cumbrous shame'

> Which makes me when with men I deal
> More powerless than the blind or lame.   (Poem 15)

In one poem Hopkins traces an omnipresent sense of sin in his friends and above all in himself:

> Myself unholy, from myself unholy
> To the sweet living of my friends I look.

He now discovers that each friend has one sin, while he himself accumulates all sins:

> And they are purer, but alas! not solely
> The unquestion'd readings of a blotless book—

for in each friend he finds a fault, this 'fault in one . . . that in another', 'though each have one while I have all'. This discovery comes to him as a moral shock:

> And so my trust, confusèd, struck, and shook
> Yields to the sultry siege of melancholy.

He resolves to turn to the divine affection, for nothing mortal is to be trusted:

> And so, though each have one while I have all,
> No *better* serves me now, save *best*: no other
> Save Christ: to Christ I look, on Christ I call.   (Poem 16)

Deploring 'the waste done in unreticent youth' (Poem 17), Hopkins is now caught halfway between heaven and hell, unable to rest in the world of men and of nature that had once brought him such delight and comfort. Now his 'heaven is brass', his 'earth' is 'iron' (Poem 18). His sense of isolation during these months is prophetic of the late sonnets:

> Hear yet my paradox: Love, when all is given,
> To see Thee I must see Thee, to love, love.   (Poem 20)

And his sense of creative failure is as poignant as anything he will know later:

> Trees by their yield
> Are known; but I—
> My sap is sealed,
> My root is dry.   (Poem 127)

And with the despairing cry: 'Therefore how bitter, and learnt how late, the truth!' (Poem 17), he foreswears all past loyalties, commitments, and affections, and resolves to listen to the 'authentic cadence . . . which ends those only strains' he can 'approve' (Poem 19).

It was on 12 March 1865, only a few weeks after Dolben had left Oxford for good, that Hopkins made this entry in his journal: 'A day of the great mercy of God.' On the next page the journal contains the entry: 'I confessed on Saturday, Lady Day, March 25', as though the rite were new to him. On 6 November he made one of his most dramatic yet enigmatic entries: 'On this day by God's grace I resolved to give up all beauty until I had his leave for it;—also Dolben's letter came for which Glory to God.' By December, Hopkins was in confession with Pusey (*JP*, 58–9, 71).

Two years after Digby Dolben left Oxford he was drowned at the age of nineteen. There was no reason to suppose he had committed suicide, yet nobody could explain his collapse in shallow water. Even the relatively unemotional Bridges was apparently moved by Dolben's life and death; he published Dolben's poems posthumously and he provided an affectionate biography as a preface to the poems. For Hopkins the shock of Dolben's death was greater than mere loss. Dolben had not yet become a Catholic, although, as he wrote Dr Newman just before he was drowned, Hopkins's conversion had persuaded him to do so (*JP*, 326). Years later Hopkins was still pursued by anxiety about his friend's eternal salvation (*JP*, 236, 1873), and he could only pray that Dolben's intention to be received into the Roman community would save him.

As soon as Hopkins heard of Dolben's death, he wrote to Bridges enclosing Dolben's translation of an Italian epitaph, and in Dolben's translation, Hopkins confessed, 'Digby might have written for his own restless, lonely life':

> I, living, drew thee from the vale,
> Parnassus' height to climb with me.
> I dying, bid thee turn and scale
> Alone, the hill of Calvary.

Hopkins was abroad when Dolben was drowned in June 1867, and by the time he heard of it, he had been a Catholic for almost a year; and Dolben's poem must then have sounded to him like a prophetic voice from his friend's tomb.[103]

By 1868 Hopkins seemed to have reached a temporary plateau of peace about his friend's salvation, if another posthumous poem printed in Lahey's life of Hopkins concerns Dolben. The poem describes two young men separated by the death of one of them. Though the poet cannot now get much beyond 'the story of my life/That he should die and I should live', his grief is made bearable by the reminder of the brevity of life and the hope that when he dies 'by his Priest God then should make' the two men 'one for all eternity' in the fellowship of Christian devotion.[104]

As long as Hopkins officially remained in the Tractarian fold, Christ Church, with her impressive cathedral, her aristocratic traditions, and her caution toward all university reform, was as much a refuge as he could hope for. But once his doubts about the validity of the Church of England began to overwhelm him, one watches him undergoing the classical struggle of all the Tractarians who converted to Rome. He had convinced himself long before his conversion that he would not be risking his immortal soul if he were to become a Roman Catholic. But the moment he was convinced that he would be risking his soul if he did not, he could no longer fool himself with the Tractarian fiction that the Church of England was the Catholic Church in England, that Oxford, as the headquarters of the Oxford movement, was 'the head and fount of Catholicism in England and the heart' as well (*FL*, 16, 1864), or that Rome, not England, was in a state of schism; 'such people' who believed things of this sort were themselves schismatics, he informed Liddon respectfully but firmly, and therefore they were 'under sentence of loss of their souls' (*FL*, 32, 1866).

Under these conditions speedy reception into the Roman Catholic Church was not only deeply to be desired, but entirely logical. As he wrote Liddon, 'I can hardly believe anyone ever became a Catholic because two and two make four more fully than I have' (*FL*, 31, 1866). And once he had found his way to Rome both by faith and by reason, he felt compelled to warn his father: 'if I were to delay and die in the meantime I shd. have no plea why my soul was not forfeit.'

Only an exile could imagine how unbearable Hopkins's spiritual loneliness must then have been. When his father begged him to delay his reception and to consult Pusey and Liddon, it must have been an ordeal to be forced to say:

> Dr. Pusey and Mr. Liddon were the only two men in the world who cd. avail to detain me: the fact that they were Anglicans kept me one, for arguments for the Church of England I had long ago felt there were none that wd. hold water, and when that influence gave way everything was gone.

Hopkins was forced to administer even more unpleasant medicine to his father. The Roman Catholic Church, he wrote, 'strictly forbids all communion in sacred things with non-Catholics'. By 'communion' Hopkins meant not only the sacraments, but religious arguments; and then he was driven by his very isolation to do the forbidden thing and to argue with his father:

> You speak of the claims of the Church of England, but it is to me the strange thing that the Church of England makes no claims: it is true that Tractarians make them for her and find them faintly or only in a few instances borne out for them by her liturgy, and are strongly assailed for their extravagances while they do it (*FL*, 92, 94, 93, 1866).

This paragraph suggests how skilful a polemicist Hopkins had become and how much he had learned from Victorian Oxford. For he had summed up the dogmatic weaknesses in both warring Anglican parties represented at Oxford; Broad Churchmen such as Jowett claimed far too little for the Church of England to satisfy the emotions and the minds of profoundly devout men who required infallibility, whereas the Tractarian priests, such as Pusey and Liddon, claimed far too much. The day before Hopkins was received at Birmingham, he wrote his mother that Liddon was 'intellectually inconsistent', and as for Dr Pusey, whom Hopkins revered 'most of all men in the world', Pusey was guilty of a 'confusion of mind' that was downright 'puzzle-headed' (*FL*, 98, 1866).

Of all the figures in the Oxford movement, Dr Pusey was the most tragic. For all his formidable talents, he lacked Newman's wit and urbanity; he also lacked Liddon's serene charm and his ability to melt crowds from the pulpit. Over the years Pusey had become embittered by a series of private and public catastrophes; the first of these was the loss of Newman, his closest friend, to Rome. His wife, his daughter, and his only son had all died young, and after his wife's death, he 'never after ceased to pray as he daily passed her grave, never dropped his black crape stole, never again would attend a chapter dinner'.[105] His latest grief had occurred only six months before Hopkins's reception; the death of John Keble, who with Newman and himself had made up the awesome triumvirate of the eighteen-thirties and -forties, had been a most 'stunning blow',[106] and all the more so because Pusey interpreted all deaths and desertions to Rome as divine punishments visited upon his unworthy self.

Pusey's reaction to each death and each wave of conversions was to assign himself greater and greater penances. 'When he took Keble as his confessor, one of his self-imposed rules, happily rejected, was "not to smile, if I can help it, except with children".' Some of his more austere suggestions for penance were adopted by the Brotherhood of the Holy Trinity, the society of Tractarian dons and students that had attracted Hopkins for a time; but two proposals, 'that members should always walk with their eyes turned to the ground (as he did), or failing that, wear round their loins a girdle of flannel as a token of self-restraint, were not adopted'.[107]

Pusey's confusion, the 'puzzle-headedness' of which Hopkins spoke, was of course, common to all Tractarian priests; they wanted to choose that part of Catholic dogma they could accept, and reject what they did not care for—in short, they wanted Catholicism without Papal infallibility. In certain ways they aped the selectivity of the Broad Churchmen, although it would have shocked them to think so, for while Broad Churchmen rejected their literal readings of the Bible, they, in turn, rejected the literal interpretation of Christ's command to Peter, that he build a Church on Roman stone.

In other ways Pusey suffered the fate of all fellow-travellers. He had been wounded in his expectations of eventual unity between Anglo-Catholics and Roman Catholics; this movement, with himself as one of its founders and its principal supporter, was designed to stem individual conversions to Rome on the one hand, and to check wholesale infidelity on the other. When the movement collapsed ignominiously during the eighteen-sixties, Pusey's distress was pitiful. His heart was always numbed with each individual secession to Rome, particularly with the departure of his most ardent students whose souls he brooded over and whom he called 'my sons'.[108] And now he felt more impotent than before the collapse of the unity movement to stem the flow to Rome.

Hopkins's secession to Rome, and that of his four close Oxonian friends,[109] taught Pusey afresh how perennially the Anglican sowing became a Roman harvest. To Pusey, as to all Tractarians, it was a sickening spectacle to watch men whom he had brought to a new flush of Christian worship, deserting the Anglican Church, one by one; and it must have begun to dawn upon him that the more devout they were, and the more they trusted Tractarian evangelicalism, the more likely conversion to Rome became. Hopkins had clearly been one of the most devout of Pusey's 'sons', and after Pusey had rejected him, Hopkins rather pathetically tried to urge this role upon Dr Newman, for he closed his second letter to Newman with the valediction: 'Believe me, dear Father, your affectionate son in Christ, Gerard Manley Hopkins' (*FL*, 30, 1866).

Hopkins must have been particularly feeling the need of a father in Christ just then, for Pusey never forgave a convert. And it must have made matters all the more terrible for Pusey to think of Newman, once his own brother in Christ, now his most dangerous enemy, sitting like a spider in its web at the Birmingham Oratory, waiting to catch the ardent young Tractarian flies from Oxford. Nothing else excuses the brutality of Pusey's last letter to Hopkins (*FL*, 400, 1866). In it Pusey refused to see Hopkins, called him a 'pervert', an ugly Tractarian nickname for Roman converts, and accused him of supporting the cause of infidelity. The slovenly spelling and punctuation, and the violently accusatory tone all reveal a man sick with pain at the ripping open of old wounds. Hopkins could not have known the particular nature of Pusey's shock; but he had learned his 'Puseyism' right from its source, and he too could be obdurate, even brutal. Thereafter he spoke contemptuously of anything that reminded him of Pusey, the 'Puseyites', and indeed, the whole Tractarian movement. Pusey himself was to live on in his isolation until 1882, attacked from the left and the right, counter-attacking heresy wherever he saw it, 'ever resistant, protesting, excommunicating'.[110]

If Pusey clearly lacked 'the sense of gentle fellowship' that was then a significant feature of the Oxonian ethos, Liddon equally clearly exemplified it. And so, for all the shock of it, Pusey's brutality to Hopkins may have been a blessing compared to Liddon's affectionate pleadings to Hopkins to stay where he was in their common Church. Although Hopkins often begged or ordered his friends to convert, and thus to save their souls, with the Rev. Henry Parry Liddon of Christ Church and past Vice-Principal of St Edmund's Hall, he would not dare to do so, no matter how great the risk he feared for Liddon's soul. In fact, he was subjected to a dose of counter-proselytizing that must have added immeasurably to his sufferings. Liddon's letters contained the typical Oxonian endearments, allusions to Hopkins's sorrowing father, dogmatic forays, and finally the familiar Tractarian argument that the would-be convert to Rome was guilty of wilfulness and of the sin of private judgment (*FL*, 402–4, 1866).

Despite his own obvious distress at the step Hopkins was about to take, Liddon's generosity contrasted sharply with Pusey's rage, for he ended all his pleading letters 'affectionately'. Yet for him, as for all Tractarians, these conversions opened up old wounds of which Hopkins could have no knowledge. Wherever moderate Anglicans

were in power, Tractarians were made to suffer professionally with
each wave of successions to Rome. To the Broad Churchmen, as to the
Anglicans at large and to the dissenting sects, the Tractarians were the
Trojan horses who had brought about the re-establishment of the
Catholic hierarchy in England, while Parliament stood impotently
watching. Liddon had been one of the Tractarians who had been
professionally punished because of the numbers of Roman converts
who had first tasted Tractarian practices under his care. And now, as
before, he was torn between duty and affection; he knew he should
release dangerous Tractarians to Rome as swiftly as they would go,
possibly for his own sake, but above all in order to prevent possible
infection for the other penitents under his care, and yet he longed to
keep these wayward Anglicans with him, not only because he loved
them, but in hopes that the Catholic ardour he had induced in them
might be contained within the English Church.[111]

Liddon must have been one of the most winsome men in a place
abounding in them. Not only was he extremely good-looking[112]—and
Hopkins frankly adored good looks in men—but he possessed qualities
that Hopkins prized most of all in close friends: 'in the heart such a
deep insight into what is earnest, tender, and pathetic in human life and
feeling' (CD, 9, 1878). This particular catalogue of Victorian virtues
Hopkins had assigned to Canon Dixon's poetry, but he was assigning
them to Dixon the Anglican priest as well as Dixon the poet, and he
could equally have assigned them to Liddon's ministry at Oxford. It
was at Liddon's feet that Hopkins had first learned how much feeling,
and 'love in particular, is the great moving power and spring of verse'
(LB, 66, 1879), or of any other art whose practitioner wishes to sway
souls rather than to commandeer them. Great poetry must 'touch you'
(FL, 218, 1864), Hopkins had indicated to Baillie when he was still
under Liddon's spell. And that spell must have been 'Beyond saying
sweet', and Liddon must have appeared to Hopkins as the earthly
counterpart of the Christ who emerges out of the waters in The Wreck
of the Deutschland, a 'Father and fondler of heart thou hast wrung'
(Poem 28, 1876). Even one of Liddon's detractors could say of him:
'neither you nor I will ever hear such preaching again.'

A Jesuit poet and an Oxonian of Hopkins's intense religious passion
could hardly have failed to be swayed by the drama of Liddon's Lenten
sermons,[113]

the swarms of undergraduates, herded in galleries, in deep rows, or
crowded into every nook and corner on the floor ... the mighty

hush of expectation; and then the thrill of that vibrant voice, vehement, searching, appealing, pleading. . . . We lived on the memory of it till next Lent came around, and then there we all were again, the same scene enacted itself, the same voice pleaded with us for our souls.

Perhaps far more than Pusey, Liddon was a maker of priests, Roman and Anglican. Apparently he was as persuasive with individuals as with crowds, for he would artlessly stop men he barely knew in the street, in order to discuss the state of their souls;[114] yet nowhere in contemporary accounts of Liddon's ministry was he ever accused of eccentricity. Nor is there any hint of eccentricity in his letters; they breathe a spirit of deep pastoral concern and a genuine humility. In a century of attractive correspondences, these letters are among the most intelligent, the most fair-minded, and the most humane. Combining as he did so much charity and so much intelligence, Liddon must have represented one of the greatest losses to Hopkins of all those appealing young men at Oxford.

Hopkins's poetry may owe something even more specific to Liddon than the Oxonian desire to sway souls by sweetness as well as by light. From the safety of his Anglican fastness, Liddon was an admirer of St Ignatius Loyola, the founder of the Society of Jesus. He was once accused of patterning the greater portion of some of his university sermons upon Loyola's *Spiritual Exercises*. This scandal broke just after Hopkins left Oxford in 1867, and Liddon was forced to offer a public explanation and an apology.[115] Liddon's crime was not so much that he took material from other sources and failed to acknowledge them, for this was not an uncommon practice, even in written sermons; his real offence was that he took material from such a tainted source, with or without awareness. In any case, Hopkins must have 'lived on the memory' of these sermons, and when he came to pick his religious order, his past confessor's admiration for St Ignatius may have weighed more heavily with him than he knew.

Pusey and Liddon are characteristic of two sorts of Tractarians— perhaps two distinct sorts of Christians—the one fierce and prophetic, as though he saw himself as the human agent of God the wrathful Father, and the other the prototype of the ardent Paraclete, come down to earth in the shape of a man to save mankind. Hopkins himself adopted both models in his poetry and in his ministry, for he too was God's agent, and God for him was both God the Father and rebel wringer, and God the Son, comforter and Saviour. Hopkins's poetry reflects this apparent conflict of roles quite consciously; and wherever he first learned these two Biblical models, he saw each one separately re-enacted in the flesh by his first two confessors who taught him penance at Oxford.

When one considers alone the loss of a man like Liddon, there was considerable heroism in Hopkins's determination to preserve his sanity and keep at his books. That he was able to do so he owed partly to Dr Newman's vast experience with the shocks of conversion and with the total losses it entailed. After Newman's conversion, the world of converted Anglo-Catholics had come in ever greater numbers to consult him. And as an old Oxonian, he was able to comfort them and to assure them that what they now anticipated missing, almost with the grief of widowhood, they would not always miss so sorely. But Newman never underestimated what the Oxonian convert gave up. He admitted openly in the *Apologia* that the years at Oxford were 'in a human point of view, the happiest times' in his life. Here, he said, he 'was truly at home'.[116]

Newman's hero in the autobiographical novel *Loss and Gain* expresses the full flavour of the title:[117]

> Whatever he was to gain by becoming a Catholic, this he had lost; whatever he was to gain higher and better, at least this and such as this he never could have again. He could not have another Oxford, he could not have the friends of his boyhood and youth in the choice of his manhood.

Once Hopkins had made 'the choice of his manhood', he yearned for some legitimate and immediate escape from Oxford. Newman understood the longing for retreat, while at the same time he cut down the only legitimate retreat possible. Admittedly, Newman wrote: 'It is not wonderful that you should not be able to take so great a step without trouble and pain.' Yet Newman's next comforting letter urged Hopkins to stay at Oxford for the time being:

> As to your retreat, I think we may have misunderstood each other ... it does not seem to me that there is any hurry about it—your duty is to make a good class. Show your friends at home that your becoming a Catholic has not unsettled you in the plain duty that lies before you.   (*FL*, 405, 1866)

Newman's call for 'the plain duty that lies before' a Balliol man, discreet as it was, came as a familiar directive to Hopkins, and he responded appropriately. Six months later he took his first class in the schools, and shortly afterward left for a trip to the Continent.

Although as a Roman Catholic and later as a Jesuit priest, Hopkins 'could not have another Oxford', for 'this and such as this he never could have again', there was one insatiable interest that he could take with him, an interest he had discovered as a schoolboy and cultivated at Oxford. Under the silent tutelage of Ruskin, Hopkins had continued all through his ordeal to make verbal sketches and pen and pencil drawings of everything interesting that came before his eyes. His analyses of leaves and berries, of wheat fields, wheat stalks, or of streams, wet and dry, were rhapsodic yet precise, as though the pane-gyric accuracy that Ruskin demanded of the artist was beneficial in times of trouble. Hopkins went on sketching and describing the city and the countryside, whenever a particular penance did not prevent it (*JP*, 190, 1869), until his final journal entry, broken off in the middle of a sentence; that broken sentence occurs in 1875, the year that he started to work on *The Wreck of the Deutschland*. These Ruskinian sketches and verbal descriptions thus form a bridge between Hopkins's last undergraduate poem and his first mature work as a Jesuit, and they helped him to develop as a poet during the nine years of poetic silence.

Hopkins needed the solace of his quick accurate eye and his rich imagination as he waited in discomfort for the call to his vocation, a call that must have seemed at times as though it would never come. But on 5 May 1868, a year and a half after his reception as a Roman Catholic, he 'resolved to be a religious' (*JP*, 165, 1868). On 1 September and 16 September there are more Ruskinian descriptions of cathedral windows, bays, towers, and transepts, as well as comments about rows of cedar flakes and the precise way they hung upon their boughs (*JP*, 187, 189, 1868).

In between these September entries, which had obviously given Hopkins much innocent pleasure and undoubtedly some courage, he recorded all the natural hesitation he must have been feeling, for the entries for 6 and 7 September in his journal repeat the phrase 'said good by' three times. But his courage was high: the descriptions of the various farewells were laconic, as though he did not wish to dwell on them, and the last entry for 7 September ended with the short resolute phrase: '—Then to the Novitiate, Roehampton' (*JP*, 188, 189, 1868).

Ruskin had performed an inestimable service for his young disciple of whom he had never heard. Hopkins's Ruskinian exercises kept his eye and hand active and his imagination supple and responsive to the ways of nature. In this manner,

> The vault and scope and schooling
> And mastery in the mind,
> In silk-ash kept from cooling,
> And ripest under rind—   (Poem 49, 1879),

was Ruskin's gift to Hopkins during the most distressing time at Oxford and the time when he was learning to become a good Catholic. For nine years Hopkins's poetic talents, 'in silk-ash kept from cooling', now ripened 'under rind', until the day his superior gave him permission to embark upon *The Wreck of the Deutschland.*

'Heaven's Sweet Gift':
Hopkins, Ruskin, and the
Plenitude of God

Hopkins   God's utterance of himself in himself is God the Word, outside himself is this world. This world then is word, expression, news of God. Therefore its end, its purpose, its purport, its meaning, is God and its life or work to name and praise him. Therefore praise [is] put before reverence and service.

(S, 129, 1882)

Ruskin   ALL GREAT ART IS PRAISE
The art of man is the expression of his rational and disciplined delight in the forms and laws of the Creation of which he forms a part.   (XV, 351)

Hopkins   I am sketching (in pencil chiefly) a good deal. I venture to hope you will approve of some of the sketches in a Ruskinese point of view:—if you do not, who will, my sole congenial thinker on art?   (*FL*, 202, 1863)

Hopkins   What do then? how meet beauty? Merely meet it; own,
Home at heart, heaven's sweet gift; then leave, let that alone.
Yea, wish that though, wish all, God's better beauty, grace.   (Poem 62, 1885)

Hopkins's critics have often remarked, and rightly so, that without the *Exercises of St. Ignatius*, the poems would not be what they are, but something entirely different. The text of St Ignatius, that man 'was created for this end: to praise, reverence and serve the Lord his God, and by this means to arrive at eternal salvation',[1] shaped Hopkins's life and his poetry with its peremptory purpose, and the discipline within the Society of Jesus trained him in many of the 'means' to 'this end'.

It is equally true that without Ruskin's works, Hopkins's poems would also not be what they are, but something entirely different. Hopkins's schoolboy experiments with Ruskinian realism and his lifelong shaping and reshaping of Ruskin's principles according to his own religious ends, are thus as great a tribute to the 'Ruskinese point of view' as the serious praise Ruskin drew from eminent Victorians, or the lighthearted vogue of quoting—or misquoting—Ruskin's sonorous prose in popular novels.[2]

The influence of one man upon another is a difficult and delicate matter to assess. It would be an impossible task, and hardly a profitable one, to attempt to delimit the exact areas of Hopkins's debt to Ruskin, from one moment to the next throughout this chapter, or to decide where the uncanny shock of the 'Ruskinese point of view' in Hopkins's prose and poetry is attributable to direct imitation, as Hopkins several times said it was, and where it ought to be explained as a mere startling similarity of vision, bred, perhaps, of a common temperament, a common intellectual climate, or similar education and reading.

One may fairly argue, for example, that Hopkins learned to trust his own passionate social anger from Carlyle, Ruskin's master, and what Victorian did not? One might say that the Platonic pairs of opposites—such as hot and cold, swiftness and slowness, dimness and dazzle, sweet and sour—that Hopkins and Ruskin both discovered throughout the phenomenal and the spiritual world would have seemed as natural to Hopkins, the Oxonian Platonist, as to Ruskin, the Oxonian Platonist. One may look to a common familiarity with the great English and European classics and with the Bible to explain their joint preoccupation with principles such as the mimetic function of religious art, nature's infinite variety and nature's specificity, and the great chain of paradoxes throughout creation. But it may be sufficient for our purposes to know that to be steeped in the work of either man is to have come a long way in understanding the work of the other.

It would have been strange indeed if a man of Hopkins's intellectual curiosity had not been saturated with Ruskin's works. George Eliot insisted that Ruskin had taught his contemporaries 'a truth of infinite value', and that truth was 'realism—the doctrine that all truth and beauty are to be attained by a humble and faithful study of nature, and not by substituting vague forms, bred by imagination on the mists of feeling, in place of definite, substantial reality'.[3] And George Eliot was but one voice in a considerable chorus. The first volume of *Modern*

Painters, published anonymously as the work of 'A Graduate of Oxford', created a 'sensation in the artistic and even in the literary world',[4] said a contemporary later on in the century. Ruskin had hurled a 'bombshell upon the world of painting',[5] and his arguments in favour of the Victorian painter Turner were 'so forcibly put as to fall like a charge of dynamite', not only 'into the camp of the somnolent critics of the day',[6] said another contemporary, but into the camp of the great and the near-great as well. Tennyson,[7] Wordsworth,[8] Charlotte Brontë, George Eliot, William Morris and the Pre-Raphaelites, Cardinal Wiseman, Octavia Hill,[9] all admired the book or went on a campaign to borrow a copy if they could not afford it. Benjamin Jowett, chary of praise for Oxonians, even graduates, was both quick and warm in his commendations of *Modern Painters*, I, and unwittingly he helped to set the fashion in early Ruskin criticism: Ruskin, his admirers all claimed, had made them see the world around them with a totally new pair of eyes. This aesthetic awakening must have been something of a shock to the omniscient Jowett, who was normally quite contemptuous of the moral claims of poets and painters or their champions:[10]

> I have read it all through with the greatest delight; the minute observation and power of description it shows are truly admirable. . . . Since I have read it I fancy I have a keener perception of the symmetry of natural scenery. The book was written by Ruskin, a child of genius, certainly.

By the late eighteen-fifties, 'Oxford was a stronghold of Ruskin worship, and year by year sent out fresh recruits to join his crusade'. There were, of course, dissenters and a large party of indifferent critics, and there were the inevitable mockers and caricaturists of a suddenly successful man; but a distinct party of the cultivated people inside and outside of Oxford, or those who wished to be considered cultivated, 'professed (if they did not possess) an intimate knowledge of his books and an enthusiastic agreement with his principles'.[11]

Professor John Rosenberg has succinctly described the dimensions of Ruskin's gifts to his countrymen: 'By writing sermons he got the Victorians to lend him their ears that he might open their eyes.'[12] How lovely it must have been for the heirs of a Calvinist past to feel themselves entitled, even more, required, to open their eyes and free their senses in order to prove to the civilized world and to themselves that they were exercising their consciences. For how else, Ruskin demanded, is the truth of nature, which is also the truth of God revealed to man, 'to be ascertained and accumulated? Evidently, and only, by perception and feeling.' The artist's 'sight' and his 'soul' must be the tools with which he witnesses 'Nature' and 'the universe': no other considerations were to shape his reproductions of nature:

> The whole of that witness depends on its being eye-witness; the whole genuineness, acceptableness, and dominion of it depend on the personal assurance of the man who utters it. All its victory depends on the veracity of the one preceding word, 'Vidi'. (xi, 49)

Ruskin called this aesthetic law 'the *innocence of the eye*', by which he meant 'a sort of childish perception' of nature, as a blind man would see the world around him 'if suddenly gifted with sight' (xv, 27n).

As an undergraduate, Hopkins used almost the same phrase, including the italics, to describe 'the *innocence of the eye*'. The artist who lacked this first Ruskinian prerequisite, Hopkins said, was one whose 'eye had not been trained to look severely at things, apart from their associations, *innocently* or *purely* as painters say' (*JP*, 77, 1864). Hopkins also said that 'when the innocent eye of the uneducated or of children is spoken of in art it is understood that their sense is correct, that is that they are free from fallacies implying some education, but not that it is strong or definite' (*JP*, 80, 1865). Hopkins meant that the artist must start with the innocent eye of children or the uneducated, but must add moral and aesthetic excitement and technical control as part of the three steps Ruskin outlined for the Christian artist.

Some of Ruskin's profound hold upon his disciples probably sprang from his knowledge of their reading habits (xxix, 501), for he extolled not only 'the pleasure of sight', as gifts of heaven, but the pleasures 'of hearing'; and the gifts of heaven in which Christians could take legitimate pleasure were 'the melody in the voice' and the 'majesty in the thunder' (iv, 45–6). Attending lectures was almost as fashionable a pursuit among the middle classes as reading aloud was among most classes, and many of Ruskin's works were first delivered as lectures. He designed his sonorous style to appeal as fully to the ear as to the eye and the conscience. George Eliot described her intense pleasure in reading Ruskin aloud to George Lewes 'for an hour or so after dinner'.[13] Canon Dixon, Hopkins's friend, enjoyed reminiscing over many a pleasant reading party at Oxford. 'Fulford, Burne-Jones, and Morris were all fine readers' who liked reading to each other.[14]

Morris would often read Ruskin aloud. He had a mighty singing voice, and chanted rather than read those weltering oceans of eloquence as they have never been given before or since, it is most certain. The description of the Slave Ship, or of Turner's skies, with the burden, 'Has Claude given this?' was declaimed by him in a manner that made them seem as if they had been written for no end but that he should hurl them in thunder on the head of the base criminal who had never seen what Turner saw in the sky.

From first to last Hopkins was conscious of his debt to Ruskin. Even while he lay on his deathbed, he dictated a letter in which he casually referred to Ruskin's colour emblems (*FL*, 198, 1889); but even while he was an undergraduate, his championship of Ruskin was almost as partisan and as aggressive as his growing championship of Roman Catholicism. He went on a deliberate campaign to convert Alexander Baillie to the 'Ruskinese point of view', describing to Baillie how much Ruskin was involved in his own development, coining Ruskinian phrases such as 'Nature's self', and informing Baillie that although 'Ruskin often goes astray', nevertheless this man, whose whole life had been devoted entirely to criticism, possessed 'powers which in their line are perhaps equal to those of the men whose works he criticises' (*FL*, 200–4, 1863).

What 'Nature's self' meant to Hopkins is suggested by his remarks to Baillie immediately following the casual announcement of his Ruskinian discipleship:

> I think I have told you that I have particular periods of admiration for particular things in Nature; for a certain time I am astonished at the beauty of a tree, shape, effect etc, then when the passion so to speak has subsided, it is consigned to my treasure of explored beauty and acknowledged admiration and interest ever after, while something new takes its place in my enthusiasm. The present fury is the ash, and perhaps barley and two shapes of growth in leaves and one in tree boughs and also a confirmation of fine-weather cloud.
>
> (*FL*, 202)

This statement would have served notice on any Ruskin lover— which Baillie was not—that Hopkins had been looking at Ruskin's chapter headings in the first volume of *Modern Painters* and had obediently been making exact studies according to the instructions in chapters such as 'Of Truth of Vegetation' or 'Of Truth of Clouds' in particular, and of Ruskin's principles of nature's infinite variety. The twin principles of accuracy and passion are here in this letter: Hopkins admits to being possessed of a 'fury', an 'enthusiasm', a 'passion, so to speak' for what he sees, but he sees precisely. He does not merely see 'leaves'; he sees two specific 'shapes of growth in leaves'. He does not go into rhapsodies over a whole sky full of clouds; he is enthusiastic over a particular conformation of one 'fine-weather cloud'. In these letters to the recalcitrant Baillie, Hopkins was proudly placing himself in the ranks of those who could honestly claim with Ruskin 'the veracity of the one preceding word, "Vidi" '.

The first volume of Ruskin's *Modern Painters* particularly stressed the three essential steps the artist must take in his work, without which Ruskin refused to call him an artist. The first step is to see what is before him, and to see it quietly, and accurately, that is to say, 'innocently'. The second step is to respond, and the third is to reproduce what he sees. The response, of course, depends on what the artist honestly sees with his innocent eye; the honest response to something awesome would be awe, and the honest response to something ugly would be disgust.

Ruskin called the properties in natural and man-made objects 'the word of truth'; and the 'word of truth' about nature is that she is 'one infinite variety': 'There is no bush on the face of the globe exactly like another bush;—there are no two trees in the forest whose boughs bend in the same network, nor two leaves on the same tree which could not be told one from the other, nor two waves in the sea exactly alike.' But 'the word of truth', or what the artist sees before him, contains a double truth—'material truth' and ideal truth; 'material truth' resides in the exact properties in things, in the actual lines, colours, spaces, over-lappings, clashes, and harmonies of still objects and objects often in motion. Ideal truth is not a distortion of material truth, nor is it in conflict with material truth; it is drawn from material truth even while it transcends this truth of exact properties, because it is the 'ideal form' of material truth, 'fixed upon the imagination for its standard of truth'.

In step one, the artist uses his innocent eye to see material truth or the truth of exact properties in things. In step two, he begins to distinguish between material truth and ideal truth; but in step two, he must make an even further distinction, and that is the distinction between material truth and ideal truth emanating from objects before him, and the truth of 'emotions, impressions, and thoughts' that material and ideal truth have simultaneously elicited from him (III, 104, 145–6). And for profoundly important moral reasons, the second step momentarily frees the heart, the mind, and the senses, or the organs of moral and aesthetic enthusiasm, from the innocent eye, or the tabulating organ. Only then can the artist proceed to take step three. Now he is free to reproduce on his canvas or with his pen exactly what he has seen and something else as well, the ideal form as it is derived not only from what he has seen, but from the moral and aesthetic energy with which he has seen it.

To achieve Ruskin's three steps, the candidate for the title of God's artist in residence must accomplish a complex psychological feat. Ruskin was painfully aware that most human beings can separate seeing, feeling, and doing all too easily—Victorian society produced organization men fully as often as it produced their opposites, men armed with nothing but loose sensibility and bathetic good will. One of the ways an industrial society disciplines its members into efficient acquiescence is by inducing them to type-cast themselves and then punishing them if they refuse to live entirely within this limited role. Two of the most common Victorian types were proud to have turned themselves into perceiving and tabulating machines after the model of James Mill or Gradgrind, machines without moral vision and without charity, or into inefficient skinfuls of formless, if noble emotions. Ruskin's great gift to his contemporaries, and to all artists and peda-gogues, is his insistence that the perceiving and tabulating faculties are not the same as the moral and emotional faculties, nor are either of these the same as the technical skills needed for reproducing nature. All three talents are essential for the artist who is searching for the hint of God's soul upon the flesh of things; and artists must separate step one from step two, and step two from step three, not so that they can choose between seeing, loving, copying, and forever afterward keep these faculties in watertight compartments, but so that they might feel the distinction and be profoundly aware that to have achieved the one is not to have achieved all three.

The first two steps, then, of seeing and responding appropriately, should be momentarily separated only so that the exact quality of things to be praised or condemned and the vital release of feeling can be savoured and valued, each for its own sake. Step three presupposes that accurate perception and unabashed response—adoration, awe, fear, disgust—come together in full technical strength in a work of art. Ruskin dared to say something that ought not to have been radical to his generation, or to any other, and yet it was. Man, Ruskin claimed, has the right to the benevolent exercise of *all* his God-given faculties, his perceptions, his affections, his honest feelings, and his technical proficiencies. All three are to be placed at the service of the single task, each in its proper amount and each at the proper moment in sequence.

Any man who denies this right on any pretext whatsoever, except for the most lofty aim imaginable, and who denies it either to himself, to his peers, or to his inferiors, will have performed upon himself or upon another human being a mutilation ultimately fatal either for technical verve or for spiritual energy.

Hopkins's terms 'inscape' and 'instress' correspond roughly to Ruskin's three steps toward a completed art work. 'Inscape' is what the innocent eye sees; 'instress' is God's plan behind nature's inscapes and man's submission to that plan. In step one Hopkins quietly sketched or described natural things. During step two he became aware of his 'fury', 'passion', 'admiration', or 'enthusiasm' for 'Nature's self'. Hopkins's nature poems represent the final step; they are lyric descriptions of what Ruskin called the 'four great component parts of landscape—sky, earth, water, and vegetation'. Far more even than the Pre-Raphaelite painters and poets, whom Hopkins admired as much as Ruskin did, he accepted Ruskin's mighty challenge to contemporary artists: he spent his poetic energies commemorating nature's infinite variety and 'embracing one by one every feeling and lesson of the creation' (III, 253n).

It is almost impossible to exaggerate the importance of the innocent eye in Hopkins's poetry or Ruskin's concomitant principle: 'ALL GREAT ART IS PRAISE' (XV, 351). Nature is the 'art of God' (XXIX, 157) Ruskin had taught his disciples, and reverence for the lovely things God has made suited Hopkins's ardent temper: 'As we drove home the stars came out thick: I leant back to look at them and my heart opening more than usual praised our Lord to and in whom all that beauty comes home' (*JP*, 254, 1874).

It is Hopkins's enormous strength as an artist, as it is Ruskin's, that emotions, feelings, delicate replies of the soul and the senses, as well as creative 'fury' were all admitted as part of an inclusive methodology, the more chaste because it demanded objectivity, and the richer and the more humane because it permitted subjective emotions. This healthy readjustment of Platonism is founded in a legitimate paradox. The real and the particular must lead to Ruskin's 'constant character—the ideal form' (III, 146), but it must never lead away from it. Conversely the ideal must never lead away from the real, since there is a vital yet mysterious relation between them. And there is even a readjustment of Aristotle's theories of art here, for the Ruskinian twin principles of mimetic and laudatory art include nature as well as men, because natural objects, like humans, were capable of actions worthy of the artist's imitations.

Since Ruskin lived in a blatantly predatory society, and since he was intensely aware of it, he was equally aware that he was asking all artists to run a race with time. For the faster nature, the mother of us all, disappeared under the rape of industry, the more it behoved artists to praise her and to imitate her, so that they might fill their canvases and cram their pages with memories of her generous profusion and her beneficent powers. Partly for that reason, Ruskin believed that the 'function of architecture', as of all art, is, as far as may be, to 'replace' nature, not only in her patterns, her growth, and her actions, but in her moods (IX, 411).

Hopkins announced to the world that he intended to follow Ruskin's twin principles of mimetic and laudatory art in his first poem, 'The Escorial'. In the sixth stanza of this schoolboy poem, Hopkins makes a graceful bow to Ruskin. He describes a fictional Gothic frieze, so filled 'with flowing tracery of engemmed rays' that one beauty melted into another. Hopkins's imaginary 'foliag'd crownals (pointing how the ways/Of art best follow nature)' are carrying out art's mimetic function, since they are imitating nature's lovely, careless profusion (Poem 1, 1860). In 'The Escorial', Hopkins's fictional architect has taken all three of Ruskin's steps, albeit a little self-consciously, and thus qualified as one of God's artists in residence: he has seen nature's generous profusion and her infinite variety. First he reproduced her profusion and her variety, and then he praised what he saw.

If there were any danger that Hopkins's 'furies' would lead him into pantheistic raptures unbecoming to a Tractarian or a Jesuit, the very precision of Ruskin's innocent eye would have prevented anything of the sort. For a man of firm dogma, such as Hopkins, Ruskin may have been unsatisfactorily vague about the characteristics of God, the Planner, but he was absolutely trustworthy about the plan itself, and he never confused the plan with the Planner, as Romantic poets were apt to do. In one of his lectures on the ash spray, he described for his audience, in minute and copious detail, exactly how ash sprays look, leaf by leaf and spray by spray, and he demonstrated how one deduced thereby examples both of the laws of generic plenitude and of specific creation. The doctrine of generic plenitude is an ancient commonplace implicit in both Plato's *Timaeus* and the first book of Genesis. It suggests nature's infinite variety according to types. God was generous to man in providing him with an infinite profusion of animal and vegetable types, all meant for his joy and his use. The doctrine of specific creation, which Hopkins first came upon in Ruskin and later in Duns Scotus, teaches that God created each living thing with its own specific peculiarities that would never be exactly recapitulated in another created thing. There is another paradox in these twin laws, for just as all creatures must live according to the laws of their type, they must also live according to the laws of their specific being. Equally, all artists must try to reproduce not only the laws of generic plenitude in picturing nature, but also the laws of each creature's specific being.

'Now nature abhors equality and similarity', Ruskin informed his audience, thus hinting at the doctrine of specific creation or the laws of individuality in each created thing. Yet each leaf and each spray conformed simultaneously to the doctrine of generic plenitude, that is, it illustrated the principles of nature's infinite variety as to types or genera. Ash sprays, Ruskin explained, grow in even-numbered pairs of leaves, that is, there will be two, four, or six pairs of leaves to a stalk, let us say, with an odd leaf invariably forming an elongated apex at the tip of the spray. Each spray, with its pairs of leaves and its tip leaf is itself paired with its own numerical type or genus: a five-leaved spray—two pairs and a tip leaf—will be paired on the other side of the stalk with another five-leaved spray, whereas a thirteen-leaved spray, six pairs and a tip leaf, will be paired on the other side of the stalk with another thirteen-leaved spray, and so on. Specific creation and generic plenitude are both exemplified, for each leaf is a different shape from every other one, and each spray differs from the one above or below as to numbers of leaves. Yet the pairing not only of leaves but of sprays exemplifies generic plenitude. And this doctrine is further demonstrated by the arrangement of neighbouring pairs of stalks. Pairs of seven-leaved sprays will have as their immediate neighbour on the bough only pairs of nine-leaved sprays or five-leaved sprays, that is, the odd number immediately below or above their own (XII, 25–6).

In the last volume of *Modern Painters*, published three years before Hopkins arrived at Oxford, Ruskin again reverted to the problem of growth in the ash leaf. There are two sides to the leaf, separated by the lobe, a thin filament marking one side of the leaf from the other. The two sides, Ruskin reported, invariably differ impressively as to size, contour, colour, or place of attachment to the lobe, just as each leaf differs in these particulars from every other leaf, thus carrying out the laws of specific creation. But the rule of simultaneous subordination both to the doctrine of specific creation and the doctrine of generic plenitude is not suspended even here (VII, 38–9). Ruskin revealed in another work 'that universally one lobe of a lateral leaf is always larger than the other and the smaller lobe is that which is nearer the central mass'; and he drew some moral lessons about the divine principles of authority and subordination as they apply to human affairs, for the 'lower leaf, as it were, by courtesy', consistently subdued 'some of its own dignity or power, in the immediate presence of the greater or captain leaf', as though it were 'expressing therefore, its own subordination and secondary character' (xv, 186). Each leaf is demonstrating how ordered and restrained it is, even while it avails itself of its divine permission to differ from all other leaves. It thus bears witness to the twin laws of nature's infinite variety, the law of generic plenitude and the law of specific creation.

In 1865 Hopkins also turned to the problem of growth in leaves, and by a natural transition, to the problem of beauty, what it is, and how we recognize it. His undergraduate essay 'On the Origin of Beauty' (1865) is in dialogue form, and like most Socratic imitations, it has a primitive plot and an embryonic cast of characters grouped around a master:

> It was at the beginning of the Long Vacation, and Oxford was nearly empty. The Professor of the newly founded chair of Aesthetics . . . came one day in the evening to New College gardens and found John Hanbury a scholar of the college walking there. They knew each other, and had taken two or three turns under the chestnuts together, when a stranger came up to them and asked if these were the Worcester Gardens. (*JP*, 86)

The stranger introduced himself as 'Middleton', a painter, who had come up to Oxford to paint some frescoes, which were 'being added to the new smoking-room at the Union' (*JP*, 91). The appeal of this essay depends partly upon the quiet way Hopkins used the Socratic dialogue to discuss Ruskinian aesthetics for almost forty pages, and partly upon the way he combined history and local gossip. In 1857 and 1858 the Pre-Raphaelite painters had made themselves much talked about with their Arthurian frescoes on the walls of the new Union debating hall, and for over twenty years there had been a movement on foot to create three endowed chairs of aesthetics at Oxford, Cambridge, and the University of London; when Felix Slade endowed one chair of fine arts at each of these universities, Ruskin, who had several times been mentioned as a candidate for one of the chairs, accepted the Oxford chair in 1870.[15]

Ruskin loved to use the chestnut leaf as an example of nature's infinite variety. Hopkins's imaginary new Professor of Aesthetics began the evening's discussion by pulling off 'one of the large lowest fans of the chestnuts' and demanding of the scholar John Hanbury, 'Do you think this beautiful?' Hanbury answered that it was, and

Hopkins launched his readers into a leisurely exposition of Ruskinian 'Truth of Vegetation': 'You see it consists of seven leaves, the middle largest, diminishing toward the stalk, so that those nearest the stalk are smallest.' 'I see', said Hanbury; 'I had never noticed there were seven before.' But the Professor's lecture on the truth of vegetation was by no means over:

> 'Now if we look about we shall find—yes there is one. There is a fan, do you see? with only six leaves. Nature is irregular in these things. Can you reach it? Now which do you think the more beautiful, the one with six, or the one with seven leaves?'   (*JP*, 87)

Just as Ruskin frequently progressed from nature, to the arts, to morality and thence to divine laws, and just as he probed each example, hoping to deduce both principles of order and principles of legitimate freedom, so the Professor and his two new friends began their discussion with an examination of symmetry and asymmetry in chestnut fans and from there moved to nature's infinite variety and Ruskinian 'Truth of Skies', then to order and freedom in music, painting, drama, and prosody, and finally to the mystery behind the grand scheme. The whole discussion turned upon the Ruskinian antitheses between likeness and difference, smoothness and ruggedness, unity and diversity, restraint and liberty, dominion and subordination.

As the three fictional conversationalists strolled up and down in the scholars' gardens and later went in to drink a companionable dish of tea together, they hardly paused in their search for the grand comprehensive plan behind the antitheses and similarities. 'And the beauty of rhythm is traced to the same causes as that of the chestnut fan, is it not so?' asked the Professor. And Hanbury, the willing disciple, replied, 'Yes, it is' (*JP*, 101).

The whole dialogue turns again and again upon the principle of the innocent eye: 'but perhaps when I have shown you how to look.' 'Do you see?' 'But now, look at this.' 'Now if we look about we shall find. . . .' 'Look here for instance.' 'If you had analysed your admiration of it I think. . . .' The little injunctions to open the eyes to nature's infinite variety, and to synthesize facts into principles, all come from the Professor, as well as the little professorial remarks of reassurance: 'That is very good', or 'Very observant'. The grateful cries of '*Vidi*' all come from the newly sighted pupil Hanbury: 'No, I had never noticed it. . . .' 'Yes, it is so. Well but—No: you are right. How could I not see that, I wonder?'

Despite the rigorous search for the principles of beauty, there is a

strong hint of some unspecified truth of beauty behind human discovery, and whatever it is, it troubles the normally urbane Hanbury:

> 'I really do not know what to say to the contrary; but I am sure
> there is in the higher forms of beauty—at least I seem to feel—
> something mystical, something I don't know how to call it. Is not
> there something beyond what you have explained?'

The Professor gently teases Hanbury over his thirst for a supernatural
explanation. The three conversationalists then discover that their feet
are wet, and they decide to go indoors for tea and more conversation
'by the aid of candlelight'. In the remaining dialogue they keep to 'the
logical ground' (*JP*, 95) with the most scrupulous concern, but
Hopkins's hint of 'something mystical' in the truth of beauty lingers
in the mind, as one suspects it was supposed to do. For instead of
using the Professor to proclaim in Ruskinian sonorities the divine
origins of nature's mysteries, Hopkins slyly puts the suspicion in the
mouth of the fool—or in this case the student—so that the reader can
accept it or not as he chooses.

The 'something mystical' corresponds to Ruskin's principle of a
deliberate mystery in nature behind all her ascertainable laws of
similarity and diversity. It is a Ruskinian paradox of profound importance for the artist. 'There is a continual mystery throughout *all*
spaces, caused by the absolute infinity of things' (VI, 75), yet artists must
'keep organization in the midst of mystery'. They can only do so if they
'lean always to the definite side', and seldom *deliberately* strive for
vagueness, at least in their apprentice years (XV, 87).

No Ruskin scholar would claim for him an easily schematized
philosophy; but there is a schema behind the fluid and rapturous
prose; and the years of 'The Darkening Glass', when Ruskin's utterances were not quite sane, reveal, nonetheless, how intimately and how
firmly the dark side of Ruskin's schema is related to the joy. For even
when it is joyous, 'the Ruskinese point of view' is filled with paradoxes
and contradictions, in imitation of the complex world of fact and value
he surveyed.

When Hopkins discussed art, life, or morals, he too slipped into all
kinds of Ruskinian paradoxes; and his undergraduate essays are obvious
attempts to avoid simplistic answers to complex matters and to burst
asunder arbitrary divisions between life and art and between one
discipline and another. For him, as for Ruskin, the restless search for
laws and principles underlying the flux of things represented a pursuit
of the didactic principles in a divine plan. Since each man claimed for

the artist the role of mediator between the world of the senses and the world beyond the senses, they both possessed—or were possessed by—as insatiable a curiosity about the temporal world and their role in it as was theirs about the Creator of this world. This frenetic desire to apprehend isolated phenomena and to synthesize laws of being that could be related to other laws, expressed a consuming need, common to both men, a creative thrust through the finite world toward the infinite, a longing to peel back the mysteries behind what Ruskin called 'The Earth Veil'[16] so that they might discover a trustworthy world of reality behind it. And so their works reveal not only nature's infinite variety and all her bewildering paradoxes, but her perennial steadiness and purpose as well.

In order to satisfy simultaneously the claims of the ideal and the real, as well as other antitheses, paradoxes, and contradictions throughout nature, Ruskin and Hopkins sought a position of moral and intellectual poise that was not easy to maintain. The search for truth as it was before the Fall and as it actually is *now*, occupied them both until the end of their lives. The search for that perilous poise did not produce in either man a bland emulsion of principles, for they knew that according to the laws of nature, antitheses cannot be synthesized. Only the mind of God can reconcile the unreconcilable, and yet there are hints of these divine reconciliations scattered here and there throughout the world of nature and human nature. It is the artist's duty to search for them and to incorporate them in his work.

In both men, the hints of syntheses, such as they were, encompassed all the painful and craggy elements of life itself, for neither man would consent to falsify 'Nature's self' for the sake of dishonest syntheses. Therefore, in fidelity to the principle of mimetic art, the antitheses they admitted to consciousness and struggled to reconcile in their work were often fiercely polarized, like the natural world they wanted to recreate; and the polarizations inevitably appear in the creative tools they adopted to express 'Nature's self'. Their style and tone is at once sensitive and rugged, capable of blinding clarity and exasperating turbidity. They preached peace and serenity, and their works are full of racking grief and the acknowledgment of man's violence and bestiality. Their mode of address to their readers is both arrogant and humble. They saw the role of the artist as divinely sanctioned, and at the same time, a threat to salvation: sometimes the artist appears as the interpreter of God's will, sometimes as the man most likely to flout it.

Both men sensed that whatever syntheses were to emerge out of the paradoxes in nature and in their own hearts would have to come out of the struggle itself. Their common puritan inheritance had bequeathed to them 'two worlds of flesh and spirit, earth and heaven', as Alan Heuser said of Hopkins,[17] and they both set themselves to reconcile these two worlds in their art and in their lives. But before we can undertake a fuller analysis of the solidity they both discovered behind the apparent flux and paradox of the material world, and before we can appreciate how intimately the Ruskinian cosmology became a part of the fabric of Hopkins's poetry, we ought to describe more fully what that cosmology was.

Since Ruskin's arch-principle that all great art is praise touches every one of his subordinate principles and maxims, as every one of them touches the others, he never felt the necessity to make careful distinctions between his arch-principle and the subordinate ones. But his cosmology can be neatly divided into two parts—the objects of praise and the tools of praise.[18] The objects of praise, as we already know, are God, and nature, the art of God; but Ruskinian realism insisted that man, the artist, must praise nature in all her paradoxes and antitheses—in order and chaos, in benevolence and in violence, in growth and decay, even in the post-lapsarian punishment of death that ends all life.

Whenever Ruskin and Hopkins dealt with such concepts as the sacrament of energy in nature,[19] or mass and detail in nature, or the doctrines of generic plenitude and specific creation in nature, or paradoxes such as the need for restraint and the need for liberty in nature's creatures, or nature's utter clarity of purpose and her wilful mystery and obscurity, we know they were discussing the objects of praise, that is, nature's selves in all their infinite variety, or what Ruskin also called 'things as they ARE' (III, 57). Things as they ARE in Hopkins's essay on the subject 'may be roughly expressed by *things are*, or *there is truth*. Grammatically it = *it is* or *there is*' (*JP*, 127, 1868). In another essay Hopkins used the phrase 'the co-existent perception of things as they are' (*JP*, 77, 1864), a perception that in no way is to prevent the search for idealism. '*It is* or *there is*' and 'things as they ARE' try to account for how living things look, act, grow, and decay under every conceivable circumstance, and in the case of man, the highest of the sentient creatures, what his moral composition is. Hopkins's term 'inscape' is most useful here, for the artist was to reveal not only the inscape of each individual thing as it comes before his artistic scrutiny, but the physical and moral inscape of the whole phenomenal world, and whenever possible, of the Creator behind it all.

The second intrinsic part of Ruskin's and Hopkins's cosmology describes the tools of praise, first the artist's innocent eye, then the heart and the moral energies and affections, and last, the trained hand or mind. This category is coequal with the objects of praise or things as they are outside the artist, and both men use it to treat the problem of apprehension—of *how* we see and praise what we see and praise, what precise attitudes we must adopt in order to be simultaneously accurate and exultant: how, in short, we may best carry out art's great functions of praise through disciplined imitation and praise through spontaneous enthusiasm. The tools of praise are the artist's self and the moral and technical training he needs to record nature's infinite variety with the awe and the utter fidelity she deserves. Ruskin discusses the tools of praise in little phrases and concepts like 'the *innocence of the eye*' and the theoretic faculty, and it corresponds to Hopkins's 'instress', the capacity to love unabashedly the inscapes of things we have just scrutinized carefully. When Hopkins deals with this category in his prose essays he uses little 'Ruskinese' phrases like 'the eye that is trained to look at things *innocently* or *purely* as painters say' (*JP*, 77, 1864).

Stanza 5 from *The Wreck of the Deutschland* allusively sums up both the objects of praise and the tools of praise, careful and loving scrutiny of things as they ARE and love of the Maker of all this beauty, whose 'mystery must be instressed, stressed':

> I kiss my hand
> To the stars, lovely-asunder
> Starlight, wafting him out of it; and
> Glow, glory in thunder;
> Kiss my hand to the dappled-with-damson west:
> Since, tho' he is under the world's splendour and wonder,
> His mystery must be instressed, stressed;
> For I greet him the days I meet him, and bless when I understand.
>
> (Poem 28, 1876)

The 'dappled-with-damson west' describes the 'violet' colour of sunset just before the sun hits the horizon and turns everything to blazing colours, or the moment it has sunk beyond the horizon. But it is a particular evening: the sky is not a solid mantle of damson or plum colour; the wind creates the 'dappled-with-damson' mottling of clouds in a particular pattern.

In a single stanza Hopkins has moved from particular objects of praise—stars, clouds—to the principles of creation behind them, and then to a frank acknowledgment of *his* duty and joy as an artist: he uses his tools of praise, his 'eye, heart, soul', and pen, to 'greet', 'bless', and 'understand' these phenomena and their Creator. The poet sees not only the 'splendour and wonder' of these things and joyously acknowledges them, that is, he 'instresses, stresses' them, but he also acknowledges the divine mystery behind all that beauty at the very moment he is expressing his own delight and awe in the scene before his eyes.

With both men this cyclical fusion between the Creator, the created thing, and the artist often occurs, and it results in a legitimate blurring of the two categories, the objects of praise and the tools of praise, or what we praise and the spirit in which we do so. They both felt that if the artist does not accept this blurring, he is not accomplishing his full task. For although man, as a natural creature, must obey the laws of his kind, he has a highly idiosyncratic self, a precise 'inscape' of his own, like every other created thing. And this 'self' becomes the tool of instress: man tabulates and loves what there is before him out of what there is inside him.

One of the most characteristic features of Ruskin's prose and Hopkins's poetry is the energy of their praise for God and His gifts to man. Here again, there is a legitimate blurring between the objects of praise and the tools of praise, for if nature seems to be engaged in an almost universal dance, and if, as Hopkins and Ruskin both said, the art of man must imitate nature, which is the art of God, then the artist must devise striking ways to reproduce all this energy in his art. His works must be exultant when he describes exultant nature and he must actively mourn when she does.

The sacrament of energy in nature flows naturally from nature's infinite variety; for a world in constant movement provides as much variety as a world of sharply individuated things and creatures. The sacrament of energy in nature is thus one of the objects of praise. The sacrament of energy in the art of man flows equally naturally from the mimetic principle of art; energy in art is a tool of praise imitating energy in nature.

If God is a Prime Mover, and nature mirrors God, then nature, Ruskin said, will be found most pure, most alive, and most Godlike when she is in motion. Mould and dust may be as interesting to study as petrified rocks that have been chipped, pounded, and cleansed by erosion; and still waters may be as attractive as running waters. Mould, dust, and stagnant waters are part of things as they ARE, and are thus to be respected; nonetheless the 'purity of the rock' must be morally 'contrasted with the foulness of dust or mould', and 'flowing water' is healthier than 'stagnant water'. And 'again, in colour', Ruskin imagined 'that the quality which we term purity is dependent on the full energizing of the rays that compose it'.

'Foulness', 'disorder', and 'decay' were 'always indicative of the withdrawal of Divine support'. Ruskin saw divine analogies between human 'sloth and degradation as well as bodily lethargy and disease' and sluggishness in nature. He read supernatural purposes into 'the contrary indications of freshness and purity belonging to every healthy and active organic frame', and the 'effort of young leaves when first their inward energy prevails over the earth, pierces its corruption and shakes its dust away from their own white purity of life' (IV, 133–4).

And so Ruskin elevated the motion, change, and energy he found in all living things into that divine law he called 'Vital Beauty'. He preached that the breath of God, or what he called 'the majesty of motion' (III, 554) had a benevolent effect upon brute matter. A world of constantly moving and growing objects—shifting cloud formations, earth trickling away under the inexorable wash of vapour and water, foliage in perpetual choreography under wind and rain, the sun in its prescribed orbit around the globe, casting kaleidoscopic tints, spots, and dapples upon the earth, painting trees, grass, mountains and clouds with imperceptible gradations of glorious colour—all this planned energy and change provided Ruskin with the hope that from the 'majesty of motion' man caught elusive proofs of the majesty of God.

Hopkins never discussed Ruskin's principle of sacramental energy, but one can watch him groping to express it even as a schoolboy and an undergraduate. Rainswept gullies do not passively echo the noise of the shower; they themselves become '*clattering* gullies' (Poem 1, 1860). During a purple sunset, '*spikes* of light/*Spear'd* open lustrous gashes' (Poem 2, 1862), and a bat is described as the possessor of 'tender and air-*crisping* wings' (Poem 19, 1865). By the time he started to write *The Wreck of the Deutschland*, the sacramental energy he needed for his role as a Jesuit missionary had become inseparable from the sacramental energy required of a Ruskinian artist. Almost all of his Catholic poems are lyric embellishments of this principle, not only in their energy of tone, image, and metaphor, but in their subject— nature's choreography as an evidence of God's affection for man. The world is not filled with the grandeur of God; it is '*charged*' with it; God's grandeur will '*flame* out, like shining from shook foil' (Poem 31, 1877). Weeds do not grow quietly; they '*shoot*' up, 'long and lovely and lush' (Poem 33, 1877). The '*meaning motion*' of great art, and particularly great art dedicated to God, '*fans* fresh our wits with wonder'

(Poem 45, 1879). The sea-tide *'ramps* against the shore' (Poem 35, 1877); a 'cheerless wind' is urged to *'Strike,* churl; *hurl'*, while a *'heltering* hail' demolishes 'May's beauty' (Poem 154, n.d.). And in a passage reminiscent of the sacramental energy with which *The Wreck of the Deutschland* 'is *charged'*, 'crumbling, fore-foundering, thundering all-surfy seas' are compared to the 'jaunting vaunting vaulting assaulting trumpet telling' truth of some awe-inspiring cosmic plan (Poem 141, n.d.). And in one of the most attractive tributes to the sacrament of energy, Hopkins described how

> Delightfully the bright wind boisterous ropes,
>   wrestles, beats earth bare
> Of yestertempest's creases.   (Poem 72, 1888)

The sacrament of energy in nature, with its correspondences in the divine plan and in the human heart, was never stated more clearly than in 'Hurrahing in Harvest' (Poem 38, 1877). The opening stanza celebrates that moment toward the end of summer when time seems to stand still, just before the onset of the first frosts and the first turn of the leaves:

> Summer ends now; now barbarous in beauty, the stooks rise
> Around; up above, what wind-walks! what lovely behaviour
> Of silk-sack clouds! has wilder, wilful-wavier
> Meal-drift moulded ever and melted across skies?

Hopkins has endowed the whole scene with Ruskin's 'majesty of motion' by a few subtle strokes. The 'stooks' or shocks of wheat or corn do not simply stand braving the wind; they 'rise around', almost as though they spring out of their fields. The clouds are in motion with constant shift of colours, shapes, lights, and shades; they are obeying the laws of sacramental energy and of nature's infinite variety. These clouds represent two levels of clouds behaving in different ways. The 'silk-sack' clouds resemble Ruskin's cloud ranks in the upper cirrus region, made of 'excessively fine, silky parallel fibres' (III, 359) drifting high overhead like 'a swan's bosom fretted by faint wind' (III, 382). Hopkins's 'Meal-drift moulded' clouds, 'wilder, wilful-wavier' as they melt 'across skies', are similar to Ruskin's massy clouds of the central region, made into 'solid mounds' by a process of 'condensation', even though 'at sunset, the fall of dew enables the surrounding atmosphere to absorb and melt them away' (VII, 163). Hopkins's 'Meal-drift moulded' clouds exemplify both the doctrine of general plenitude and the doctrine of specific creation: they are individuated, in fact wildly so—'wilder, wilful-wavier'—but the wind drives them in a recogniz-able pattern according to certain Ruskinian laws of wind motion.

These clouds of Hopkins are also obeying Ruskin's principle of sacramental energy: 'And the result of this arrangement in masses more or less angular, varied with, and chiefly constructed of, curves of the utmost freedom and beauty, is that appearance of exhaustless and fantastic energy which gives every cloud a marked character of its own' (III, 373).

The sestet of 'Hurrahing in Harvest' is a demonstration of the principles of mimetic and laudatory art. Hopkins's images are reproduc-ing nature's infinite variety and they are themselves a sacrament of energy, in imitation of the scene Hopkins is celebrating:

And the azurous hung hills are his world-wielding shoulder
Majestic—as a stallion stalwart, very-violet-sweet!—
These things, these things were here and but the beholder
Wanting; which two when they once meet,
The heart rears wings bold and bolder
And hurls for him, O half hurls earth for him off under his feet.

(Poem 38, 1877)

Ruskin had claimed that mountains 'are to the rest of the body of earth what violent muscular action is to the body of man'. And the 'muscles and tendons of its anatomy are, in the mountain, brought out with force and convulsive energy, full of expression, passion, and strength' (III, 427). In other places, Ruskin spoke of mountains as earth cathedrals (VI, 425) and symbols of divine justice (VI, 127). In the sestet to 'Hurrahing in Harvest' the tall 'Majestic' and 'azurous hung hills', flinging and thrusting themselves up out of the earth with the muscular action of a bucking 'stallion stalwart', are symbols of Christ, with His 'world-wielding shoulder'. And with the metaphor of the heart, rearing 'wings bold and bolder' and hurling earth 'under his feet', Hopkins has carried out the function of mimetic art: the energy of the tone and metaphors mirrors the energy of the divine plan in nature's self (Poem 38, 1877).

The opening lines of *The Wreck of the Deutschland* announce that a new principle of energy has found its way into Hopkins's poetry and that we are now in the presence of an authentic new poet. The scarcely controlled excitement of the ode is one of its most pronounced features. Hopkins now saw himself and the world as fastened to God, yet revol-ving around Him in a universal charge of motion; now the awesome energy of nature and God's control over it moves Hopkins to repeated outbursts of praise in stanza after stanza. The entire ode is full of the Ruskinian 'majesty of motion' in man and in nature, in a way that is quite new to Hopkins's poetry. The poet is 'Fast, but mined with a motion, a drift' that 'crowds and combs to the fall': he is buffeted by hurtlings of hell, whirlings of wings, swoons of the heart, flashings of flames. In the actual scene of the *Deutschland*'s catastrophe, nature herself imitates the majestic terror that God visited upon the priest at his prayers earlier in the ode. The doomed ship herself 'sweeps' into the snows, driven onward by the grim winds and waters waiting to overwhelm her. The love and terror of God overwhelmed the priest at his prayers and wrung cries of fear and supplication from the giant nun. The nun's cries to Christ are also full of violent feelings, in keeping not only with her terror but also with the titanic energy of the whole apocalyptic scene upon the waters (Poem 28, 1876).

Although Ruskin, in common with his teacher, Carlyle, may be accused of patronizing condescension when he discusses working men, nonetheless he looked for some of the same complexity, yet harmony of spirit, and some of the same moral energy as he looked for in the finest artists. When they are working vigorously at some important task, they are showing 'indications of freshness and purity belonging to every healthy and active organic frame' (IV, 133). When Ruskin used the terms 'healthy and active', he was thinking of moral health as well as physical health. For purity of heart, Ruskin thought, was directly related to energy, to 'human effort', and to 'truthful knowledge of *human power* and *human worth*' (IV, 56).

Hopkins's poetry contains many little character sketches of morally energetic people. His giant nun in *The Wreck of the Deutschland*, his soldiers, sailors, labourers, and priests at their humble tasks, all belong to Ruskin's type of the pure at heart. The career of the obedient soldier corresponds most closely to the life of Christ, who also 'knows war, served this soldiering through', and who knows even better than any soldier how to 'reeve a rope' (Poem 63, 1885). Booted Tom, contented construction worker, 'rips out rockfire homeforth' (Poem 70, 1887) as he leaves his job at the end of the day. Felix Randal, 'at the random grim forge, powerful amidst peers' (Poem 53, 1880), demonstrates the moral validity of energetic toil. But all this energy, 'This, all this freshness fuming', must be consecrated to God, otherwise it is a dangerous commodity that 'death half lifts the latch of' and 'hell hopes soon the snatch of' (Poem 49, 1879).

'The Sea and the Skylark' (Poem 35, 1877) exhibits two sorts of energy, the legitimate energy of wild things that have not disobeyed their Creator and the profane energy of post-lapsarian man who has been guilty of disobedience. The three wild things are the moon, the tide, and the lark. They are described as inexorably bound to each other's motion, according to nature's laws. They demonstrate Ruskin's 'purity' as a type of divine energy. Hopkins has provided a sort of rhythmical counterpoint as part of nature's choreography; the tide's motion is diurnal and 'rampant'; it 'trenches', that is, it cuts ruthlessly, and it 'ramps against the shore' like a strong fast melody. The progress of the moon is slower and less vehement, like the ground-bass to the melody, more measured in its pace, but mathematically subject to the same laws of tempo as the sea. The lark's vehement and spontaneous song, pouring and pelting against the sky, 'till none's to spill nor spend', is closer to the voice of the Christian artist exulting in God's majesty.

The sestet shows energy gone awry. In Ruskin's terms, it is no longer 'pure'; it shames 'this shallow and frail town'. It is the evil energy behind 'our sordid turbid time'. All mankind, 'life's pride and cared-for crown',

> Have lost that cheer and charm of earth's past prime:
> Our make and making break, are breaking, down
> To man's last dust, drain fast towards man's first slime.

The sestet of 'The Sea and the Skylark' lacks the vibrant energy of the octave, in imitation of the Ruskinian principle of moral decay with which it deals. The shallow and frail town, with its soulless denizens, is like one of Ruskin's stagnant pools or mounds of dead dust, each harbouring within itself the barely moving bodies of moribund things (VII, 207). In the sestet all available energy is directed toward moral evolution in reverse.

'God's Grandeur' (Poem 31), written in the same year as 'The Sea and the Skylark', contains another dirge on modern man's perverse use of energy:

> Generations have trod, have trod, have trod;
> And all is seared with trade; bleared, smeared with toil;
> And wears man's smudge and shares man's smell: the soil
> Is bare now, nor can foot feel, being shod.

Again, according to the principles of mimetic art, Hopkins's sounds have imitated the sluggishness of decay: 'seared', 'bleared', and 'smeared with toil' are long, drawn-out syllables: the inexorability of the insensate feet that 'have trod, have trod, have trod' suggest Ruskin's most 'absolute type of impurity . . . the mud or slime of a damp, over-trodden path, in the outskirts of a manufacturing town' (VII, 207).

The moral significance of colour was as important to Hopkins and Ruskin as the moral meaning of energy. Both men loved to drench their work in colour; they loved to describe exotic colours, and soft colours, triumphant and aggressive primary colours and gentle half-shades. Constantly shifting colour was part of nature's universal dance, and the shifts of colour from moment to moment contributed to nature's infinite variety. Ruskin and Hopkins loved to use vivid colour metaphors to describe God's gifts to man. Here again, their tools of praise mimic the objects of praise: since 'Nature's self' is bathed in an infinite variety of colours, shifting not only according to whim, but also according to distinct laws, then the art of man should imitate both the whims of colour and the laws of colour.

And so, in poem after poem in Hopkins's canon, the earth's inscapes glow and flash off the page, as the ecstatic poet gives thanks for country scenes awash with vibrant moving colour. In one poem he imagines the sky like 'grey lawns cold where gold, where quick-gold lies!' (Poem 32, 1877). In the spring, leaves and blooms '*brush*/The *descending* blue' of an azure sky, 'all in a *rush* with richness' (Poem 33, 1877). The italicized words suggest that Hopkins also felt 'Of Truth of Colour' to be part of the sacrament of energy, as Ruskin did. The sky and vegetation are celebrating the rites of spring in patterned move-ment. And in May, the Virgin Mary's month,

> When drop-of-blood-and-foam-dapple
> Bloom lights the orchard-apple
> And thicket and thorp are merry
> With silver-surfèd cherry
>
> And azuring-over greybell makes
> Wood banks and brakes wash wet like lakes—

all this colour is the time for a 'star-eyed strawberry-breasted' thrush to hatch its 'Cluster of bugle blue eggs'. In 'The May Magnificat' the truth of tone and colour combine to praise nature's fecundity, as the pun in the title suggests:

> Flesh and fleece, fur and feather,
> Grass and greenworld all together.

'All things' are 'rising', 'all things' are 'sizing', that is, swelling or growing; and the growing things are performing a sacrament of energy with their own colours, for they are casting their own lights, dapples, and shadows upon each other in a sort of mock fecundity that joyfully mirrors the growth and change within them (Poem 42, 1878).

Ruskin's first volume of *Modern Painters* is full of pyrotechnical descriptions of sunsets: one such sky appeared to him as 'one molten mantling sea of colour and fire; every black bar turns into massy gold, every ripple and wave into unsullied shadowless crimson, and purple, and scarlet'. Another sunset was like a 'flood of fire which deluges the sky from the horizon to the zenith'; of another sky at noontime, after a shower he said: 'I cannot call it colour, it was conflagration' (III, 285, 287, 279).

One of the most striking contributions that Ruskinian 'Truth of Colour' made to Hopkins's poetry was the difficult principle of colour in motion. As the sun moves in its slow dance from the horizon to the zenith and back again before it disappears behind the earth-rim, it changes its own colour several times, rinsing all objects beneath it and usually changing their colours as well. On the horizon at dawn and in the evening, the sun is brown, crimson, mauve, scarlet, or rose, depending upon the moment and the degree of cloud moisture. During its ascent, the sun's colours shift by imperceptible gradations, from red to orange to yellow, finally assuming a white-gold hue at the zenith. This process of 'gradation' is recapitulated in reverse during the sun's descent (III, 268–71).

The principle of gradation was a law of nature operating throughout the universe and symbolizing benign mutability; 'for gradation is to colours what curvature is to lines, both . . . expressing the law of gradual change and progress in the human soul itself' (xv, 147). Ruskin once compared graded colour-painting to 'playing on a colour violin, seventy-times seven stringed'. On the violin string, the shift of sound is infinitesimal from second to second, as the fingers move along the string, just as in the rainbow, colour shifts from one primary colour to its related secondary colour to the next primary colour without a perceptible break (xv, 416, 422).

Ruskin believed that the principle of gradation was at odds with another universal principle. He called this conflicting principle 'chiaroscuro', by which he meant abrupt mixtures of light and shade— spotting, dappling, and pointing. According to Ruskin, Turner was the great master of chiaroscuro; he knew how to paint 'separate lights' and lights 'falling in spots, edged by shadow but not melting off into it', and he had learned as no other modern painter had, the techniques of 'sharpness, decision', in both highlights and deep shade. He could paint lights and shadows as they really are, throwing them 'one after another like transparent veils along the earth and upon the air, till the whole picture palpitates with them'. In the chapter called 'Of Truth of Chiaroscuro' Ruskin warned the apprentice that he must imitate Turner's distinction between gradation and chiaroscuro, for this 'violent decision, the great transition from sun to shade', that is to say, from gradation to chiaroscuro, faced nature whenever she took up her own palette (III, 306, 314). Since this 'violent decision' between gradation and chiaroscuro was an opposition at work throughout the universe, and since both principles, though conflicting, were true, the artist had to reconcile them and to reflect them in his work. Ruskin urged that the beginner who was searching for nature's 'violent decision' between gradation and chiaroscuro should compare 'gradated colours of the rainbow with the stripes of a target', or the 'gradual deepening of the youthful blood in the cheek with an abrupt patch of rouge or with the sharply drawn veins of old age' (IV, 89).

Hopkins was fascinated by this theory of conflicting aesthetic laws. He used Ruskin's term 'gradation' (*JP*, 85, 89, 1865) to describe the principle of 'continuous' (*JP*, 76, 1864) or 'transitional' beauty (*JP*, 104, 1865); he also used Ruskin's term 'chiaroscuro' (*JP*, 85) to mean 'abrupt' (*JP*, 104) changes of shade, colour, shape, tone, or size. Not only did he employ Ruskin's terms, but he invented a whole catalogue of his own terms to correspond to 'gradation' and 'chiaroscuro'. The universe of 'beautiful things', he said, was subject to a 'division into *chromatic* beauty and *diatonic* beauty. The diatonic scale, you know, leaves out, the chromatic puts in, the half notes' (*JP*, 104). Hopkins's chromatic beauty corresponds to gradation or to equivalent terms; diatonic corresponds to chiaroscuro and to terms equivalent to chiaroscuro:

> The division then is of abrupt and gradual, of parallelistic and continuous, or intervallary and chromatic, of quantitative and qualitative beauty. The beauty of an infinite curve is chromatic, of a system of curves, parallelistic; of deepening colour or a passing of one colour into another chromatic, of a collection of colours inter-vallary; of the change of note on the strings of a violin or in a strain of wind chromatic; of that on the keys of a piano intervallary.
>
> (*JP*, 76)

Hopkins employed Ruskin's principles of gradation and chiaroscuro in poem after poem; and so discreet was he that one might study both men for years without being aware of the Ruskinian cosmos that Hopkins recreated in a few dazzling images. Who would have thought, for example, that the haunting pair of lines:

And the azurous hung hills are his world-wielding shoulder
Majestic—as a stallion stalwart, very-violet-sweet!

(Poem 38, 1877

contain not only a salute to the sacrament of energy but to chromatic colour as well? The 'azurous hung hills ... very-violet-sweet' have picked up first the colour of one of Ruskin's 'craggy or blue mountain distances' (VI, 431) and then turned violet with the dying crimson sun upon them. Ruskin had often warned the painter about the atmospheric blue that distance lends to the local colour of green hills, which then become blue, or 'azurous', one of Ruskin's favourite words. These hills then undergo yet another colour change under the blaze of a rose-coloured fire-ball on the horizon; they become purple, for the blue distance-colour blends with the rose of the sinking sun to take on the secondary hue of mauve, purple, or violet. This phenomenon Ruskin also called 'truth of aerial effect' (III, 269); Hopkins's skill consisted in the way his two contiguous colour images suggest the passing of time. The metaphor shifts from colour to colour, from blue to violet, just as the hills imperceptibly shift colour under the rose of the sinking sun.

Some of Hopkins's poetic discussions of colour make little sense unless we are aware that he is exemplifying principles of gradation or chiaroscuro. In one poem, the little tell-tale phrase 'The seven or seven times seven/Hued sunbeam' (Poem 60, 1883) is not only reminiscent of Ruskin's 'seventy-times seven stringed' colour violin, but to another phenomenon that Ruskin called 'the effects of visible sunbeams', that is, the false colours of a solar halo (III, 268, 351, 354). 'As Kingfishers Catch Fire' muses delightedly upon both chromatic and diatonic sound. The bells finding 'tongue' and the ringing stones, 'tumbled over rim in roundy wells', provide diatonic or abrupt tone; the 'tucked string' provides chromatic or graded tone (Poem 57, n.d.).

Several of Hopkins's allusions to diatonic and chromatic beauty are so tightly fused with their symbolic meaning that they are difficult to hear even after dozens of readings. In 'St. Alphonsus Rodriguez', the poet comforts himself that the same God who 'tall trees makes more and more', thus permitting them chromatic growth and beauty, also 'Veins violets' with diatonic strips of 'trickling increment' (Poem 73, 1888). The sestet of 'Gods' Grandeur' also contains an allusion to chromatic colour phenomenon that comforts the poet when he thinks of cities 'seared with trade; bleared, smeared with toil'; Hopkins refers to 'the last lights' moving 'off the black West went/Oh, morning, at the brown brink eastward' (Poem 31, 1877). He had obviously surveyed a dawn sky and noticed that the colour of the western sky is black or inky blue, whereas the eastern sky is brown for a few seconds before the sun rises and the sky then becomes some species of rose, crimson, or scarlet.

Metaphors of colour and of energy are merely the two most obvious surface features of Hopkins's poetry and Ruskin's prose. These metaphors reflect not only the contending principles of gradation and chiaroscuro, and of moral energy and moral decay, but a whole universe of contending principles. If everywhere Hopkins and Ruskin looked in the phenomenal and the spiritual world they saw paradoxes, dichotomies, antitheses, and contradictions, they could only explain these ubiquitous contrasts as the result of man's original fall from grace. Professor Rosenberg believes that 'the paradox of the fortunate fall underlies Ruskin's whole concept of Gothic' and that it largely shaped 'his esthetic and social criticism';[20] in Hopkins's case also, the paradox of the fortunate fall informs his criticism and his poetry.

The paradox of the fortunate fall is both tragic and joyous—that is its paradox. The worship of the resurrected Christ and the hope for eternal salvation after earthly struggle does endow man with a dignity and a moral purpose not consciously present in his first parents; but the costs to mankind of that fall are incalculable. And one of the costs of the fall is that man lives in a world where good and evil struggle for supremacy, where life ends in death, where darkness and light, summer and winter, sickness and health, beauty and ugliness (IX, 306) alternate with each other as part of the post-lapsarian plan of justice (IV, 184, 186).

And so Ruskin and Hopkins both admired above all else those artists who frankly express the universal paradoxes. Their admiration extended even to pre-Christians like Plato and para-Christians like Wordsworth. As Hopkins tried to explain in an essay discussing paradoxes in the works of Plato, Shakespeare, and Wordsworth,[21]

> It is these contrasts and disparities which give complexity and interest to the lives or writings of great thinkers so clearly beyond what they would otherwise have had, making for instance their enthusiasm not free from pathos, or, if the proportions be the other way, their denunciations from hope.   (*JP*, 115, 1865)

Hopkins was overcome all his life with 'despair at the multiplicity of phenomena unexplained and unconnected', as though he could not always draw upon the coexistent vision of grace that heals the polarities in the phenomenal and the spiritual world at the very moment it illuminates them. As a Jesuit, Hopkins made heroic efforts to understand the divine synthesis in all these antitheses; for God Himself, as Hopkins once told his parishioners, 'brings together things thought opposite and incompatible, strict justice and mere mercy, free grace and binding duty' (*S*, 57, 1880).

For the artist, the problem of the universal paradoxes was obviously more complicated than for the ordinary person, since these paradoxes function simultaneously in the external world of nature and within the half-angelic, half-satanic heart of man. The artist himself, a fallible man must condemn evil, while reproducing 'things as they ARE'. He must here above all cling to the principle of mimetic art. It is his business, as a Christian artist, to reproduce not only nature as she is, but man as *he* is; and somehow the artist's works must mirror 'the Adamite curse' and 'the antagonism of the entire human system' (IV, 184, 186). Ruskin dwelt at considerable lengths on the perilous balance between truth as beauty and truth as ugliness, and he praised the famous men in art and literature who had provided the world with honest distinctions between the ideal and the real. Fra Angelico was to be admired because he offered his viewers many a 'frank portraiture' of 'ungainly sanctity' and 'the most ordinary features of his brother monks'. Paul Veronese also knew the moral value of reproducing 'beauty and its proper foils'; he opposed 'the dwarf to the soldier, and the negress to the queen', while Shakespeare placed 'Caliban beside Miranda, and Autolycus beside Perdita' (v, 55–8). This natural idealism 'is a universal principle common to all great art':

> Consider in Shakespeare how Prince Henry is opposed to Falstaff, Falstaff to Shallow, Titania to Bottom, Cordelia to Regan, Imogen to Cloten, and so on; while all the meaner idealists disdain the naturalism, and are shocked at the contrasts.   (v, 112–13)

Ruskin had called 'the Adamite curse' that moment in the human adventure when 'in some way "Sin entered into the world and Death by Sin"' (IV, 184). Hopkins naturally stood on firmer dogmatic ground than Ruskin when he discussed the paradox of the fortunate fall. For Hopkins the Adamite curse was not merely a symbol, 'in some way', of paradoxical nature and sinful human nature. It was the precise historical moment when sin and death entered into the world with Eve's sin of curiosity. In a series of sermons on pre-lapsarian and post-lapsarian justice, Hopkins informed his parishioners that before the fall there was no necessity for God to exercise His paradoxical nature as both wrathful and loving father; 'no frown of God's, no stern and threatening law was needed then; for the still and private voice of conscience, reason sovereign within the heart, spoke at the right time the Yes or No.'

Nature's post-lapsarian violence, as the arm of divine justice, would have found no place in pre-lapsarian Eden. It was not part of the divine commonwealth, nor of 'that famous original justice of which you have all heard'. And thus Eden meant life without nature's paradoxes, 'it would have been no Paradise if it were liable to drought and storm plague, blight or locusts', nor would these contrasts to nature's bounty have been needed then as admonitions. Before the fall, the simple and kindly commands, issuing from God's voice, and accompanied by one equally simple prohibition, were all the aids to virtue man needed. '*Afterwards* the same laws were published in thunder from Mount Sinai' (*S*, 57, 60–1, 1880).

Ruskin also had come to the conclusion that nature's violence toward man was a mirror of the punitive wrath of God, just as her kindness and her beauty mirrored the benevolence of God. The benevolence

> is indeed everywhere and always visible; but not alone. Wrath and threatening are invariably mingled with the love; and in the utmost solitudes of nature, the existence of Hell seems to be as legibly declared by a thousand spiritual utterances as that of Heaven.
>
> (XI, 164)

From his earliest undergraduate days, Hopkins adopted Ruskinian techniques in his struggles to resolve the problem of universal paradoxes. 'All thought is of course in a sense an effort [at] unity', he said, and he went looking for a 'golden mean' that would help man as moralist and as artist to live with nature's conflicts (*JP*, 83, 75, 1865, 1864). Hopkins's 'golden mean' could serve both as comfort and as admonition. 'If mercy tempers justice so does justice check indulgence and generosity', he warned himself in one of his religious meditations (*S*, 134, 1883). *The Wreck of the Deutschland* and 'The Loss of the Eurydice' both examine the paradox of God's mercy at the centre of every wrathful act He commits against His creatures. And in poem after poem, the argument between the octave and the sestet turns not only upon the paradoxical temper of God, but the paradoxical drives of man, his need for fame and his greater need for sanctity, his legitimate thrust toward selfhood and his conformity to the Christian type, his worship of beauty and nature and his ruthless destruction of the countryside.

According to the principles of mimetic art, Hopkins had to devise ways to imitate paradoxes in his prosody as well as in his subject matter, and he was more than equal to the task. Sprung rhythm, as he once explained to Bridges, answered this very purpose. Hopkins revealed the twin aims behind sprung rhythm in two statements, one on God's paradoxical designs and another on sprung rhythm's paradoxical designs. 'Why do I use sprung rhythm at all?' Hopkins said to Bridges, hoping to silence his fellow poet's complaints. 'Because it is nearest to the rhythm of prose', Hopkins answered, 'combining, as it seems to me, opposite and, one would have thought, incompatible excellences, markedness of rhythm—that is rhythm's self—and naturalness of expression' (*LB*, 46, 1878). With this analysis of sprung rhythm's purpose, Hopkins is describing the difficult decisions facing the mimetic artist. He must combine '*incompatible excellences*', since he must find ways not to repress any excellences. Whether or not he succeeds, he will be attempting to follow God's example, for God Himself 'brings together things thought opposite and incompatible' (*S*, 57, 1880).

Hopkins did not rely on sprung rhythm alone as a vehicle for imitating the universal paradoxes. The techniques he discovered are familiar to all of us: the chiming alliterations, assonances, and consonances almost invariably pair 'opposite and one would have thought incompatible excellences'; he also used them to bring 'together things thought opposite and incompatible', such sharp dualisms, for example, as good and evil. The paradox of God's tenderness and God's wrath is almost always couched in alliterative metaphors and images: 'Being mighty a master, being a father and fond' (Poem 34, 1877) while man's heroic efforts to understand his duty toward his Creator are often obliquely handled in discreet little alliterative or assonantal patterns: a man who is 'strung by duty, is strained to beauty' (Poem 41, 1878) suggests a conflict between beauty and the Christian's drive toward moral perfection.

The world of universal paradoxes and the principle of mimetic and laudatory art posed a great many knotty problems for Ruskin and Hopkins. For instance, in an artist's life, as in his artistic techniques, he must ever be alert to ask himself these questions: when does liberty engender licence or restraint become rigidity? May the objects of praise and the tools of praise be legitimately blurred under all circumstances? In other words, if the principles of mimetic and laudatory art are binding upon Christian artists, may paradoxical man praise his own paradoxical nature, including his propensity for sin? If 'ALL GREAT ART IS PRAISE' of nature's post-lapsarian self, or things as they now ARE, as well as things as they ought to be and were before the fall, and if man with his capacity for love and hate, wisdom and criminal stupidity, honest humility and ruinous self-deception, impressive purpose and aimless or predatory sensuality, is part of nature's post-lapsarian self, or things as they now ARE, should the Christian artist now praise evil men?

The artist had to decide not only what attitude to take toward the evil in himself, but to what extent he was to praise or to imitate nature's violence. How reliable a model was nature when she dealt out random execution to the just and the unjust alike? The answer to these problems lies in a careful distinction between praise as imitation in art and praise as imitation in life. The Christian artist with the innocent eye must record with candour whatever he sees, but the Christian moralist inside the artist's skin must attempt to live an impeccable life. The honest idealist-realist paints ugly things as they ARE because they are part of the paradoxes of the fortunate fall and thus part of the post-lapsarian plan, but he must always strive to recapitulate pre-Edenic virtue in his private and public life. In fact, the Christian artist frequently *must* paint what he would be forbidden to *do* under any circumstances.

The paradox of the fortunate fall shaped Ruskin's vision of the artist as heroic failure as it was later to shape Hopkins's. Fallen man must try to live without sin, knowing he will fail, and the Christian artist must take equal account of his post-lapsarian predicament: he must try to create perfect copies of nature's infinite variety, including all her paradoxes, knowing that his works will be full of imperfections. 'Indeed', as Professor Rosenberg stressed, Ruskin never tired of insisting 'that no architecture could be truly noble which was *not* imperfect'. The Christian artist must somehow reconcile 'Gothic "rudeness" and toleration of imperfection' with the search for that unobtainable perfection, or 'God's retributive justice' with man's 'joyous reliance on grace', or Gothic art's high aspirations with its egalitarian and Christian humility. As Rosenberg said, 'Ruskin rejected the Renaissance because in its pursuit of perfection the Renaissance denied the Fall'. And in denying the Fall, man arrogantly denies his 'lost power';[22] in so doing he falsifies not only nature and himself in nature but the divine plan.

Despite the frank admission that joy and grace lay at the heart of the universal paradoxes as well as violence, sacrifice, and grief, Ruskin and Hopkins allowed more than a touch of the Manichean spirit in their treatment of the paradoxical cosmos. They often expressed paradoxical matters, even morally neutral matters, in implacably dualistic phrases, as though revealing an unconscious urge to utter Hopkins's unambiguous 'Yes!' or more likely 'No!' When this mood came upon them, all paradoxes seemed to mirror the Manichean Prince of Darkness, who lurked in the body of all created things, opposing his principle of evil to the good in the Prince of Light, who lived only in the soul. Hopkins had come to believe that salvation might depend upon this distinction. Therefore he had to oppose mere 'good', which might contain seeds of evil, to absolute 'right', which could contain no evil. 'Right' therefore always came before mere 'good', and might have to eliminate mere 'good':

> For good grows wild and wide,
> Has shades, is nowhere none;
> But right must seek a side
> And choose for chieftain one.

Art, 'this masterhood,/This piece of perfect song' is no more 'right nor wrong' than nature herself:

> No more than red and blue,
> No more than Re and Mi,
> Or sweet the golden glue
> That's built for by the bee.   (Poem 148, n.d.)

In this Manichean mood both men brooded over the principle of generic plenitude and of specific creation. Which was more reliably the recipient of divine favour, they asked themselves, the type, or the individual? Fairly early in his career Ruskin concluded that the type was more likely to be in favour (IV, 182–92). Hopkins also said he was inclined to believe that the type, 'or the form of the whole species', was 'nearer being a true Self than the individual', even though specific creation was a gift of the Holy Trinity, 'in bringing into play with infinite charity Their personality':

> Being personal They see as if with sympathy the play of personality
> in man below Them, for in his personality his freedom lies and this
> same personality playing in its freedom not only exerts and displays
> the riches and capacities of his nature . . . but unhappily disunites it,
> rends it, and almost tears it to pieces.   (S, 128, 171, 1882, n.d.)

As Hopkins saw matters, post-lapsarian man was 'the heir/To his own selfbent so bound, so tied to his turn' (Poem 58, 1882), so uniformly abusive of the great gift of specific creation, that he ought hardly to be trusted with it. Nonetheless, whether in joy or in pain, Hopkins could not resist tasting his own selfhood with frank interest:

> I find myself both as man and as myself something most determined and distinctive, at pitch, more distinctive and higher pitched than anything else I see; I find myself with my pleasures and pains, my powers and my experiences, my deserts and guilt, my shame and sense of beauty, my dangers, hopes, fears, and all my fate, more important than anything I see.

For a man who feared the satanic presence in the hint of selfhood, Hopkins was courageously honest in examining his own unique inscape:

> when I consider my selfbeing, my consciousness and feeling of myself, of *I* and *me* above and in all things, which is more distinctive than the taste of ale or alum, more distinctive than the smell of walnutleaf or camphor,

then nothing else in the universe

> comes near this unspeakable stress of pitch, distinctiveness and selving, this selfbeing of my own. Nothing explains it or resembles it, except so far as this, that other men to themselves have the same feeling. But this only multiplies the phenomena to be explained.
>
> (*S*, 122, 123, 1880)

'As Kingfishers Catch Fire' shows how circular the Ruskinian principles are. In this poem Hopkins makes lyric metaphors of the sacrament of energy and its paradox, the sacrament of restraint, and the principle of diatonic beauty and its opposite, the principle of chromatic beauty; and with some discreet and little metaphors he turns the doctrines of generic plenitude and of specific creation into a benign paradox rather than a stark dualism. In the first quatrain Hopkins had already offered the sacramental energy as diatonic sound in bells and tones, and as chromatic sound in strings. The second quatrain frankly exults in the selfhood of all things:

> Each mortal thing does one thing and the same:
> Deals out that being indoors each one dwells;
> Selves—goes itself; *myself* it speaks and spells,
> Crying *What I do is me: for that I came.*

But with the abrupt little clause—'Í say móre':—and even the colon after 'móre': is firmly, if subtly importunate—the sestet begins to bring the principles of energy and of specific creation under the repose of grace:

> Í say móre: the just man justices;
>   Keeps gráce: thát keeps all his goings graces;
> Acts in God's eye what in God's eye he is—
>   Chríst. For Christ plays in ten thousand places,
> Lovely in limbs, and lovely in eyes not his
>   To the Father through the features of men's faces.
>
>   (Poem 57, n.d.)

In the sonnet on mortal beauty, Hopkins progressed through the same pattern of reconciliation. Specific mortal beauty is first described as full of energy: it sets the blood to dancing, it flings out proud forms, it is the originator of the arts; it even appears to be benevolent, for 'See: it does this: keeps warm/Men's wits to the things that are' and 'what good means', yet it is 'dangerous'. The specific 'feature' of a Purcell tune pays homage to specific creation in the arts, while the handsome Anglo-Saxon slaves, 'Those lovely lads once, wet-fresh windfalls of war's storm' are types of human beauty whose unwitting glory it was to play a part in the conversion of England to Christianity.

In the octave we have seen the dance of nature and the dance of art, all beautiful, all containing good, but not right. By a familiar hierarchy of values the sestet moves from a world of generically and specifically created things, 'To man, that needs would worship block or barren stone', to 'World's loveliest—men's selves', to the principle of beauty itself, admittedly 'heaven's sweet gift', and finally, to man's only safe resting place, 'God's better beauty, grace' (Poem 62, 1885).

Like all other Ruskinian principles, the theory of universal paradoxes had to be reflected in the Christian artist's work. How, then, does an artist create his own specific art form, full of mimetic energy, yet disciplined, as all great art is, so that it might reflect the 'principle, Christ's gift' that Hopkins celebrated in *The Wreck of the Deutschland,* the principle of spiritual poise under grace? Ruskin said that artists with energetic style and idiosyncratic techniques should avoid 'violence or extravagance': they should not indulge in 'want of moderation and restraint'. Nature might appear to run riot in her own energy and in her profusion of types and individuated creatures, she might pile leaf upon leaf, cloud mass upon cloud mass, and pebble upon pebble in gracious profusion, yet a distinct pattern can be discerned in her giving, for she moved in an 'orderly succession of motions and times' (IV, 139, 95). And these paradoxical impulses toward prodigality and generosity on the one hand, and toward measured parsimony on the other, are to be found not only in nature, but in man himself and must be found in the work of the Christian artist.

The artist's mimetic ornamentation, then, must be generous and close-packed, like nature's, but it must not be 'overcharged', Ruskin warned. The artist must run the risk of a 'measure of license'—and to pit 'measure' against 'license' is paradoxical enough, to begin with—but if he is to release the innocent, the spontaneous gestures of imitation and love, he must run the risk of his own 'human energies' (VIII, 52, 250, 194).

Ruskin and Hopkins both used two of the three classical pillars, the Corinthian and the Doric, as symbols of prodigality and parsimony. The Corinthian order, with its rich convex bas-relief and its profuse employment of 'the earth leaf of the acanthus' (XXXI, 26), imitated the sacrament of energy and specific creation as well as the principle of prodigality, for in the finest Corinthian pillars each leaf was distinguishable from another, no matter how closely packed they were. The Doric pillars, on the other hand, with their chaste classical lines, sparse decoration and concave bas-relief, were keynotes for morality. These pillars did not stand for 'the power of art', but for the power 'of *conduct* or harmony' (XXXI, 25).

Ruskin spent as much time seeking for the right balance between these paradoxical impulses as Hopkins was to do upon the search for his 'golden mean'. For these two orders of architecture represented for Ruskin,

> the two great influences which must for ever divide the heart of man: the one of Lawful Discipline, with its perfection and order, but with its danger of degeneracy into Formalism; the other, of Lawful Freedom, with its vigour and variety, but its danger of degeneracy into Licentiousness. (IX, 383)

The principle of lawful freedom contained memories of nature's pre-lapsarian feast in Eden; one could not imagine there either licentiousness or rigid formalism.

Hopkins's many discussions of freedom and discipline in nature, life, and art are reminiscent of Ruskin's. All men need boundaries, Hopkins discovered, and 'genius', especially, 'works more powerfully under the constraints of metre and rhyme and so on than without' (*JP*, 108, 1865). Two years after Hopkins had insisted to his friend

Baillie, in defence of Ruskin, that no critic ought 'to cramp and hedge in by rules the free movements of genius' (*FL*, 204, 1863), we find him admitting that genius is nonetheless 'more effective when conditioned than when unconditioned' (*JP*, 108). The secret, of course, is that the artist must condition himself, and the golden mean between redundancy and niggardliness must arise organically out of the selving of the poet's own moral and artistic purposes.

'The Escorial', Hopkins's first schoolboy poem, encapsulates a comparative history of architecture in two stanzas. Hopkins compared the freedom and profusion of the Gothic and Corinthian pillars with the classic restraint of the Doric. We can now see why his Gothic pillars are so full of tracery 'that fills the eye' as 'one beauty strays/And melts amidst another'. His imaginary Corinthian pillars are likewise profuse with vegetation: their 'shafts acanthus-crown'd' and their 'golden fillets and rich blazonry' are in a state of vibrant energy and 'fiery chivalry' (Poem 1, 1860).

Hopkins has marvellously captured the chaste *hauteur* of the Doric order; his imaginary Doric architecture offers to the equally imaginary spectator 'massy pillars of the Doric mood', surrounding a 'classic temple'; the severity of the Doric line is 'Broad-fluted', like many of Ruskin's illustrations in *Stones of Venice* (Poem 1).

In order to maintain some semblance of Doric severity in his poetry, Hopkins chastened his poems with a strict Petrarchan rhyme scheme; his plan results in occasionally forced or ugly rhymes, and their appearance is otherwise inexplicable in a poet with as exquisite an ear as Hopkins's. He allowed himself no off or slant rhymes, possibly because he felt he could not afford both quantitative profusion of rhyming sound and excess feet. His poetry already exhibited a preponderance of the Corinthian temper since sprung rhythm imperiously calls for freedom, profusion, and vigour. The sheer numbers of weak or slack syllables in such poems as 'The Windhover' provide exactly the feeling of awe, sacramental energy, and moral urgency so essential to a Jesuit and a Ruskinian disciple. They represent Hopkins's need to crowd into the confines of lyric poetry the free, expansive, 'Corinthian' side of the universal paradox, while his strict Petrarchan rhyme scheme and the rhetorical opposition of octave and sestet provide the 'Doric' conditioning he also sought.

Nature presented the mimetic artist with yet another paradox to solve. Just as she is simultaneously profuse and ordered, and just as she creates both types and individuals, she is simultaneously clear and mysterious. Ruskin did not mean that by the principle of mimetic art the artist must be simultaneously clear and obscure. He meant that the artist should be clear in his lights, spots, dapples, and so forth, where nature was, and cloudy where she was. But the apprentice should first practise clarity until his techniques were refined, for the right of being obscure, Ruskin warned, 'is not one to be lightly claimed; it can only be founded on long effort to be intelligible, and on the present power of *being* intelligible to the exact degree which the nature of the thing permits'.

The Christian artist's yearning for perfect fidelity and his inevitable failures reduplicate the loss of man's first home, 'WE NEVER SEE ANY-THING CLEARLY', Ruskin insisted, and any great artist 'will puzzle you, if you look close, to know what he means'; and since there is 'no exception to this rule', then 'EXCELLENCE OF THE HIGHEST KIND, WITHOUT OBSCURITY CANNOT EXIST' (VI, 75, 80, 81). Hopkins's wild, 'wilful wavier' clouds in 'Hurrahing in Harvest' are not only obeying the principles of specific creation; they are behaving according to the principles of nature's wilful mystery.[23] And when Hopkins begged Bridges over and over to be more patient with sprung rhythm and the novelties and imperfections it contained, he was arguing according to Ruskin's theory of legitimate obscurity. Hopkins had faithfully moved from the relative facility and intelligibility of his early poetry to the tense and gnomic language of his mature style because the sacred mystery of his subject warranted a more complex style. Ruskin had warned beginners 'how easy it is for dull artists to mistake the mystery of the great masters for carelessness, and their subtle concealment of intention for want of intention' (VI, 86). Nowhere had Ruskin expressed the principle of mimetic art more clearly than when he discussed the imitation of nature's wilful mystery: 'As all subjects have a mystery in *them*, so all drawing must have a mystery in it' (VI, 83). But even here, nature may be imperious and 'wilful' merely because she wishes to; it is her right. The artist is not wilful in imitating her; he is merely imitating her mystery with all the accuracy and the humility he can muster: 'That execution which is least comprehensible, and which there defies imitation (other qualities being supposed alike) is the best' (III, 123).

Hopkins's pleas that Bridges try to respect stylistic obscurities contain a number of arguments that could well have been drawn from various volumes of *Modern Painters*. Nature's mystery, Ruskin inevitably claimed, was a reflection of the divine mysteries. And Hopkins admitted to Bridges that his prosodic experiment 'needs study and is obscure, for indeed I was not over-desirous that the meaning of all should be quite clear, at least unmistakable' (*LB*, 50, 1878). Almost ten years later Hopkins was still pleading for his Ruskinian principle of legitimate obscurity.

> Plainly if it is possible to express a sub[t]le and recondite thought on a subtle and recondite subject in a subtle and recondite way, with great felicity and perfection, in the end, something must be sacrificed, with so trying a task, in the process.   (*LB*, 265, 1887)

'Obscurity', he admitted once again to Bridges, 'I do and will try to avoid as far as it is consistent with excellences higher than clearness at first reading. This question of obscurity we will some time speak of but not now' (*LB*, 54, 1878). His most crushing remark to Bridges was that shallow criticisms of the sort Bridges had to offer 'are barbarous and like what the ignorant and the ruck say' (*LB*, 50). Hopkins never did explain to Bridges exactly what he meant by 'excellences higher than clearness at first reading', but it seems fairly clear that he was hinting at Ruskin's paradoxical rule that all true excellence implied failure. Young artists should not grieve if their works are full of failures, 'for these are the signs of efforts' (III, 141), just as they are also the sign of man's humility, his acceptance of his fallen state.

Perhaps the most puzzling aspect of the world of paradoxes, and the one that caused Ruskin and Hopkins the most pain, was their common fear that the term 'Christian' and the term 'artist' might contain a hidden dualism. When they discussed art and the making of the artist, they both assumed that all artists worthy of the name were also to be Christian gentlemen, and therefore relatively safe from the temptations art might pose. And yet, so used were they to slipping from reconcilable paradoxes to unrecognizable dualism that they asked themselves frequently whether there was not something morally impossible in coupling the term 'Christian' at all with the term 'artist'. And with considerable anguish, they both concluded that there was. Their strict Calvinistic training would inevitably make them suspicious of the sensible world as worthy of study in and for itself, rather than as a mirror of God. Certainly they proclaimed often that art and the Christian artist needed no vindication in the courts of moral opinion beyond his own gifts rightly employed in praising God. They went even further and they suggested that the artists who sought always to justify the ways of God and nature performed a moral service to their readers and their viewers that other men could not accomplish.* Yet

---

* There is no question in my mind that Hopkins wrote his poems with imaginary readers in mind, and that he hoped—no doubt against hope—to be published after his death.

But since there has been so much discussion about Hopkins's supposedly unconscious motivation where his poetry was concerned, motivation that was supposedly dishonest precisely because it *was* supposedly unconscious, that a few words on his behalf are even now in order. In the first place, Hopkins's attitudes toward fame and toward his own aesthetic creations, and those of other people, were always openly and frankly ambivalent, rather than secretly or dishonestly so. Fame, he said, over and over, is essential for the poet, but dangerous to the immortal soul of the priest, or indeed, to the immortal soul of any human being.

In the second place, contemporary critics, particularly aetheists, often tend to hint that the Jesuits were somehow responsible for the supposed dishonest brokerage that Hopkins exhibited towards his muse and his reasons for its relative neglect. But if this study of Hopkins and the Victorian temper has taught me anything about Hopkins, as priest and poet, it has suggested that Hopkins's ambivalence in the matter of fame and art was as much a part of Hopkins, the ex-Tractarian, Hopkins, the scholar of Jowett, Balliol and Oxford, Hopkins, the Ruskinian aesthetician, and Hopkins, the paradigm of the new Victorian gentleman, as it was of Hopkins, the convert to Catholicism and Jesuit priest. As a matter of fact, his life as a Jesuit had taught him to engage regularly in a scrupulous examination of all his motives, the benign, the pseudo-benign, and the evil; for this reason he was able to bring to the surface in a clear and logical fashion the essential ambivalence toward fame and the aesthetic life that is characteristic, in far more inchoate form, of a great many Victorian artists. Yes, Hopkins wanted to be published, and he said so, but if this were to happen, he wished it to happen at a time, which would have had to be after his death, when any fame his poems might have won for him would no longer endanger his profession or his soul.

There are many indications, both subtle and open, that Hopkins hoped we would some day be reading his poems. For example, his elaborate and frequent explanations to Dixon, and particularly to Bridges, as to what sprung rhythm was all about, suggest a man preparing a new critical terminology whereby future readers such as ourselves might come to understand and appreciate his poems. And then, some reason must be forth-coming as to why Hopkins was so anxious that Bridges keep copies of his poems, when Bridges had proved himself—or so Hopkins continually complained—totally unsympathetic not only to Hopkins's profession, but also to the poetry, which dealt largely with that profession. But Hopkins did not dare leave his poems to the more sympathetic Dixon or to Coventry Patmore; both these poets were considerably older than Hopkins, and he naturally would have supposed that they would predecease him. For his hopes and purposes he had to take an enormous chance; the guardian of his poems would have to be another poet, one his own age, who could, if Hopkins could only persuade him, keep the poems together in one place and, if Hopkins should die before him, publish them.

All of these hopes Hopkins was quite open about, in his letters to Bridges. He once said to Bridges 'I cannot think of altering anything. Why shd. I? I do not write for the public. You are my public and I hope to convert you' (*LB*, 46, 1877). As I have suggested elsewhere, Hopkins wanted to convert Bridges not only to the way he wrote poetry, but to Catholicism. What he also meant was that he was not writing for any large *present* public, but for a possible future one, to which Bridges, and only Bridges, could gain him access. For, in another letter written a year and a half later (*LB*, 66, 1879), Hopkins referred once again to the painful problem of publication:

When I say that I do not mean to publish I speak the truth. I have taken and mean to take no steps to do so beyond the attempt I made to print my two wrecks in the *Month*. If some one in authority knew of my having some poems printable and suggested my doing it I shd. not refuse, I should be partly, though not altogether, glad. But that is very unlikely. All therefore that I think of doing is to keep my verses together in one place—at present I have not even correct copies—, that, if anyone shd. like, they might be published after my death. And that again is unlikely as well as remote.

Hopkins had not needed the cautious approach of Tractarians like Pusey and Liddon, or liberals like Jowett, or his colleagues in the Society of Jesus toward art and the artist's life to come to the stricken conclusion that the creative life did hold snares for him. Ruskin had taught his disciples to rejoice over each star, mountain, cloud, bud, bloom, and berry, as though the whole world were bathed in a fresh radiance unknown since Adam and Eve first surveyed their private domain; yet even in Ruskin Hopkins had encountered a sick discomfort in the presence of the sensible world and in the artist's most reverent efforts to recreate it; and this unease eventually found its counterpart in his own racked conscience. In *Stones of Venice*, which celebrated equally nature's riches, ecclesiastical art, and the spirit of worship in the great Christian artists, Ruskin suddenly paused to express a fear totally at variance with the mood of these volumes:

> I cannot answer for the experience of others, but I never yet met with a Christian whose heart was thoroughly set upon the world to come, and so far as human judgment could pronounce, perfect and right before God, who cared about art at all.

There are tremendous risks for the lovers of art, no matter how Christian their aims:

> I have known several very noble Christian men who loved it intensely, but in them there was always traceable some entanglement of the thoughts with the matters of this world, causing them to fall into strange distress and doubts, and often leading them into what they themselves would confess to be errors in understandings, or even failures in duty. (X, 124–5)

Hopkins was to put the matter more doctrinally, with a paraphrase from Revelation on lukewarm Christians: 'And this is what Father Whitty says is the meaning of tepidity, the state of a soul, that being in God's grace, is content to live not according to grace but according to nature.' Fervour, Hopkins warned himself, 'is properly the being on the boil, the shewing of stir of life, of a life not shared by all other things, and the being ready to pass, by evaporation, into a wholly spiritual condition' (*S*, 208, 1882). That was the crux of the dualism

---

As we all know, no matter how profoundly the two poets may have quarrelled about prosody, and about faith and morals during Hopkins's lifetime, Hopkins's faint hopes were realized; Bridges did keep 'correct copies' of all the poems that Hopkins sent him, and the first edition of 1918, with Bridges as editor, was the result.

for Hopkins: no matter how praiseworthy a man was, a natural object was, or a work of art was, no talent, no natural beauty, no charm of any sort counted one single jot beside 'a life not shared by all other things'. And Ruskin also feared that although many artists might 'be in very deed nobler than those whose conduct is more consistent; they may be more tender in the tone of all their feelings, and farther-sighted in soul', and for these very reasons 'exposed to greater trials and fears, than whose hardier frame and naturally narrower vision enabled them with less effort to give their hands to God and walk with him' (x, 125).

In a harrowing correspondence with Canon Dixon, who begged Hopkins not to give up poetry, Hopkins said that God might already be preparing a 'severe judgment' against him, for the very 'lothness' he had shown in giving up poetry, for the very 'backward glances' he had 'given' with his 'hand upon the plough', and for the 'waste of time the very compositions' Dixon was pleading for 'may have caused and their preoccupation of the mind which belonged to more sacred or more biding duties, for the disquiet and the thoughts of vainglory they have given rise to'. Hopkins then closed this painful discussion with a simple and dignified statement similar to Ruskin's own conclusions: 'A purpose may look smooth and perfect from without but be frayed and faltering within' (*CD*, 88, 1881). And so Hopkins, obviously remembering *The Spiritual Exercises of St. Ignatius* and possibly paraphrasing Ruskin on the grave risks even to 'very noble Christian men' and of fatal 'entanglement of the thoughts with the matters of this world', had to accept that for himself,

> in the midst of outward occupations not only the mind is drawn from God, which may be at the call of duty and be God's will, but unhappily the will to is entangled, wordly interests freshen, and wordly ambitions revive. The man who in the world is as dead to the world as if he were buried in the cloister is already a saint. But this is our ideal. (*CD*, 75–6, 1881)

In the third volume of *Modern Painters* Ruskin outlined three archetypal attitudes toward art and nature. There is the man who despises them or ignores them, and he is the lowest of 'the three orders of being'; he is closer to an animal than a man. The second lowest—or second highest—order of being is the Christian artist. The highest order of being is a man who had once given his heart to the delights and the truth of nature, but who now, yearning to accomplish some divine purpose, 'loses sight in resolution, and feeling in work', and who deliberately calls up in himself 'the stern energy which disdains' all art, nature, and beauty, braced as he now is with 'the wisdom of purpose which represses emotion in action' (v, 361).

Under circumstances such as these, the whole principle of the innocent eye may even partake of the satanic. Whether it was conscious or not, the conflict between the innocent eye and Ruskin's 'highest order of being' is usually observable in the structure of Hopkins's sonnets. The octaves usually suggest the undeniable attractions of this world, while the sestets reconcile the priest to his sterner tasks. And so, at the very moment of writing these poems, Hopkins often urges upon himself the higher sanctity of silence.

The full shock of the 'Ruskinese point of view' is never more startling than when one stumbles upon it in Hopkins's most popular poems. 'Pied Beauty', for example, honours the truth of chiaroscuro or diatonic beauty, generic plenitude and specific creation, the sacrament of energy, the theory of universal paradoxes, and the Christian artist's proper role as exultant imitator of nature's infinite variety. This is a curtal sonnet of ten lines and a coda; the opening sestet compresses into six lines almost as many Ruskinian concerns:

> Glory be to God for dappled things—
> > For skies of couple-colour as a brinded cow;
> > For rose-moles all in stipple upon trout that swim;
> Fresh-firecoal chestnut-falls; finches' wings;
> > Landscape plotted and pieced—fold, fallow, and plough;
> > And áll trádes, their gear and tackle and trim.

The opening line celebrates nature's infinite variety and the grand Ruskinian aphorism that ALL GREAT ART IS PRAISE. The first line implies praise of specific creation and the second line describes it. Hopkins is illustrating Ruskin's truth of chiaroscuro; the skies are 'couple-coloured' in a very specific way—they are 'brinded', meaning 'brindled' or streaked or spotted, that is, 'dappled' with very small portions of colour.

In the third line, the 'trout that swim' are not there merely for the sake of the rhyme to come. These trout, each one darting and flashing through the stream, as their 'rose-moles all in stipple' catch the innocent eye of the onlooker, are obeying not only the principle of specific creation, since, like the couple-coloured skies, they are each stippled in a different pattern, but they are celebrating the sacrament of energy in their generic behaviour, typical of trout. Most of the 'dappled' and stippled things are on the move; 'Pied Beauty' is a hymn to Ruskin's 'majesty of motion'.

The last two lines of the opening sestet move imperceptibly toward a moral judgment based on the world of nature, just as Ruskin almost invariably progressed toward some principle of divine ordination after one of his paeans of praise to specificity. To the human eye, landscapes 'plotted and pieced—fold, fallow, and plough', do appear to carry out the look of nature's variety in all things, but here the hand of man has done the plotting. Hopkins's farmer, in ploughing according to immemorial custom, has thus obeyed two of Ruskin's principles: that the work of man should imitate nature as far as possible, and that a humble man, doing the work of his station with a good will, contributes to the praise of the Lord as fully as though he were painting or praying.

As a Ruskinian document the last quatrain is a marvel of condensation. In this four-line stanza and its two-word coda, Hopkins unobtrusively introduces four of Ruskin's favourite corollaries to the principle of specific creation: the principles of stability behind flux, of sacramental energy, of nature's wilful mystery, and of natural antitheses in all things:

> All things counter, original, spare, strange;
>   Whatever is fickle, freckled (who knows how?)
>   With swift, slow; sweet, sour; adazzle, dim;
> He fathers-forth whose beauty is past change:
>   Praise him.   (Poem 37, 1877)

The first three lines of the quatrain proclaim the beauty and righteousness of specific creation and the sacrament of energy. Hopkins has neatly encompassed the sacrament of energy and of flux with three adjectives: 'fickle'—meaning here merely shifting and changeable, 'swift', and 'slow'. He discreetly praises nature's wilful mystery with the parenthetical clause '(who knows how?)'. The admission of universal antagonisms is contained in the line 'with swift, slow; sweet, sour; adazzle, dim'; here even the alliteration and the parallel punctuation imitate nature's benign reconciliation between 'things usually thought incompatible'. 'Adazzle, dim' also sums up Turnerian mystery of tone, as Ruskin called Turner's 'power of dazzling' his viewers with fantastically brilliant scenes (III, 291) at the very moment he was teaching them the 'noble dimness' (VI, 91) at the divine heart of all this dazzle. 'Adazzle, dim' symbolized for Hopkins, as Turner's landscapes had for Ruskin, both the blinding glory and the eternal secrecy of God (VI, 90).

'Pied Beauty' quite naturally begins and ends with a salute to God, the changeless origin of beauty in all its flux and its variety. The first

line of the sestet—'Glory be to God for dappled things'—and the last
line of the poem with its coda:

> He fathers-forth whose beauty is past change:
> Praise him.

thus place the apotheosis of flux within a framework of stability. The
delighted shock that greets the listeners every time they arrive at the
two grave yet joyous monosyllables, 'Praise him', has its origin in this
artful framework. The sonnet begins in exhilaration and ends in solemnity. The two monosyllables are, in a sense, themselves examples of
specific creations, as so much of Hopkins's poetry is; they are 'counter,
original, spare, strange', for they throw the ten-line sonnet off balance
in a most satisfactory way, even while they are introducing the listeners
to a world of changeless values beyond the world of 'fickle' sensible
things. And so Hopkins has wonderfully resolved the tension between
man's need for infinite variety, for change and for selving, and his
equal need for order, discipline, and permanence. And the whole
sonnet vibrates with an implicit contrast between 'swift, slow'; creatures
are moving at different rates of speed, and the patient ploughman moves
at an even slower rate than fish and finches. And so in the sky, under
the waters, and on the rich earth, the whole universe is swaying in
shifting patterns of movement to the dictates of some unseen orchestra.
And for Hopkins, as for Ruskin, behind the orchestra was a silent God,
Who caused all flux and all majesty of motion, and all binding to
principles beyond flux and motion.

Hopkins once said of his enigmatic sonnet, 'The Windhover' (Poem
36, 1877), that it was the best thing he had ever written (*LB*, 85,
1879). Neither his affection for it nor its enigmatic quality should
surprise us entirely. He was trying 'to express a sub[t]le and recondite
thought on a subtle and recondite subject in a subtle and recondite
way'; he appeared to accept that this subtlety might be 'consistent with
excellences higher than clearness at first reading', and that 'great
felicity and perfection' might result 'in the end' (*LB*, 265, 54, 1887,
1878). More than any other poem in Hopkins's canon, this one satisfies
Ruskin's claims upon the artist, especially Ruskin's demand for
legitimate obscurity in art. 'The Windhover' is 'no exception to this
rule. EXCELLENCE OF THE HIGHEST KIND, WITHOUT OBSCURITY, CANNOT
EXIST' (VI, 81). And Hopkins himself hints at a far more paradoxical
reading than is generally accorded 'The Windhover' by pairing the
title with a subtitle, 'To Christ our Lord', as though the windhover
were a Ruskinian foil for Christ, as he clearly is for the ploughman

lumbering down the furrows at a patient speed quite distinguishable from the windhover's free and exuberant flight.

In order to qualify as a Ruskinian poem, 'The Windhover' must exemplify Ruskin's twin principles of mimetic and laudatory art, without blurring the difference between good and evil. This sonnet goes out of its way to praise and imitate two creatures, the windhover and the ploughman; but the greatest praise is offered to their Creator, to whom the sonnet is dedicated. The sonnet celebrates things as they ARE in nature, or that windhover as he IS in nature, without any judgment of *him*. But this vision is deliberately paired with a far more trustworthy Ignatian vision of man as he ought to be, a vision strikingly similar to Ruskin's vision of the highest order of men, who 'lose sight in resolution and feeling in work' (v, 361). The two creatures, the almost invisible ploughman and the dazzlingly visible windhover, are 'two prototypes', one of work and one of play, or in more severe terms, one 'of obedience' and one 'of disobedience' (*S*, 115, n.d.).[24]

In a later poem, appropriately titled 'To what serves Mortal Beauty?' (Poem 62, 1885), Hopkins was to put the matter less obscurely than he did in 'The Windhover'; this poem advises the lover of natural beautiful things to do exactly what the windhover's admirer does; he must acknowledge beautiful things with open-hearted generosity. But he must then ask himself what all this beauty is for, and whether one ought not invariably seek out the more authentic sort of beauty that the onlooker finds in the sestet of 'The Windhover':

> What do then? how meet beauty? Merely meet it; own,
> Home at heart, heaven's sweet gift; then *leave, let that alone.*
> Yea, wish that though, wish all, God's better beauty, grace.
>
> [Italics mine]

Thus, in 'The Windhover', Hopkins is risking what the Ruskinian artist must risk; he is faithfully describing as an artist what he would be forbidden to do as a man. It is essential to emphasize again that the Ruskinian artist must make symbols of nature, but in doing so, he must not tell untruths about nature, or hopelessly confuse the Planner with the plan. And the truth about the windhover is that he is part of the plan, not the Planner. Although he is an example of Ruskinian VITAL BEAUTY, and therefore, as part of the plan, he is worthy of imitation in art, he is also a proud and ostentatious beast, and therefore dangerous as a living model for man.

The sonnet's title announces the falcon's presence according to generic behaviour; he is hovering,[25] as that species of falcon does—

hence his name. But he is also an example of specific diatonic beauty, since his chiaroscuro, or dappling, will never be precisely repeated in another windhover. For it was above all, in such matters as speckling, stippling, dappling, spotting, and streaking, Ruskin reiterated, that nature contrives never to repeat herself. The windhover's glorious sweeping motions in the sky, his 'off, off forth on swing', like a skater's curves on fresh ice, even exemplify chromatic or graded beauty, reminding us of the pleasure both Ruskin and Hopkins took in curves as a symbol of infinite beauty. Hopkins's windhover is also re-enacting the sacrament of energy in natural things; he is a part of nature's choreography as he sweeps, hovers, and glides, proudly rebuffing 'the big wind'.

The entire octave of the sonnet operates upon the principle of mimetic art; it stuns readers and listeners with its Ruskinian majesty of motion. The very first verbal phrase, 'I caught this morning', sets the current of mimetic energy pulsing through the sonnet. The verb 'caught' is a vigorous one, indicating how spontaneously and how generously the onlooker in the poem has completed step one and step two that Ruskin required of the Christian artist. He does not say 'I saw', which would have been a pallid response unfitting for a Ruskinian artist; he says 'I caught'—'I committed an action imitating the vigour of what I saw.' The second line is a pell-mell rush of outriding feet and crowded syllables; it even begins with a split between the single word 'kingdom'. The first line ends with 'king-' and the second line begins with 'dom'. The reader himself is thus forced to re-enact the sacrament of energy, since the first line runs into the second, with only the breathless hyphen separating the lines; and each subsequent line runs headlong into the next until the exclamation mark in line five: 'How he rung upon the rein of a wimpling wing/In his ecstasy!' This exclamation mark is placed according to the guidelines of mimetic art, for it permits a pause just before the falcon abandons his hovering motions and sweeps himself off in his stirring series of infinite curves—'then off, off forth on swing'.

The breathless tone of the octave is that of a delighted child, his innocent eye unspoiled by fear, cynicism, or by blinding envy of the bird's freedom, a freedom not granted man as a fallen creature. Even Hopkins's punctuation indicates his delight in the sacrament of energy, and it also resembles Ruskin's hyperbolic style: the dashes, the exclamation points, the run-on lines are all Ruskinian in their frank exuberance. Yet because the bird's dappled, hovering, and swooping inscapes offer the reader a precise picture of him, this Ruskinian precision brings to the octave just the proper touch of Doric restraint beneath the Corinthian rejoicing.

What, then, accounts for the ominous quality in the windhover, a warning of some danger to man that no onlooker's joy in the falcon's splendid 'achieve' can quite submerge? For various answers we can look again at Ruskin's law governing nature's freedom, and the artist's proper response to it. Then we should look closely here and there at the language of the sonnet, and finally at some corresponding comments in Hopkins's sermons and letters.

First we might consider how different a moral symbol this imposing falcon is from Hopkins's small joyous lark in 'The Sea and the Skylark'. Hopkins calls the windhover 'Brute beauty', and this bird is a Ruskinian symbol for nature in one of her moods. Nature may sometimes be man's comfort, sometimes his scourge in her 'wrath and threatening' (xi, 164), and sometimes she is merely indifferent to him, as the windhover is. But nature is free to do and be exactly as she wishes, because she is nature, not man. In the same manner, Hopkins is using the windhover as a symbol of nature's non-lapsarian freedom, a freedom man lost after the fall. But just because the windhover symbolizes the world of free nature, untouched by human sin, this 'Brute beauty' is not the potential recipient of grace, as man is. Man's only freedom is to make a picture of the windhover, or to write a poem about him, but man must never try to imitate the windhover's conduct.

The first indication we have in the sonnet itself that the windhover's conduct contains a grave warning for man takes place in the opening two lines of the octave:

> I caught this morning morning's minion, king-
> dom of daylight's dauphin, dapple-dawn-drawn Falcon,

and this warning reveals itself partly through the apostrophe after 'daylight'. The bird is 'daylight's dauphin', or rather 'king-dom of daylight's dauphin', not the king's dauphin. The falcon is not a royal son of a king and thus a symbol for 'Christ our Lord'. He is the 'king-dom of daylight's dauphin', or the royal son of the daylight; and he is the royal son of a very precise time of day, at that, for he is *morning's* minion', a 'dapple-*dawn*-drawn Falcon', that is to say, a royal son of the morning. The windhover's earliest Biblical prototypes, whom Hopkins discussed exhaustively in his sermons and his religious notes, are Satan and Lucifer, Isaiah's 'son of the morning', who boasted that he would 'ascend into heaven' and would exalt his own false 'throne above the stars of God'.[26] Both these figures had once been under divine protection, and so they still carry the divine lineaments about themselves; but both of them had been stripped of actual divinity because they had attempted to imitate the glory of God rather than to praise it.

If we wonder how Hopkins could have brought himself to admire so mixed a figure as the windhover, with both the diabolic and the angelic lineaments about him, we need not even consider Marlowe's Faustus. It was a marked feature of Hopkins's aesthetic and critical generosity, as it was of Ruskin's, to exhibit praise and warning wherever these were due. The metaphors Hopkins uses to describe his windhover simultaneously praise the windhover and warn us of him; he is a '*Brute* beauty', full of 'valour and act, oh, air, *pride*, plume'. These metaphors are both bestial and chivalric, and they bear far more relation to Ruskin's proud Venetian Doges or his bold and active merchants, soldiers, and architects than they do Hopkins's Paraclete, the compassionate Son of Man. Ruskin enormously admired these Renaissance men of action,[27] yet they stood for potential or actual corruption as obviously as Ruskin's splendid Venice was herself a model for corrupt cities.

There are endless Victorian examples of this sort of critical and aesthetic honesty. One need only consider Matthew Arnold's repetitious injunctions to see the object before us as it *really* is, regardless of our desires, our prejudices, or our historical assumptions. And one need only think of the admiration Tennyson expressed for his self-centred Princess upon her mountain heights or his equally sybaritic soul in her lofty 'Palace of Art'. Certainly in these three cases, the Ignatian, the Tennysonian, and the Ruskinian, the same moral progress occurs—the first ecstatic encounter with beauty, then the uneasy testing of it, and finally its renunciation in favour of some more authentic aim equivalent to 'God's better beauty, grace'. Hopkins himself had once said almost wistfully that Lucifer 'was innocent and virtuous and enlightened and high in grace' before he was conquered by pride in his own talents; then Hopkins moved from praise of Lucifer to regret that this attractive, talented creature had 'entangled and "with his tail swept down", as the Scripture says, his angels themselves' (*S*, 180, 1881).[28]

In the first volume of *Stones of Venice* (IX, 343), Ruskin described a winged cherub who possesses the paradoxical qualities of Hopkins's Lucifer and Hopkins's windhover. The movement from praise of the freewheeling creature to a discomfort in its presence is implicit rather than explicit and it is far more unobtrusive than Hopkins's final rejection of the windhover. But the movement toward rejection is there, just the same:

> The most beautiful base I ever saw, on the whole, is a Byzantine one in the Baptistry of St. Marks, in which the spur profile ... is formed by a cherub, who sweeps downward on the wing. His two wings, as they half close, form the upper part of the spur, and the rise of it in the front is formed by exactly the action of Alichino, swooping on the pitch lake. . . .

In this paragraph we also encounter implicit praise of 'VITAL BEAUTY'; the rejection of the potential licence residing in 'VITAL BEAUTY' may be unconscious here, but Alichino is one of the demons in *The Divine Comedy*.

In the sestet of 'The Windhover', the distinction emerges between vital, or natural beauty and that beauty which is 'a billion/Times told lovelier, more dangerous', or more authentic than mere vital beauty.[29] Ruskin's term for beauty closer to divine principles even than vital beauty was the 'Levitical sacrifice'. God would never turn His back on a man who had humbly offered up a labour of love. Hopkins's ploughman, so quietly making 'plough down sillion/Shine' that he is present more as a humble act than a person at all, is officiating at a 'Levitical sacrifice'; and for this sacrifice to be effective, Ruskin said, there ought to be some strain in the labourer's offerings, some martyrdom of himself, and 'this costliness was *generally* a condition of the acceptableness of the sacrifice' (VIII, 33).

'God's better beauty, grace' was Hopkins's equivalent of Ruskin's 'Levitical sacrifice'. Hopkins emphasized even more than Ruskin that it should be a modest beauty, even a hidden beauty. 'My heart in hiding' in 'The Windhover' means just that; the ploughman is Ruskin's unobtrusive 'soldier of the ploughshare' (XVI, 26);[30] and his humble task brings him closer to God than if he were to imitate any 'prince of the power of the air', who symbolized for St Paul 'the spirit that now worketh in the children of disobedience'.[31] Hopkins had several times said to Canon Dixon that 'show and brilliance do not suit' the Jesuits, who prefer instead 'to cultivate the commonplace outwardly and wish the beauty of the king's daughter the soul to be from within' (*CD*, 96, 1881).

It is a Christian commonplace, as it was a Victorian commonplace, that a beautiful exterior could not hide an ugly interior from God or from a spiritually discerning soul. But it is the habit of converts to make literal patterns of spiritual truths and to frame every act and thought upon them: 'genius attracts fame and individual fame St. Ignatius looked on as the most dangerous and dazzling of all attractions', Hopkins wrote Canon Dixon (*CD*, 93–4, 1881). Dixon had begged Hopkins not to give up poetry; 'Surely', he desperately tried to reassure Hopkins, 'one vocation cannot destroy another: and such a Society as yours will not remain ignorant that you have such gifts as have seldom been given by God to man' (*CD*, 90, 1881). But pleadings of this sort frightened Hopkins more than they reassured him; the windhover's brilliance was not for him. God might even have 'a severe judgment' in store for him, because with his very 'hand upon the plough' he had been guilty of 'disquiet and thoughts of vainglory' when he wrote poetry, or thought of earning fame for his poems. And it was for these reasons that he sought to keep his 'heart in hiding', for 'there is more peace and it is the holier lot to be unknown than to be known' (*CD*, 88, 89, 1881).

The last tercet in 'The Windhover' arrives at the same resolution; the plough may be shining, but it is shining in secret, 'down sillion', that is to say, hidden by the furrows.[32] After offering to the windhover all the excited response that was his due, the ploughman, who is also probably the onlooker, has found the 'wisdom of purpose which represses emotion in action' (v, 361); this wisdom, Ruskin said, belonged only to the highest order of being, who had first loved and praised beauty, and then left it for something more authentic.

As an imitation of nature, the art of God, 'The Windhover' satisfies in every way Ruskin's demand for 'lawful freedom with vigour and variety', a freedom that risks aesthetic licence without falling into it, just as it may risk moral licence for an uncloistered virtue. The sonnet's almost total hyperbole, coupled with the restraint both of treatment and of resolution, announce that in this poem above all others, Hopkins is attempting something like Ruskin's 'noble ornamentation', a controlled lavishness that declares itself unmistakably anxious to serve as an 'expression of delight in God's works' (IX, 70). So the two parts of the sonnet, the octave and the sestet, fully display the two principles behind Ruskin's theory of religious sanity. The octave is a canticle of praise for one of God's artifacts; the sestet celebrates Ruskin's higher principle than that of artistry. For to be an artist is to praise God's works, but to labour is to praise God Himself.

'The Windhover' is a masterful 'achieve' in its fusion of Ruskinian and Ignatian principles. It sums up in fourteen lines most of the maxims and most of the paradoxes in Ruskin's canon, and finds a 'golden mean' between them. Idealism and realism, self-sacrifice and self-fulfilment, God and man, art and prayer, the beautiful phenomenal world and 'God's better beauty, grace', are all given their due. And all these paradoxes are linked together in the proper proportions by a series of metaphors whose symbolic meaning rocks and shifts from line to line and from octave to sestet; and these rocking and shifting metaphors first induce excitation and finally culminate in spiritual poise, so that according to Ruskinian principles of mimetic art, the reader may experience the same resolution as the poet. And thus the ploughman's legitimate delight in a 'Brute beauty', an arrogant darling of nature, and all possible longing to which the delight may have given rise, is quietly resolved in the contentment of the last three lines. The windhover, unimpeded by moral demands upon his natural freedom, now goes his way, while Christ's humble soldier of the ploughshare, equally refreshed by the vision he has rejected, and the vision he has accepted, goes his.

'New Nazareths in Us':
the Making of a Victorian Gentleman

Now there are three great loves that rule the souls of men: the love of what is lovely in creatures, and of what is lovely in things, and what is lovely in report. And these three loves have each their relative corruption, a lust—the lust of the flesh, the lust of the eyes, and the pride of life.

And as I have just said, a gentleman is distinguished from a churl by the purity of the sentiment he can reach in all three passions: by his imaginative love as opposed to lust; his imaginative possession of wealth as opposed to avarice; his imaginative desire of honour as opposed to pride.   (Ruskin, XXVIII, 80)

I agree then, and vehemently, that a gentleman, if there is such a thing on earth, is in the position to despise the poet, were he Dante or Shakspere, and the painter, were he Angelo or Appeles, for anything in him that shewed him *not* to be a gentleman. He is in the position to do it, I say, but if he is a gentleman perhaps this is what he will not do. Which leads me to another remark.

The quality of a gentleman is so very fine a thing that it seems to me one should not be at all hasty in concluding that one possesses it.   (Hopkins, *LB*, 175, 1883)

In their voluminous comments on the making of a Christian artist, Hopkins and Ruskin implied that they were equally concerned with another problem inseparable from it in Victorian eyes—the making of a Christian gentleman. They did not say that every Christian gentleman had to be an artist, but they agreed that every artist must attempt to develop the attributes of the ideal gentleman if he was not born with them, for without them, he would fail his public.

In their statements on the making of a gentleman, Hopkins and Ruskin stressed a subtle sense of virtue, far removed in its discrimination from the cruder judgments of the evangelizing religious parties and the Philistines. Walter Houghton calls this moral sense 'the all-inclusive virtue of magnanimity, the Aristotelian greatness of soul which raises one above everything that is petty, mean or commonplace'. Houghton suggests that the Victorian ideal of magnanimity, or humanistic perfection, 'was facilitated by the whole movement of naturalism, dating from the Renaissance, and gaining momentum rapidly in the nineteenth century'.[1]

Claude Colleer Abbott opened his introduction to the two earliest volumes of Hopkins's collected letters with a similar suggestion; significantly enough, all students of Hopkins's work thus find themselves introduced to his letters by a quotation from Spenser's preface to *The Faerie Queene*:

> 'The generall end therefore of all the boke is to fashion a gentleman or noble person in vertuous and gentle discipline.' So writes Spenser in expounding to Raleigh the whole intention of his *Faerie Queene*; and we at once associate his knightly figures with the Renaissance ideal of a complete man defined in many treatises, and made flesh and blood in our literature, by a Wyatt or a Sidney.

The idea that the virtues of a Victorian gentleman were in any way consonant with those of a Renaissance gentleman may have startled Abbott at the time he was writing, for he appeared faintly apologetic about the comparisons he was making:

> It is, indeed, with some difficulty that we look before and after the Elizabethans to find other mirrors of chivalry and courtesy, so enamoured are we of the energy abounding in that pregnant age, when
>
> > The noble heart, that harbours vertuous thought,
> > And is with child of glorious intent
> > Can never rest, vntil it forth haue brought
> > Th'eternall brood of glorie excellent.

Abbott was offering students of Hopkins's poetry, and indeed, students of the whole Victorian period, a richer and more comprehensive framework by which to appreciate the Victorian achievement than was customary in 1935:

But though the brood of glory be eternal, neither the noble heart nor the pattern of the progeny runs to one mould. Every age has its own examples. From these volumes emerge three figures worthy to adorn a concourse of chivalry however exalted, three poets whose endeavours to perform the purpose of God as they understood it witness to that diversity in excellence which is the prevailing beauty of the spirit of man.

The three gentlemen poets Abbott had in mind are Hopkins, Bridges, and Dixon, all Oxonians; they naturally remind us of two other Victorian gentlemen, both graduates of Oxford: Matthew Arnold and his father, Dr Thomas Arnold, Headmaster of Rugby and a famous maker of gentlemen in his time. Abbott's figure of the Christian gentleman, Victorian or Renaissance, with his 'diversity in excellence which is the prevailing beauty of the spirit of man', and his moral aims clearly directed toward the performance of God's purpose, is Arnoldian. And the Arnoldian figure itself expresses a freer and more ample Christian humanism than is ever yet invariably admitted to be a true measure of that most attractive human type, the new Victorian gentleman (*LB*, xv, n.d.).[2]

Victorian writers on the subject of the new chivalry stressed 'pathos',[3] by which they meant pity, a quality of sustained sympathy, particularly with the sufferings of helpless and disenfranchised people such as women and children and the inferior classes. Here again Hopkins freely drew upon Ruskin and innumerable Victorian predecessors. The necessity for 'pathos' was one moral and artistic staple upon which almost all writers and their readers could agree, since it was one of the signs by which one discovered a gentleman born or made. Furthermore, to demonstrate the capacity for pathos in oneself, or to announce that one has discovered it in a friend, might very well suggest the presence of the gentleman in oneself, without any vulgar boasting.

As many critics of Victorian society have discovered, the articulate members of this society often behaved as though they were simultaneously gazing backward at an attractive past, thought to be more gracious, more moral, and even intellectually richer than the present, and peering anxiously into a future both threatening and promising. This Janus-stance was obvious not only in the craze for things Elizabethan, but in a simultaneous craze for things medieval. The Victorian cultivation of the virtue of 'pathos' was in many ways akin to the cultivation of courtesy and 'the gentle heart' in the late medieval courts of Provence. As Maurice Valency discusses the merging of 'high nobility' and 'low' in France during the twelfth and thirteenth centuries, he describes an almost archetypal process. Upper classes and their supporting religious establishments almost invariably teach that 'nobility—and its concomitants, privilege, virtue and wealth—' are hereditary gifts of God, or rights earned in some manner impossible for the lower orders to emulate. Nothing could be more like the English aristocracy, particularly before the successive reform acts of the nineteenth century, than Professor Valency's description of the hereditary nobility of late medieval France. It is the habit of the articulate members of any ruling caste to create overt rules of precedence and a covert mystique sanctioning their power and privileges; as new classes move up, they incorporate not only the rules but the mystique. Certainly nothing could be more familiar to students of Victorian history than Valency's description of the way the classes just below the high nobility captured some of the values of the nobles above them, and with subtle modifications, turned these values to their own uses:

> But as the new chivalric class was gradually ennobled, it became useful to distinguish between the nobility of birth and the nobility of personal merit, and it was normal for those who had not the former to insist on the unique importance of the latter.

The *trouvères* of northern France, like the emerging Victorian gentlemen,

> based their idea of nobility upon the manly virtues, prowess, loyalty, and honor, those traits which would primarily recommend the fighting man to his lord. The southern troubadours grounded their concept of nobility not as much upon prowess as upon courtesy. In exemplifying the concepts, these poets developed two radically different types of poetry, the narrative of martial deeds and the song of love.

The would-be Victorian gentleman adopted not only the manly virtues of 'prowess, loyalty, and honor' typical of northern France, but also the Provençal virtues of courtesy; and courtesy and 'pathos' became the Victorian version of 'the gentle heart'. Hopkins called this sort of courtesy 'the handsome heart', and it was to be found in the gentleman and the slum-child alike, for, as the late medieval southern troubadours also had insisted, some virtues took no account of genes or of social hierarchies:[4]

For the troubadour, therefore, nobility was the capacity to love and to acquire worth through love. This was possible only to those who had a natural predisposition, and this disposition was the gentle heart. The gentle heart was not something one inherited. It was the gift of God.

For the rising knight in medieval France, courtesy and the gentle heart were ideally placed at the service of womankind, and especially the one lifelong lady of one's heart. The Victorian 'handsome heart' throbbed for all mankind, especially for the members of the community in need of a strong man's protection. Although the recipients of a Victorian gentleman's compassion would naturally include his frail wife and tender children, the pathos in his heart served a national need: it alleviated public misery, and it was intended as a substitute for revolution.[5]

As educated sons of mercantile families, Hopkins and Ruskin were typical of innumerable Victorians who had to come to terms with the social values of the classes above them. Oxford had left them both thoroughly imbued with the lessons of England's medieval past, as well as her classical and Renaissance heritage, and despite their distinctly middle-class origins—or even perhaps because of these origins—they were fascinated with the pageantry of aristocratic breeding and hereditary wealth. They were both anxious to see ancient chivalric values blended with the sturdy morality sifting up from the lower middle classes. The two Balliol classicists, Jowett and Matthew Arnold, might have trusted in hellenism to civilize the Philistines, but Hopkins, the ex-Tractarian, wanted something equally beautiful, but safer, more Christian, and he joined Ruskin and the rest of the latter-day medievalists in trying to subdue the romance of chivalry for domestic consumption.

But Hopkins had not been a pupil of Jowett and a Balliol scholar for nothing, and furthermore, like most intelligent Victorians, he had developed an omnivorous taste for reading. In his attempts to create a manageable synthesis of all his miscellaneous readings, particularly the classical and the medieval, he had provided himself with a hierarchy of values by which he could admire whatever was attractive in books and people, without yearning for attributes dangerous to his faith and his vocation. Lowest on his hierarchic ladder of virtues was the artist who was neither a Christian nor a gentleman:

As a [matter of?] fact poets and men of art are, I am sorry to say, by no means necessarily or commonly gentlemen. For gentlemen

do not pander to lust or other baseness, nor as you say, give themselves airs and affectations nor do other things to be found in modern
works. And this adds charm to everything Canon Dixon writes,
that you feel he is a gentleman and thinks like one.

(*LB*, 176, 1883)

And yet the artist, Hopkins wholeheartedly believed, has a vital
place in the Christian and the English scheme of things:[6]

> What are works of art for? to educate, to be standards. Education is
> meant for the many, standards are for public use. . . . Besides we are
> Englishmen. A great work by an Englishman is like a great battle
> won by England. It is an unfading bay tree. (*LB*, 231, 1886)

But the gentleman who is no artist is a finer tribute to the English
way of doing things than the artist who is no gentleman: 'By the by if
the English race had done nothing else, yet if they left the world the
notion of a gentleman, they would have done a great service to
mankind.'
At the top of Hopkins's ladder of virtue was the Christian, whose
divine model in all things was Christ, as St Ignatius was the human
model. In the middle of a long discussion on the features of a gentleman, Hopkins suggested that Christ was the surest archetype. 'Christ's
life and character are such as appeal to all the world's admiration', and
to be a gentleman, a mere gentleman,

> is but on the brim of morals and rather a thing of manners than of
> morals properly—then how much more must art and philosophy
> and manners and breeding and everything else in the world be below
> the least degree of true virtue. This is that chastity of mind which
> seems to lie at the very heart and be the parent of all other good, the
> seeing at once what is best, the holding to that, and the not allowing
> anything else whatever to be even heard pleading to the contrary.
> (*LB*, 176, 174, 1883)

Christian morality was highest in the hierarchy of virtues, gracious
gentility second, creativity third, and the lowest two virtues on the
list were to be jettisoned, whenever necessary, in favour of the highest.
Nothing could be more Victorian, and nothing could have been more
reassuring to St Ignatius Loyola or to Hopkins's colleagues in the
Society of Jesus.
Ruskin also fashioned a similar hierarchy of virtues that he hoped
would serve as a guide to the aspiring lower middle classes. Perhaps

out of loyalty to his own peasant ancestors and his vintner father,[7] Ruskin admitted certain decent and well-educated people into the company of gentlemen made, if not gentlemen born:

I do not in the least see why courtesy, and gravity, and sympathy with the feelings of others, and courage, and truth, and piety, and what else goes to make up a gentleman's character, should not be found behind a counter as well as elsewhere, if they were demanded, or even hoped for there. (XII, 343)

As a carrot to the lower orders and a stick to the reckless members of the upper classes, Ruskin had worked out a form of social Darwinism to his own satisfaction. Although normally the descendants of the carefully bred classes would exhibit moral and physical signs of their superior breeding, careless conduct and consistent abuses of the mind and the body over a number of generations would eventually result in debasement of the descendants. Equally so, if lower-class families took care of their health—or were given wages that would permit them to do so—if they married prudently, and taught their sons manners and good conduct, the family would improve, physically and morally, within a few generations. 'And the knowledge of this great fact ought to regulate the education of our youth, and the entire conduct of the nation.'

At other times Ruskin did not appear to be altogether sure that the attributes of breeding could be readily acquired, and whether, or how firmly, they could be transplanted:

Gentlemanliness, however, in ordinary parlance, must be taken to signify those qualities which are usually the evidence of high breeding, and which, so far as they can be acquired, it should be every man's effort to acquire, or if he has them by nature, to preserve and exalt. (VII, 345)

For all England's citizens, then, gentle or simple, Ruskin stressed the primacy of moral education, whether he was considering the moral welfare of the individual, the genetic welfare of the family, or the social welfare of the nation: 'All education must be moral first: intellectual secondarily. Intellectual before—(much more without)—moral education, is incompleteness, impossible, and in incompleteness, a calamity' (XXVIII, 655). What was fitting for the churl was equally fitting for the gentleman:

the main thing to be understood is that a man is not educated, in any sense whatever, because he can read Latin, or write English, or can behave well in a drawing-room; but that he is only educated if he is happy, busy, beneficent, and effective in the world.   (XI, 263)

Ruskin's hierarchic ladder of virtues—Christian morality on the highest rung, gentility, with all it entails in sensitive manners, breeding, and education next, and creativity on the lowest—emerges piecemeal:

just because we are intended, as long as we live, to be in a state of intense moral effort, we are *not* intended to be in intense physical or intellectual effort. Our full energies are to be given to the soul's work—to the great fight with the Dragon—the taking the kingdom of heaven by force.   (XII, 344)

Ruskin echoed the beliefs of Newman and Hopkins that it was possible to be a Christian without being a gentleman, but that it was impossible to be a true gentleman without being a Christian. Anyone who wished to make himself 'a scholar and a gentleman' must first make himself a Christian by reading Genesis (XXVIII, 496). To Ruskin, Adam Smith was the dread example of a man who had thrown over gentility when he forswore the gospel; after that, he was simply no gentleman. And what went for the gentleman went also for the artist. One could practise the artist's profession without being a Christian, but one could not *be* an artist in Ruskin's terms, without being a Christian, any more than one could be a gentleman without being a Christian, for 'whenever the Christian falls back out of the bright light of the Resurrection, even the Orpheus song is forbidden him' (XXXIV, 314, 313).

It is obviously possible to be a Christian day-labourer without being a gentleman, but Ruskin and Hopkins both wondered, along with many of their contemporaries, whether it was possible to be a Christian gentleman without having been a day-labourer at some time or another. True gentlemen, Ruskin thought, ought to do some work, preferably hard manual labour or work that usually carries the stigma of incivility with it, for 'it is no part of their duty or privilege to live on other people's toil':

They have to learn that there is no degradation in the hardest manual, or the humblest servile labour, when it is honest. But that there *is* degradation, and that deep, in extravagance, in bribery, in indolence, in pride, in taking places they are not fit for, or in coining places for which there is no need. It does not disgrace a gentleman to become

an errand boy, or a day labourer; but it disgraces him much to
become a knave, or a thief.   (VII, 344)

Ruskin's injunctions concerning the things a Victorian gentleman
would *not* do, and Hopkins's also, sum up what the Regency bucks—
presumably gentlemen—*did* do without a single moral qualm or a
moment's anxiety about losing social caste. But as James Laver describes 'the new ideal of the gentleman' in Victorian England,[8] he might
almost have had Hopkins's or Ruskin's model in mind:

> It is necessary to stress the word 'new' for many who would have
> passed as gentlemen in the earlier years of the century would have
> been considered howling cads before Victoria's reign was over. The
> Prince Regent himself was called the First Gentleman of Europe,
> and he delivered himself of the opinion that a gentleman was a
> man who knew Greek, that is, had had a certain kind of education.

In other words, 'the new ideal of gentleman' included the necessity for
conspicuously pure morals as well as exquisite manners and conspicuous money and prestige. Ruskin's gentleman parasite, like
Hopkins's base panderer to lust, was a 'howling cad', and according to
Laver,

> Long before the end of the century 'gentlemen' like this were an
> anachronism. The word gentleman had come to mean something
> quite different: it had come to mean the standard product of the
> Public Schools, and this is perhaps the most striking social phenom-
> enon in the history of Victorian England.

But not every Victorian gentleman in the making went to one of the
great public schools, or to a public school at all; for many the standard
product was to be found at one of the great Tudor day-schools or one
of the two historic universities, where responsibility to the community
also stamped a gentleman, as no amount of artistic or intellectual
prowess alone could have done. In praising the beautiful gentleman
who saw his duty and did it, and in opposing him to the mere artist
or the mere hereditary gentleman who was often assumed to shirk
responsibilities, Ruskin was simply elucidating his highly coloured
version of a moral commonplace. Hopkins also had urged the duty of
community service upon Bridges, Hallam upon Tennyson, Dr Arnold
upon his pupils, and Jowett upon his. The populace, Ruskin insisted,
were entitled to exact something from the privileged classes in exchange
for the protected life these classes lead:

And it is, perhaps, better to build a beautiful human creature than a beautiful dome or steeple—and more delightful to look up reverently to a creature far above us, than to a wall; and the beautiful creature will have some duties to do in return—duties of living belfry and rampart.

Ruskin's metaphor of the 'living belfry and rampart' suggests how conscious the Victorians themselves were of the historic strands in the new code of chivalry. The new Victorian gentleman was to combine the purity of a saint with the steadfastness of a medieval Knight Templar and the beauty and colour of a Renaissance courtier. And Ruskin made it quite plain that this beautiful creature need not be a mere insular product; he would find his counterparts all over Europe:

A highly-bred and trained English, French, Austrian, or Italian gentleman (much more a lady), is a great production,—a better production than most statues; a being beautifully coloured as well as shaped, and plus all the brains; a glorious thing to look at, a wonderful thing to talk to; and you cannot have it, any more than a pyramid or a church, but by sacrifice of much contributed life. (XVIII, 107–8)

Ruskin, who was an ardent admirer of Edmund Spenser, said several times that for him, St George, the humble soldier of plebeian origin, who rose to prominence although he did not disdain the arts of husbandry, was the ideal 'type of gentleman'.[9] If so, Ruskin's St George had obviously been through some of the Platonizing Schools at Oxford, and possibly taken a look at *The Book of the Courtier* while he was there. Certainly Ruskin's ideal gentleman owed as much to Socrates and to Castiglione as he did to St George:

A gentleman's first characteristic is that fineness of structure in the body, which renders it capable of the most delicate sensations; and of structure in the mind which renders it capable of the most delicate sympathies—one may say, simply, 'fineness of nature'. This is, of course, compatible with heroic bodily strength and mental firmness; in fact, heroic strength is not conceivable without such delicacy.

Like most Victorian models of the gentleman, Ruskin's blending of classical, medieval, Renaissance, and chastened Romantic figures combines more than a touch of the Victorian fondness for 'pathos' in his moral features:

a vulgar man having some heart at the bottom of him, if you can by talk or by sight fairly force the pathos of anything down to his heart, will be excited about it and demonstrative; the sensation of pity being strange to him and wonderful. But your gentleman has walked in pity all day long; the tears have never been out of his eyes; you thought his eyes were bright only; but they were wet.

So sensitive a creature, so alert to the sufferings of others as to weep, and to the comfort and ease of others as to treat all men with deference, was, like the equally finely honed and poised Christian artist, a far greater prey to temptation than his less sensitive compatriots:

> And, though rightness of moral conduct is ultimately the great purifier of race, the sign of nobleness is not in this rightness of moral conduct, but in sensitiveness. When the make of the creature is fine, its temptations are strong, as well as its perceptions; it is liable to all kinds of impressions in their most violent form; liable therefore to be abused and hurt by all kinds of rough things which would do a coarser creature little harm, and thus to fall into frightful wrong if its fate will have it so. (VII, 345, 348, 346)

Ruskin's gentleman model typifies the manner in which these Platonizing Oxonians revised Plato to suit the needs of their society. In his model republic, Socrates' gentlemen were to be taught that there was inevitable 'degradation in the hardest manual, or the humblest servile labour', and that it did indeed 'disgrace a gentleman to become an errand boy or a day labourer' (VII, 344). Perhaps the new Victorian gentleman had too much respect for the source of his wealth to deny the validity of labour. In any case, Jowett's classical scholar, capable of earning his firsts and his double firsts in the schools for the greater glory of Balliol, and equally capable of working beside his tenant peasants in the piggery, or digging ditches to improve the drainage on his property, is just such another Victorian knight of the plough. Hopkins's ploughman is obviously a gentleman born or made, despite his humble occupation: he has the educated taste and the generosity to adore the windhover's artistry. The windhover himself is like one of Ruskin's 'highly-bred' beings before he has submitted to the 'duties of living belfry and rampart'; he is 'beautifully coloured as well as shaped' and he is a 'glorious thing to look at'. The ploughman, on the other hand, is one of Ruskin's gentlemen brushed by temptation; for 'since the make of the creature is fine, its temptations are strong as well as its perceptions', and for a moment Hopkins's knight of the plough is tempted to envy the windhover's freedom and the personal achievement that went with it. As Matthew Arnold repeatedly warned generations of Philistines, a crude dissenter, debarred by his class and his religion from the seats of learning, would have turned his envy into contempt, and as Hopkins told Bridges, 'a gentleman would be in a position to do it, but if he is a gentleman, perhaps this is what he will not do'.

However it came about, Hopkins's beautiful creature, wheeling in the sky, and his ploughman, quietly digging the earth, are like two sides of the Ruskinian gentleman: the man who achieves an aristocratic bearing or an artistic technique worthy of emulation, and the man who renounces these virtues for the common weal. Hopkins had delivered the same kind of warning to his readers as Ruskin, Carlyle, Newman, Disraeli, and many another Victorian medievalist had delivered to theirs. What England needed from its beautifully bred creatures was less beauty and more sweat.

But there were some makers of the new gentleman, Matthew Arnold among them, who believed that if England were to survive as a civilized power, then the English gentleman would have to dispense with some of the sweat and the piety and cultivate far greater intellectual and aesthetic discernment than was at present fashionable, even at Oxford. And Hopkins's ploughman, despite his austere resolutions, is a paradigm of Arnold's gentleman critic; he possesses both 'sweetness' and 'light'. By 'sweetness' Arnold meant generosity and largeness of vision. By 'light' he meant the discrimination without which vision and generosity are flabby. That is why Arnold thought of criticism as a gentleman's profession, for only a gentleman combines the generosity and the fearlessness 'to see the object as in itself it really is'. Those talismanic phrases of Arnold's, so often reiterated, are, finally, his touchstones for all model citizens who would pattern themselves after the new gentleman.[10] Only a gentleman is secure enough to put aside prejudice, fear, self-justifying envy and spite, in order to praise what he may not have the talent to emulate. And for a Christian martyr like Hopkins, who was also an Arnoldian classicist and a Ruskinian aesthetician, this was the most important lesson he learned from his Oxonian predecessors—only a Christian who is also a gentleman can admit that he dearly loves what he believes he ought to abandon. He loves it because its beauty, as beauty, is good, though its solicitations may be dangerous for him.

As a schoolboy and an undergraduate, Hopkins saw many varieties of the new Victorian gentleman in the flesh. Twenty years after Dr

Arnold's death, 'the Rugby prigs', as they were often dubbed at Oxford,[11] still bore the imprint of their school. Dr Arnold had indeed done what he had set out to do: he had changed the face of the English public school. Just as his friend Jowett had colonized the intellectual and parliamentary world, and eventually other continents, with Balliol men, so Dr Arnold had imbued his Rugby pupils with the new gentlemanly ideal, part scholar, part gentleman missionary for Christ. He had colonized other public and day-schools and the two great universities, and he had seen to it that the new ideal of the Christian gentleman spread from the middle classes to the upper, so that it eventually reached even a few normally inaccessible peers of the realm.

All around him, as he grew to manhood, Hopkins encountered writers deeply concerned with the creation of new gentlemen heroes. Tennyson's King Arthur supported the new gentlemanly ideal by stressing the importance of the world's work. The escape of his knights into a feckless quest initiated the downfall of the realm. Sir Galahad and Sir Launcelot were foils for each other, the one too withdrawn from the world to be a successful model for the average Christian gentleman, the other too worldly.

Matthew Arnold's vision of rich totality as a supplement to piety and Christian conduct, and Newman's equally complex vision of a university man, socially and intellectually poised, yet morally on guard, were both aspects of the new gentleman hero for troubled times. Carlyle's heroes were not altogether Oxonian types; still less were they Balliol types—urbane, yet eager, polished, yet concealing under demure black gowns a passion for public service. Carlyle's heroes, on the contrary, were often rather crude mythic types, vigorous and even violent, and always interesting and idiosyncratic, but none-theless in their own rough way they were gentlemen because they were leaders. They knew they had been put in the world to be their brothers' keepers, though for heroes like Frederick the Great, service to their fellow men seemed to have an uncomfortable affinity with service to themselves. But they shared with other Victorian models, and what is of particular interest to us, they shared with Hopkins's models a deep distrust of most political reform. They exhibited a strong sense of selfhood; they had vigorously developed their own talents, or as Hopkins would have put the matter, they had 'tasted themselves' as leaders or as artists. They did not totally repress their talents, but rather turned them outward into the community in order that the world's work might be more efficiently and more attractively accomplished.

Nonetheless, moral and civic leadership, even leadership emanating from a realized self, required long training, considerable sacrifice of personal needs, and only so much 'selving' of the self, to use Hopkins's phrase again, as to ensure the completion of the task at hand. Tennyson's poetry often mediates unconsciously between the artist's need for privacy and a personal vision and the public's need for leadership.[12] His well-bred heroes and heroines move uneasily between two types: the hermits of one kind or another, who always fail the public; and the leaders, who finally accept the rules of the establishment, and somehow, despite Tennyson's eager support for them, often lose something of their vitality when they descend into the valley of the working world. Matthew Arnold, on the other hand, lacked vitality on the Parnassian heights; his poetry with its sad lucidity of soul may reveal the pain of an isolated being trying to find its way back to the community, and thus it speaks to a common Victorian distress. But he found his own vigorous voice only by addressing himself directly in prose to the complex issues of his time; and only in his prose did he become a witness, like Claude Colleer Abbott's models, Hopkins, Bridges, and Dixon, to the Victorian ideal of 'diversity in excellence which is the prevailing beauty of the spirit of man'.

These difficulties touching the formation of the new Christian gentleman at every point in his education, and the daily choices forced upon him, choices both subtle and obvious, troubled almost all the morally sophisticated Victorians at one time or another. In fact, Hopkins joins a particular company of eight writers and educators,[13] as he joins hosts of others less prominent, just because he encountered many of the same problems, and where solutions were possible for him, he solved them in similar ways. There are certain poems that yield some of their ambiguities only if we discover, behind the gnarled syntax and the cascade of metaphors, the new Victorian gentleman, struggling to adapt himself to the diverse responsibilities he had assumed. Although Hopkins prayed for a Catholic revival in England that would bring her once again under Roman dominion, he wanted from this return to Rome all the other auxiliary goods that other gentleman prophets considered prime goods, and that they wanted from submission to other authorities than Rome. Yet he spoke with their voices when he called for 'New Nazareths' in the ordinary Englishman, 'New Bethlems', so that England would be peopled by a new and finer breed:

> New self and nobler me
> In each one and each one.

He wanted for every morally reawakened Englishman a

> happier world, wherein
> To wend and meet no sin.   (Poem 60, 1883)

The making of the new Christian gentleman was as delicate and as complex a feat as the making of a Christian artist. In his manners, his morals, his dress, voice, and carriage, in everything he thought and did, and in the way he addressed his public in his writings, a man betrayed whether he had been born to the gentry, or if not born to them, at least educated by them. If he were interested in the new sciences, and above all in the monstrous new natural sciences, he had to decide how far he could go in his championship of Darwin before he would lose caste as a Christian or a social and moral arbiter among his peers. If he were a military officer, a Foreign Officer, or a member of the Diplomatic Service, he had to adopt a prescribed tone with the swarthy peoples among whom he might find himself living and working, a tone indicating intelligent sympathy while it stressed his inalienable right to leadership. As the nineteenth century wore on, the new gentleman had to take his stand on the question of England's imperial mission to civilize the non-Christian world. And to cast one's vote for the white man's burden often meant exile from England, especially for younger sons. For Hopkins, as for most of the latter-day medievalists, England's imperial mission was taken for granted, and anybody who denied it could not have been among 'the true men'.

The Victorian gentleman born was expected to treat with equally delicate condescension the crude vulgarians who were struggling to be gentlemen, by various strategies such as retiring from business, buying up country estates, riding to hounds, and sending their sons to the universities. For the peers of the realm and for the landed gentry there was no question whom one had the right to snub, if one were minded to snub anyone. A gentleman born has the social right to snub anyone —but, of course, if he had begun to absorb the code of the new Christian gentleman, 'that is perhaps what he will not do'. But for the university-bred sons of mercantile families, uneasy upstarts as they were, the problem was not so simple. District and county visiting, always a feature of upper-class life, spread downward to the middle- and lower-middle-class families after the 'hungry 'forties'. New money, compassion, and respect for upper-class customs no doubt prompted much useful charity, but perhaps it was also pleasant to know there were people one could condescend to while one was being treated condescendingly from above. There was something a little anxious

about Hopkins's obsession with the making of a gentleman, and something unnecessarily hearty about his treatment of that Victorian
commodity called the 'worthy poor'. In any case, he shared this
anxiety far more with other rising figures like Carlyle and Ruskin, or
Dr Arnold and Jowett, or Newman, or Disraeli, than he did with
gentlemen born. Attractive as the composite models of these new
gentlemen were, and essential as they were for national decency, even
national survival, one suspects that they were all asserting their right
not to be snubbed, because a gentleman is as a gentleman does. The
gentlemanly mantle did not lie quite easily upon their shoulders; as
Rupert Wilkinson has pointed out:[14]

> Tacit acceptance of how to behave and how not to behave was,
> therefore, a strong public school code. It was a code well in keeping
> with the gentlemanly ideal. 'I myself am not a gentleman', writes
> Simon Raven, in the introduction to his book *The English Gentle-*
> *man.* 'If I were, I would almost certainly not be writing this book,
> for one of the marks of a gentleman is that he seldom mentions the
> questions of gentility, whether in application to others or to
> himself.'

Rupert Wilkinson is quite right about the gentleman born and his
tacit assumption of codes of honour. And what is true of the twentieth-
century public-school boy was equally true of the nineteenth-century
boy. Until the not-quite-gentlemanly types, such as Dr Arnold,
Carlyle, Ruskin, and Hopkins, preached to the gentlemen of England
that they had grave responsibilities as well as power and privilege,
Matthew Arnold's phrase for these parasites—'barbarians all at play'—
was cruelly apt.

But even for a gentleman born, nothing to do with caste and conduct
could be quite as tacitly accepted in Victorian England as heretofore,
especially if the gentleman born had read his Carlyle or his Disraeli to
while away the hours between play, and had thereby found a new
conscience stirring within him. If he were religiously inclined—and
more and more gentlemen born were touched by religious enthusiasm
—he had to make grave decisions about the quarrels among the clergy,
especially between the eighteen-thirties and the eighteen-sixties. To
what extent, if any, could a Christian gentleman, born or made, trust
the new Biblical scholarship? Since even archbishops in the making
were not immune from trials for heresy,[15] and since the scholar priests
Jowett and Colenso had also been branded as heretics in open court

procedures, how were these dangerous men to be treated? Were they still gentlemen, though no longer Christians? If they were no longer Christian gentlemen, how were their friends, colleagues, and students to treat them? With icy silence? With grave and compassionate remonstrance, as Hopkins treated Bridges? With demands for banishment from all Christian society? And as the accusations of heresy flew back and forth across party lines even into the eighteen-seventies and -eighties, the morally sensitive gentleman had to decide where his religious safety lay, among the Dissenters of one brand or another, the Evangelicals, the latitudinarian Protestants, the high and dry county-bred Anglicans or the high and fevered Tractarians. No doubt his parents might pray that he would stay safely latitudinarian or safely high, and certainly dry, for in increasing numbers at Oxford and elsewhere, gentlemen were going over to Rome. And even when they remained within the Tractarian fold, they were bound to question the claims of the Anglican Church. Was she, in fact, what she claimed to be, the legitimate Catholic Church in England and the spiritual mother of Englishmen, or, like the Virgin Queen and first Anglican-born sovereign, merely the illegitimate offspring of a wilful and reprobate monarch, himself the offspring of an upstart line of monarchs?

These were the issues presented to generations of young Victorian gentlemen for their private solutions. In searching for his solutions, the young gentleman was far more apt to seek counsel from writers and from his peers than he was from his parents. If he were a gentleman born, his parents were usually far too preoccupied doing and thinking what they and their ancestors had always done and thought to be of any assistance to him. If he had sprung from families anxious to rise in the social scale, in so far as social mobility would not interfere with personal salvation, his parents, especially his father, would be anxious to have him look, sound, and act like the tacitly comfortable sons of the gentry.[16] No matter how prevalent religious and intellectual crises were in Victorian England, they were still 'not quite nice', or 'not quite healthy', and much as George Eliot may have admired her own heroine, Dorothea Brooke, Celia Brooke's sturdy complacency was typically considered much more fitting for a gentlewoman than Dorothea's strange enthusiasms and moral alarms. If the would-be gentleman had come from chapel-going folk, and if his conversion to the Church of England had made him eligible for Oxford or Cambridge, his task of metamorphosis was infinitely more difficult and more painful. Not only were the dissenting sects scorned among the educated classes but, to do Matthew Arnold and other scorners justice, the dissenters all too often lacked the kind of moral imagination that could grasp the spiritual stresses of an Anglican son at a university.

Now we can see more clearly what the convert Hopkins had in common with this fairly diverse group of morally concerned Victorians. Carlyle called men of this stamp 'noble conservatives'.[17] We might also call them 'gentleman prophets',[18] for with the exception of Tennyson, they were all gentlemen made, and they all possessed a prophetic streak far removed from any tacit assumption of rank and privilege. They all wanted to deal with the present and the future by consulting the lessons of the past; they all wanted the best of several worlds, and like most men of reconciliatory tempers, they were also mediators. They undertook to arbitrate between opposing forces, between the ruthless money-making Philistines and the angry social reformers, between the feckless poor and Matthew Arnold's beautiful barbarians all at play, between the brimstone preachers in their sordid little chapels and the absentee Anglican bishops starving their curates; in short, they wanted to do away with all forms of ugly hebraism and decadent hedonism.

In the absence of the old reliable leadership from the upper classes, these morally braced gentleman prophets and others like them stepped into the vacuum. They all felt that England was a 'Fast foundering own generation', as Hopkins called her (Poem 41, 1878), yet they tended to propose conservative remedies rather than radical. There was to be mutual respect and mutual consideration between upper and lower classes rather than numerous legal adjustments or a significant widening of the franchise. Change was to take place individually and from the heart. Urged on by the gentleman prophets, wherever they were to be found, the new gentlemen were to take their places behind the plough, in trade, or in the schools and universities, spreading a chivalric sense of responsibility or a kindness toward England's heroic past. And so, in the manner of Jowett and Dr Arnold, the gentleman prophets undertook to change the face of the nation by the sheer persuasive power of their prophetic utterances. Even Hopkins, with a tiny public of no more than half a dozen friends for his poems and his letters, and a restricted audience for his sermons, addressed himself to his readers and his penitents in the same anxious, admonitory note as the other gentleman prophets with their wider audiences.

To be simultaneously a gentleman and a prophet is to court a double stress upon one's loyalties; and all these men shared a sense of exile at one time or another. No matter how many readers might devour their writings, or how, and how successfully they might at one time or another resolve the implicit conflicts in their various roles, they felt themselves to some extent *emigrés intérieurs*, foreigners in their native land. Even Tennyson, the poet laureate, and Carlyle and Ruskin, the acknowledged masters of the prophetic voice, would have appreciated Hopkins's lament: 'To seem the stranger lies my lot, my life/Among strangers' (Poem 66, 1885?).[19]

And yet, except for Hopkins and Newman, exiled from English society by their conversions and by their work in Ireland, all these men had better company than they knew. The success of Carlyle and Ruskin, at least in the early stages of their careers, and the instantaneous popularity of *In Memoriam*, could only have occurred among a mass audience of equally despondent or troubled Englishmen, all looking for prophets to guide them through the Victorian wilderness. And in the middle of the eighteen-sixties a storm of acclamation greeted Newman's *Apologia pro Vita Sua* from a reading public that scorned his religious beliefs where they did not fear them. But Newman understood his Victorian readers very well. His autobiography offered new gentleman readers an opportunity for disinterested pathos. And it touched another responsive chord in the hearts of educated people, trained by the novels of Kingsley, Disraeli, and Bulwer-Lytton to accept contemporary life as a domestic *Bildungsroman*, a pilgrimage in search of wisdom and experience, which took place as much inside a man's head as during the fashionable postgraduate trip to the Continent.

Pilgrimages of any sort naturally presuppose dissatisfaction with one's present self and one's present opportunities, and these dissatisfactions in turn presuppose new choices and new renunciations. Here again, the Jesuit ideal of glad submission to one's superior since that superior represents Christ, God's Vicar, is reminiscent of the educated Victorian's desire to make choices for the good of his community, since it represents the wisdom of the Christian past. Hopkins had once reminded Dixon that though the Jesuit order attracted brilliant men, it did not encourage the practice of brilliance:

> Our Society values, as you say, and has contributed to literature, to culture; but only as a means to an end. Its history and its experience show that literature proper, as poetry, has seldom been found to be to that end a very serviceable means. We have had for three centuries often the flower of the youth of a country in numbers enter our body: among these how many poets, how many artists of all sorts, there must have been! (*CD*, 93, 1881)

It has often been said that the Victorian concentration upon duty and self-sacrifice and the repression of sexual feelings accounted for much of the mental malaise suffered by every educated Victorian of whom we possess any records.[20] It has also been said that a climate of inter-necine religious inquisitions, of waning faith and burgeoning sciences, of industrial squalor and open lower-class revolt, placed Victorians with educated consciences in a constant state of tension with no relief. All these statements are true, but I venture to suggest that there were other stresses peculiar to certain sophisticated Victorians, and that these stresses stem not from poverty of experience, nor entirely from repression, but from an excess of imaginative vitality. The nine gentleman prophets and others akin to them were all men of affairs; in asking themselves to harmonize all the lessons of the books and of the past, while admitting to their consciousness the legitimate clamour of the present, and to admire diversity in excellence while renouncing many of the benefits for themselves, placed upon them a greater burden than any man could comfortably carry. It is obviously far easier for a man to adapt to a missionary life in the tropics, in the slums, or in some acrid little provincial parish, if he has not spent four years at a university polishing the intellect and the aesthetic and moral sensibilities and arranging his mental life in some delicate hierarchic balance. The Victorians who had most gladly responded to the challenges of the examined life and had developed their talents to the fullest were bound to suffer the most, no matter how gladly they might also respond to the inevitable call for duty and renunciation when it came. The deprivations from which they would suffer under these con-ditions were fully as much intellectual and social as sexual and spiritual.

One would not care to suggest that the Victorian type of gentleman prophet, with his youthful achievements and his mature sacrifices, represents something entirely new in Christendom. Hopkins's own life is partly a copy of older models, Catholic and Continental, as these, in turn, imitate the passion of Christ. But in explaining St Ignatius's rules for the Society of Jesus and in offering them as a reason for his own renunciations, Hopkins justified them as guidelines for his contemporaries, most of them non-Catholic. Hopkins obviously believed that St Ignatius's rules were general rules, applicable to all men, ancient or modern, Catholic or heretic. And his description of the dazzling young men whom the Society of Jesus had attracted and then chastened to its own ends could equally have described the dazzling young Victorians of a certain stamp whom the public schools and the universities civilized and then turned loose to work their missionary zeal upon a morally and intellectually parched nation.

Nonetheless the figure of the Victorian gentleman prophet may well represent something new in Christendom. Not only did he appear in greater numbers than ever before, and that in itself proclaimed some new moral vigour abroad, but the type seemed to flourish equally well in holy orders or in secular circles. Arthur Hallam was destined for the law, but his warnings to Tennyson on the hedonistic poet sound like the advice of a man bound for the priesthood. Almost one-third of his dazzling companions among the Cambridge Apostles went into holy orders and it was a perfectly natural place for them to go. Walter Bagehot once said:[21]

> Nothing is more unpleasant than a virtuous person with a mean mind. A highly developed moral nature joined to an undeveloped intellectual nature, an undeveloped artistic nature, and a very limited religious nature, is of necessity repulsive.

In educated circles, this diversity in excellences was expected of a man in holy orders as well as of any other gentleman. In fact, the mid-century prophet student *as student* believed in this wholesome trivium of Christian morality, courtesy, and talent; he practised it as long as he could, and painfully missed his books and his civilized companionship when more urgent duties called him away from these university delights. And no matter how much grumbling there may have been about the sterility of education at either university or any of the public schools, to profit from the finest and the fullest education these schools provided, especially from the eighteen-sixties onward, was to be fashioned by a system of almost Renaissance amplitude.

Yet the Victorian gentleman was not, after all, a Renaissance courtier or a medieval knight. Whether he was born in the eighteen-twenties or the eighteen-forties, successive waves of evangelizing movements had rolled over him, as they had rolled over his forebears. Furthermore, he now felt the anguish of the poor as personal wounds, and though his propensity for pathos would have discomfited any of Castiglione's courtiers, to whom he was often likened, it undoubtedly would not have embarrassed a Knight Templar, in whom he liked equally to see prefigurations of himself.

G. M. Young has suggested something of the social and intellectual ferment of the mid-Victorian period:[22]

> Released from fear, the English mind was recovering its power to speculate, to wonder, and to enjoy. The dissolvent elements in early

Victorian thought, romance and humour and curiosity, the Catholicism of Oxford, the satire of Dickens, the passion of Carlyle, the large historic vision of Grote and Lyell and Arnold were beginning to work.

Young also implied some of the strains to which the Victorian intellectuals, and one may add, particularly the gentleman prophets, were subjected:

One of the last survivors of the mid-century time spoke of those years as having the sustained excitement of a religious revival. Excitement was Lord Morley's word also, and all through the fifties we are aware of the increasing tension of thought. The Christian Socialists rose in ill-directed but fruitful revolt; the Pre-Raphaelites struck out for a freedom which they had not strength to reach. Tennyson in *Maud* and Dickens in *Hard Times* turned savagely on the age that had bred them.

One cannot therefore subject the Victorian period to convenient labels such as 'the age of conformity' or 'the age of revolt', for within the body politic and the individual mind of responsible Victorians, conformity and revolt were both present, sometimes in equipoise and sometimes in conflict. Hopkins's political conservatism and his radical prosody are typical admixtures. And this combination hints at another peculiar feature of the Victorian gentleman and especially the Victorian gentleman prophet. The gentleman, bent simultaneously upon submission and rebellion, possessed a curious freedom—and his very freedom added to his tensions. He could choose his own brand of martyrdom and of rebellion, and, to some degree, the limits of both. Tennyson did not give up poetry, only poetry dedicated to pure aestheticism. Ruskin, taking his cue from Carlyle, often spoke as scornfully of self-examining verse as Matthew Arnold was to do, and Ruskin admired the Society of Jesus precisely because it offered his slothful contemporaries 'a splendid proof of the power of obedience' (XXXVII, 207). Yet Ruskin was as scornful as Arnold of absolutely raw Puritan morality because the raw Puritan's stunted aesthetic sense crippled his moral sense. Ruskin turned from art criticism not because it was morally wrong, but because he encountered a sick society no longer fit for Christian art, and because he came to believe that to preach the moral values of art to a nation half-starved and half-choked with industrial offal was not only irrelevant, but ethically obtuse.

Jowett could not always maintain his utilitarian attitude about the ends of a liberal education; what Platonist could? And although he supported the husbandman farmer and the public servant over the poet every time, we remember his admiration for Ruskin and the patient support and criticism he offered Tennyson and Swinburne.

Matthew Arnold's reasons for his poetic retrenchment are still obscure, but his public explanations were quite compatible with the arguments of other gentleman prophets: for a sturdy and purposeful national aesthetic, the times were simply out of joint. And as his statements in the preface to the poems of 1853 imply, Arnold must have come to dread the phantom of an incomplete and mutilated man revealed to him in his own poems. Although he appeared to suffer less over his renunciation of poetry than Hopkins was later to do, in some respects it may have cost him more. With infinite anguish Hopkins could suppress his own diversity in excellence and endure to become a eunuch because, as he said to Bridges, 'it is for the kingdom of heaven's sake' (*LB*, 270, 1888). But Arnold sought his own hellenic kingdom of heaven here on earth, in rounded human perfection, and he could not have found much evidence of that in his own poetry.

Hopkins the artist, poet, linguist, musician, and priest was no more diversely accomplished than Kingsley, the sometime poet and lifetime novelist, scientist, and priest, or Ruskin, the encyclopedic critic, whose talents, Hopkins had admiringly claimed, were equal to the gigantic men he criticized. Disraeli, the novelist turned parliamentarian, obviously felt that if 'the serf' were to be 'physically emancipated' and the 'aristocrat' to be 'spiritually emancipated',[23] the arts of debate were not enough, and he continued to write novels during breathing-spells in his parliamentary career. And when Hopkins begged Bridges to become a country magistrate as well as a poet (*LB*, 152, 1882), he was using the arguments of the gentleman prophet as well as the Jesuit priest. Bridges was not only refusing the chance of a levitical sacrifice, which should be part of the experience of every gentleman prophet; he had given up medicine and was doing nothing but writing poetry, and so was in danger of losing diversity in excellence.

Because Hopkins was born a generation later than most of the new gentlemen in whose company I have placed him, and because he is therefore usually discussed later than all of his eight prophetic predecessors in Victorian courses, we should experience a sharp sense of *déjà vu* as we approach his poetry and watch the figure of the Victorian gentleman gradually taking shape once more in poem after poem. For Hopkins's gentlemanly paradigm, with all his colour and his restraint, his self-confidence and his anxieties, his achievements and his renunciations, his generous enthusiasms and his dogmatic pronouncements, will already have appeared in the works of Hopkins's predecessors. And we may discover how close the parallel is between the Victorian gentleman and the Jesuit priest. And so, before we examine the new gentleman prophet in Hopkins's poetry, we should look even more closely at some of the sources upon which Hopkins the Victorian Jesuit appeared to have drawn for his complex, yet conventional, model of the new Victorian gentleman.

As we know, Hopkins devised a hierarchic ladder of virtues identical with Ruskin's. But Ruskin's ladder of virtues was not new in the nineteenth century. Jerome Buckley believes that almost without exception, 'every Victorian thesis produced its own antithesis, as a ceaseless dialectic worked out its own designs'.[24] Buckley's Hegelian metaphor is an especially apt description of the gentleman prophets, struggling throughout the century to bring to order all the unabsorbed portions of jagged experience. For the Romantic period had left the articulate Englishman far more openly sensitive to experience than before, and the Ruskinian version of the 'handsome heart' is always vulnerable to fresh ideas, as Matthew Arnold's model of the incomplete and mutilated evangelist is not. Again and again during the century, the hierarchic ladder of virtue was pressed into service to provide guidance and comfort for the generous heart and the divided mind.[25] And the first of the Victorian prophets to preach this hierarchy of virtues to intelligent Englishmen was Thomas Arnold, whose ladder of virtues was as acceptable, as far as it went, to orthodox Catholics like Newman and Hopkins as to lapsed or marginal Christians like Ruskin, Matthew Arnold, and Jowett.

When Dr Arnold solemnly surveyed his cadre of schoolboy leaders[26] gathered around him in his study at Rugby, and warned them that he intended to see his own hierarchy of virtues prevail at Rugby, he was inaugurating what was to become a Victorian commonplace: 'And what I have often said before I repeat now; what we must look for here is, 1st, religious and moral principle; 2ndly, gentlemanly conduct; 3rdly, intellectual ability.'[27]

In Dean Stanley's record of Dr Arnold's headmastership, one may well be struck with the similarity of Arnold's vision to that of his son, Matthew Arnold. One of Matthew Arnold's favourite concepts was 'the spirit of the whole', a spirit that could be counted upon to keep man free from rigidity or the meanness of parochialism. Dr Arnold called these 'comprehensive and great and good' qualities that he thought essential to 'Christian gentlemen',[28] 'moral thoughtfulness—the enquiring love of truth going along with the devoted love of good-ness'.[29] Although Arnold often employed military metaphors to induce chivalric loyalty in his pupils,[30] he wanted no mere automatic obedience from them; instead he wanted them to be as fascinated by 'the romance of antiquity'[31] as by the romance of modernity,[32] and even his 'passion for the past'[33] encompassed both the Biblical past and the classical past so admired by his son. Dr Arnold wanted to set before his boys a vision of their companionship in the company of 'God's scholars',[34] whose intellectual understanding was at once 'clear, rich, versatile in its powers',[35] yet always under the benevolent reign of duty and piety. But clarity, richness, and versatility have always been presumed to be hellenic virtues, rather than hebraic; Dr Arnold insisted that one set of virtues need not exclude the other.

Dr Arnold's hierarchy of virtues naturally included pathos. Walter Houghton believes that the sense of pathos may have been strongest in those Victorians who tended to disapprove of legal steps for ameliorat-ing the disgraceful conditions under which the lower classes lived.[36] Certainly Dr Arnold was no egalitarian, and certainly he indicated that sympathy for the sufferings of the poor was one of the marks of a gentleman. He once said to Carlyle that 'the condition of the poor throughout the kingdom' should be brought 'to public attention ... by every possible means';[37] but he often seemed anxious to relieve public suffering even more because it afforded 'the boys', and anyone else who practised it, 'an opportunity for self-denial and alms-giving',[38] than because he was profoundly disturbed by public suffering itself.

Valency has argued that the virtue of self-denial is typically valued by subordinate classes on the rise. The would-be gentleman naturally stressed 'the nobility of merit', since he was in no position to stress 'the nobility of birth'. For the same reason he stressed service as a badge of nobility: 'the service of his lord, his country, his king, his faith, his church, and in times, his lady; he was not especially encouraged to serve himself.'[39]

Victorian schoolboys of the Rugby stamp were never encouraged to serve themselves either, nor were their headmasters, as Matthew Arnold's 'Rugby Chapel' bears witness. 'Rugby Chapel' also bears witness to Dr Arnold's flair for moral 'magic', a 'mysterious aura of differentness which distinguishes certain leaders and makes them respected for what they are rather than what they do'. Wilkinson explains that this sense of the morally dramatic was one of the 'com-ponents to the gentleman ideal', and that 'it was more easily attained by the medieval lord than it was by the business man'.[40] But Dr

Arnold was fully as anxious to place the model of the 'comprehensive' man before the sons of business men as before the sons of the landed gentry, since more and more members of the middle and lower middle classes now constituted a sizable proportion of the student body at Rugby.[41]

Dr Arnold was known as 'the hero-schoolmaster', and his favourite pupils might hope to earn Dean Stanley's title of 'the hero-pupil'.[42] And indeed, Arnold had emerged from exactly the kind of heroic mould that Carlyle wished to make the national archetype. As Arnold bent his consuming eyes[43] upon his hearers, he must have seemed to his young masters and his pupils alike a semi-divine figure, Mosaic and Socratic at once. For he too had discovered in himself an 'extraordinary sense of the reality of the invisible world', a reality that thoroughly formed his mind and his conduct, and it was this quality in him that accounted for much of his magic.[44] To Arnold, as to those who worshipped him, all virtue emanated from the intensely felt 'reality of the invisible world', and for this reason, virtue was far more than a barren duty; it was a state of enchantment. It may well be true that the greatest beneficiaries of his 'zealous' and 'beneficent' strength were meagrely talented students, as Stanley suggested, or dream walkers, stumbling along the 'border land' between 'vice and virtue', as Matthew Arnold suggested. But under Dr Arnold's 'radiant vigour',[45] any boy, whether quick or slow, who was able 'to believe in the sentiment of the ideal life transforming the life which now is, to believe in it and come to serve it', became a legitimate candidate for 'the Kingdom of God'.[46]

Although Rugby had fallen upon grim days when Thomas Arnold became headmaster, it had never lost its membership in the famous 'Seven Public Schools' that defined the collective ethos of the Victorian old-boy. Highgate, Hopkins's preparatory school, was not among the elite 'Seven', nor was it even among the 'greater day schools' like St Paul's or Merchant Taylors', which had turned out enough illustrious alumni in past centuries to have acquired an imposing mystique of their own.[47] As Hopkins hinted to Dixon,[48] his school possessed no mystique, and his relief at escaping to one of the most impressive intellectual and social centres in the country, where a man might hope to acquire diversity in excellence, is only too apparent in his first year at Balliol.

Even if Hopkins had not wistfully caught some of 'the spirit of Thomas Arnold', as decade by decade, it 'eddied out through the public schools',[49] he could hardly have failed to be swayed by Carlyle's hortatory voice. As usual, Hopkins was most judicious in his comments upon Carlyle, precisely because he considered Carlyle a heretic, 'an extreme enemy' of Catholicism,[50] 'morally an imposter', and 'worst of all imposters a false prophet'. Under the circumstances, all the civilized fairness and justice of the 'comprehensive' man is summed up in Hopkins's final assessment of Carlyle: 'the force of his genius seems to me gigantic.'[51]

This hoarse northern prophet, whose 'gigantic genius' would have been dangerous to any dogmatic Christian, was the more so to a generous critic like Hopkins, who found Carlyle's opinions all too congenial. Hopkins's capacity for hero worship was, if anything, greater than Carlyle's, because he passionately preached and practised fidelity to a faith and to his Hero, Christ,[52] while Carlyle merely preached with passion. But Hopkins possessed the same awareness of both past and present, the same missionary zeal, the same capacity for self-subordination, the same hierarchical view of the universe[53]—even couched in the same military metaphors[54]—that he found in Carlyle's works. They both thought that religious belief was the highest good and the only virtue one may demand of all men. To be sure, Carlyle never stipulated any particular belief, and Hopkins was bound to consider this moral fuzziness heresy.

Despite Carlyle's moral laziness and his dogmatic tone, his diffuse statements resemble the Arnoldian hierarchy in kind, while they helped to popularize it. 'The noble priest was always a noble *Aristos* to begin with', and under ideal conditions, the priest and the aristocrat are one. But if the functions of priest and aristocrat become separated, 'there can be no doubt but the Priest class is the more dignified' of the two classes;[55] in other words, the priest, who stands for faith, virtue, and morality, is superior to the nobility, who in corrupt times, may stand merely for social grace. In common with all the Victorian gentleman prophets, Carlyle placed talents of all sorts, particularly talents of the intellect, at the bottom of his ladder of virtues. Yet even in his most fiercely strident tones, Carlyle is describing the Arnoldian comprehensive hero, who 'is to be in turns Apprentice and Workman; or say rather Scholar, Teacher, Discoverer'.[56] It was not necessary, Carlyle thought, that the 'gallant battle-hosts and work-hosts' be comprehensive men, but they must respond to the magic of a comprehensive leader. The hero who has become a leader must in turn possess compassion for his followers; he must remember that 'without love men cannot endure to be together', and this version of 'the handsome heart' should inspire his followers 'to give their life for him if need came'. This was the model from antiquity to which most of the gentleman prophets aspired. 'It was beautiful; it was human!'[57]

As we might expect, since Hopkins himself was one of the 'gallant battle-hosts and work-hosts', he allowed far greater urbanity in his soldier of the plough than Carlyle thought necessary in his Caledonian model of the sturdy, loyal peasant. But Hopkins had been touched by Newman, another legendary swayer of souls, equipped with both pulpit magic and the Arnoldian spirit of the whole. It may be a considerable puzzle to us how Newman's classical urbanity could coexist not only with charismatic powers, but also with the 'animal sensibility of conscience' and the 'super-morality of the nerves and sense, of bodily repulsion and social alarm' that G. M. Young considered the 'peculiar element' of the nineteenth-century English temper.[58] But the Arnoldian spirit of the whole was an attempt to blend just this sort of hebraism with hellenism, to make faith less distrustful, more gracious. And so Newman could not and would not expunge the evidences of his classical training and Oxonian breeding from his discourses on the model university, not for all the criticism it might have brought down upon him from Catholic sources in and out of Ireland.[59] For Newman's *beau ideal* of a gentleman offers clues to his hopes that greater comprehensiveness might prevail among English and Irish Catholics: he wanted social grace and urbanity, not at the cost of faith, but in addition to faith, and he saw no reason why a Christian gentleman need spurn the one in order to obtain the other. As he remarked with the sort of unanswerable logic we usually credit only to empiricists like John Stuart Mill: 'even what is supernatural need not be liberal, nor need a hero be a gentleman, for the plain reason that one idea is not another idea.'

Newman's passages on the nature and training of the cultivated gentleman are very poignant, because, by seducing himself with the power and beauty of his Oxonian memories, he hoped to seduce the suspicious minds of the Dublin listeners to his own Arnoldian version of sweetness and light. As he warmed to his radiant *beau ideal* of a gentleman, his prose in *The Idea of a University* became increasingly ardent; it moves in waves of emotion, troughs of coolly descriptive logic, and then ever higher waves of passionate rhetoric; evocative adjectives and abstract nouns abound, as though Newman wished to cast a spell upon his listeners.

Newman wished to make his listeners aware of the hierarchical distinction between a man of mental genius and a man who has dutifully and industriously equipped himself with the intellectual accoutrements of a gentleman. It seems at first reading as though Newman wanted to enchant his listeners with the spectacle of natural genius; men of this stamp are capable of 'vast ideas or dazzling projects'. Such men 'have sudden presence of mind equal to any emergency, rising with the occasion, and an undaunted magnanimous bearing, and an energy and keenness' that irradiates 'almost as if from inspiration' any subjects they touch. This, Newman informed his listeners, is intellectual genius; 'this is heroism', but it is an 'exhibition of a natural gift, which no culture can teach, at which no Institution can aim; here, on the contrary, we are concerned, not with mere nature, but with training and teaching'.

The educated gentleman, as opposed to the intellectual hero, should quietly make his mind capable of an 'analytical, distributive, harmonizing process'; he should seek 'perfection of the Intellect, which is the result of Education, and its *beau ideal*'. Newman echoes the modest assumptions of Carlyle, and Dr Arnold, which Hopkins was later to duplicate; we are not all similarly endowed, but under the spur of some magic hero, we may all come to love the *'beau ideal'*. Since it is 'to be imparted to individuals in their respective measure', we may all seek it, and since it 'is the clear, calm, accurate vision and comprehension of all things as far as the finite mind can embrace them, each in its place and with its own characteristics upon it',[60] the *'beau ideal'* requires self-denial and the spirit of the whole far more than those 'dazzling' gifts of the intellectual hero. There are several prototypes of Hopkins's windhover and ploughman and similar Victorian models in these passages. There is the stunning creature, whose gifts are the product of 'mere nature', and who is capable of 'vast ideas or dazzling projects'; this natural genius makes no levitical sacrifice of himself for the common weal. But by the unobtrusive insertion of the adjective 'mere' in support of the noun 'nature', Newman has started to raise the commonplace Victorian ladder of virtues. His caution against pride in 'mere' genius is akin to his insistent damnation of the witty and imaginative Burkeian gentleman, who feared the appearance of sin more than sin itself, and whose very breeding and 'prestige of rank' had become 'a screen, an instrument and an apology for vice and irreligion'.[61]

Newman was walking a tightrope in these passages, and he was well aware of it. Look, he urged his audience, look what happens to the mind of the average Anglican, provided he is industrious and touched by the *'beau ideal'*. And Catholic students could have all this beauty and faith as well. Newman was thus demonstrating considerable courage—unless he was merely foolhardy—for it is never safe to inform new friends that old friends who are now enemies possess virtues the new friends lack. But nevertheless, in the interests of comprehensiveness, Newman had to say[62] that even without faith, his *'beau ideal'* is

> almost prophetic from its knowledge of history; it is almost heart-searching from its knowledge of human-nature; it has almost supernatural charity from its freedom from littleness; it has almost the repose of faith, because nothing can startle it; it has almost the beauty and harmony of heavenly contemplation, so intimate is it with the eternal order of things and the music of the spheres.

This was the secular beauty of the mind so appealing to Hopkins that he returned to the subject again and again in his letters, most poignantly perhaps after Digby Dolben's death:

> You know there can very seldom have happened the loss of so much beauty (in mind and body and life) and of the promise of still more as there was in his case—seldom I mean, in the whole world, for the conditions wd. not easily come together.   (*LB*, 16–17, 1867)

On another occasion Hopkins paraphrased whole passages from *The Idea of a University*:

> I think then no one can admire beauty of the body more than I do, and it is of course a comfort to find beauty in a friend or a friend in beauty. But this kind of beauty is dangerous. Then comes the beauty of the mind, such as genius, and this is greater than the beauty of the body, and not to call dangerous. And more than the beauty of the mind is beauty of character, the 'handsome heart.' Now every beauty is not a wit or genius nor has every wit or genius beauty.
>
> (*LB*, 95, 1879)

Hopkins might have added with Newman: 'for the plain reason that one idea is not another idea'; but this passage epitomizes Victorian concepts about the making of a Christian gentleman. For all the diversity of the typical gentleman prophet's experience and the vitality of his imaginative life, he was usually clear on the distinction between beauty in art and moral beauty in human beings. One idea is *not* another idea; Newman might share that pragmatic, almost Baconian insistence with Victorians as diverse as John Stuart Mill, the Darwinian scientists, Matthew Arnold, or Hopkins himself, yet none of these men would indulge in sloppy realism. One idea may possess equal charm or equal theoretical value with another idea, as part of a diverse and comprehensive whole, but each man revealed where his preference lay, and why. Matthew Arnold might urge that for the time being far more hellenic virtue than hebraic was needed to cure the predominant sourness of English life, whereas for men of Hopkins's and Newman's stamp, physical and mental beauty are not only evanescent without predominant spiritual beauty; they alone are decadent, and therefore, paradoxically they are but 'beauty-in-the-ghost'. But beauty for Hopkins and Newman was still beauty; an honest Oxonian Platonist could no more deny beauty than scientists could ignore facts. Beauty, as Hopkins never tired of saying, even when he was fleeing from it, is still 'flower of beauty' and 'fleece of beauty', no matter how 'dearly and dangerously sweet' it is when the mere natural man first confronts it. The ephemeral quality of natural beauty may even enhance its charms and its dangers, since human beings without grace long for what they will soon lose; and when a man is bereft of grace, 'wisdom is early to despair' (Poem 59, 1882).

For Hopkins, the Christian hierarchy of virtues rescues the lover of natural beauty from confusion, even from 'despair'; the Christian gentleman is safe as long as 'thought and thew', or talents of the 'Head, heart, hand, heel, and shoulder' are abstracted from the realm of mere nature and held 'at Christ's employment' (Poem 49, 1879). In this way the Christian gentleman is reminded of the beauty of servitude, which is Christ's example and His gift to man. By a divine inversion, natural beauty, which seems so palpable, becomes ghostly, as spiritual as a puff of breath because it is so ephemeral, whereas the fact of the Resurrection, a fact beyond the comprehension of our five senses, takes on the undeniable quality of palpable things: it is 'immortal diamond' (Poem 72, 1888).

In finding solutions for the making of the Christian gentleman, Hopkins piled paradox upon paradox: Christ's sacrifice, which seemed to him 'more touching and constraining than everything else is', consisted in His behaving more like a man than like God, and 'taking the form of servant'; Christ

emptied or exhausted himself as far as that was possible of godhead and behaved only as God's slave, as his creature, as man, which also he was, and then being in the guise of man humbled himself to death, the death of the cross. It is this holding of himself back, and not snatching at the truest and highest good that was his right, nay his possession from a past eternity in his other nature, his own being and self, which seems to me the root of all his holiness and the imitation of this the root of all moral good in other men.   (*LB*, 175, 1883)

And so by a paradox that is as Victorian as it is Christian, the true gentleman must become a servant of others rather than their master, their entertainer, or their parasite. It is no levitical sacrifice to give up ugly or meaningless things; to be as Christ was, one must give up what one loves as one's natural right. Man's greatest natural dilemma is therefore his greatest spiritual opportunity; and almost all of Hopkins's mature poetry deals with aspects of this Christian paradox.

As a Jesuit and a Victorian priest, Hopkins lived by antique abstractions such as 'dignity', 'self-sacrifice', 'self-restraint', and by constant admonitions to himself and his parishioners. As a Victorian gentleman prophet Hopkins followed his predecessors and deliberately set out to enchant his readers with the glory of his vision, while warning of its difficulties. When his poems on the making of the prophetic gentleman enchant us most, the tension between nature and the supernatural may even be at its highest, so that the reader is plunged into the sensations of Hopkins's affliction. But the solutions will take place through dazzling images and metaphors, as they do in 'The Windhover', rather than through rhetoric or excess pathos. Where his taste slips, and the emotions move toward the sort of pathos he often condemned in his contemporaries, one can only respect the complexity of his vision and the weight of its burden, and marvel that spiritual solutions, to say nothing of prosodic solutions, were possible at all.

'The Handsome Heart: at a Gracious Answer' (Poem 47, 1879) is the earliest poem to have as its explicit subject a Christian gentleman in the making. Bridges liked it, somewhat to Hopkins's surprise; and in truth it is not one of Hopkins's greatest successes. Of another poem written about the same time on another young gentleman in the making, Hopkins said uneasily: 'pathos has a point as precise as jest has and its happiness "lives ever in the heart of him that hears, not in the mouth of him that makes" ' (*LB*, 86, 1879). There is more than a touch of Pre-Raphaelite moral posing in 'The Handsome Heart'; 'the Hero of it', as Hopkins called another of his proletarian gentlemen (*LB*, 92, 1879), has the saccharine perfection of some of Dickens's children:

> 'But tell me, child, your choice; what shall I buy
> You?'—'Father, what you buy me I like best.'
> With the sweetest air that said, still plied and pressed,
> He swung to his first poised purport of reply.

What the heart is! which, like carriers let fly—
Doff darkness, homing nature knows the rest—
To its own fine function, wild and self-instressed,
Falls light as ten years long taught how to and why.

Mannerly-hearted! more than handsome face—
Beauty's bearing or muse of mounting vein,
All, in this case, bathed in high hallowing grace. . .

Of heaven what boon to buy you, boy, or gain
Not granted!—Only . . . O on that path you pace
Run all your race, O brace sterner that strain!

The little Acolyte, the hero of 'The Handsome Heart', exhibits the highest virtue in the hierarchy; he trusts his priest, who represents his betters, he will be pleased with what pleases his betters and he serves without looking for any reward. The 'high hallowing grace' enveloping him is explicitly opposed to what is 'wild and self-instressed', that is, 'Beauty's bearing or muse of mounting vein'. The ten-year-old Acolyte possesses beauty and talent, but he does not need them or cherish them. His low breeding does not matter either, although his 'father is Italian and therefore sells ices'. 'The Handsome Heart' is about the apotheosis of street urchin into modest, deferential Christian gentleman. Hopkins later reported a further apotheosis: 'The little hero of the Handsome Heart has gone to school at Boulogne to be bred for a priest and he is bent on being a Jesuit' (*LB*, 86, 92).

Hopkins obviously felt that the making of a Christian gentleman was a permissible topic, for in the same letter to Bridges in which he took up the subject of taste and pathos, he remarked, 'I find within my professional experience now a good deal of matter to write on. I hope to enclose a little scene that touched me at Mount St. Mary's' (*LB*, 86). The poem was called 'Brothers' (Poem 54, 1880) and the comradely title itself suggests what it is, a little sermon on the handsome heart. It is one of many Victorian poems reminiscent of the contemporary Pre-Raphaelite parables, where the painter captures the moment of moral decision on canvas. 'Brothers' is a comparative study of mere natural talent in opposition to self-forgetful Christian love. It is a narrative in forty-three lines of blunt tetrameter couplets, most unlike Hopkins's usual tight Petrarchan rhetoric, and it tells the story of two brothers involved in a school play. The elder brother, Henry, is a member of the audience; the younger boy, John, is one of the actors:

> How lovely the elder brother's
> Life all laced in the other's,
> Lóve-laced!—what once I well
> Witnessed; so fortune fell.
> When Shrovetide, two years gone,
> Our boys' plays brought on
> Part was picked for John,
> Young Jóhn; then fear, then joy
> Ran revel in the elder boy.

In 'Brothers', Henry, the awestruck onlooker below the stage, watching his brother's thespian prowess on the stage above him, plays a role similar to that of the humble and dazzled ploughman watching the windhover circling and swooping above him. Hopkins has even preserved the same spatial paradoxes in 'Brothers' as he used in 'The Windhover'. Henry, the patient, adoring onlooker *below* the stage, turns out to be playing the more 'dangerous', the more authentic role of the Christian gentleman than John, the dazzling performer, who is heedlessly selving himself *above* his audience like some latter-day Lucifer. But in 'Brothers' Hopkins warns of the dangers of talent in terms that Newman, Carlyle, Ruskin, or Dr Arnold would have recognized, and his treatment of the subject is far less enigmatic than in 'The Windhover'. He also warns far less enigmatically than theretofore of a concomitant danger, that the proud, beautiful, talented creature is dangerous not only to himself but to others. The humble Christian gentleman may be drawn into the proud one's net just because the gentleman, as a gentleman, recognizes talent and beauty and is generous toward it. More than any other Christian, as Ruskin had warned, he must be taught the distinction between sacred and secular beauty. Henry was in the process of learning that distinction. He was capable of unabashed and disinterested admiration for his younger brother's public glory; indeed, he 'hung on the imp's success'. But at the approach of 'the imp's success', he seemed troubled by his admiration and he beckoned Father Hopkins 'beside him'. 'I came where called', said Hopkins, 'and eyed him'

> By meanwhiles; making my play
> Turn most on tender byplay.

Hopkins himself is quite clear that he infinitely prefers the moral spectacle of Henry's conduct to that of John's, and he reserves all his admiration for Henry, obsessively 'lóve-laced' in the younger brother's exploits. All the images describing Henry's fraternal anxiety are designed to enlist our sympathy for Henry and to restrict it for John. Hopkins calls Henry 'My lad' in distinct opposition to John. Henry is vividly pictured as undergoing the torture of empathy as he awaits his brother's cue, supposing the younger boy to be as nervous as he, or any other modest boy would be. Henry is 'wrung all on love's rack' with suspense; 'lost in Jack', he smiles, blushes, bites his lip, and clutches his hands through his clenched knees. When John finally appears on cue, not only does Henry reveal his 'heart's stress' by dropping his eyes, but suddenly

> —in his hands he has flung
> His tear-tricked cheeks of flame
> For fond love and for shame.

Hopkins clearly understands Henry's 'shame' at John's 'bráss-bóld' performance and shares it, without sharing Henry's admiration for the 'achieve of, the mastery of the thing!' (Poem 36). Hopkins does not respond to John's 'achieve' as Henry does and as the ploughman could for the windhover; in 'Brothers' the priest clearly rejects ambivalent love for dangerous talent. He is very careful to describe John in a series of satirical images, now belittling, now faintly brutish. The younger boy is called 'Jack', always a synonym for corrupt man with Hopkins.[63] 'Jack' is an 'imp', a young 'Dog' who 'did give tongue'. He is a self-seeking actor, who

> had no work to hold
> His heart up at the strain;
> Nay, roguish ran the vein.

In 'The Windhover' the opposition between a mere 'brute beauty', incapable of making a levitical sacrifice, and the handsome heart of a Christian gentleman, is probably more ambiguous because Hopkins had not yet resolved the tension between the lovely things of this world as they appear to mirror God's better beauty, grace, and his own dire visions of the cracks in that very mirror. He was still simultaneously 'strung by duty' and 'strained to beauty' (Poem 41, 1878); and the three symbolic figures of the dazzling windhover, dangerously imitating God's majesty, the martyred Christ, and the ploughman onlooker who yearns first after the one, then the other, are admittedly somewhat fused. But in 'Brothers' the three figures, the actor, the admiring onlooker, and the priest, Christ's agent on earth, are severely polarized and firmly, if unobtrusively judged. All during the poem we are forcibly swung back and forth from the cocky, swaggering gestures onstage, to the private morality play in the audience, from the confident young 'Dog' awaiting his cue, completely unaware of his brother's anguished concern, back to the elder boy, awkwardly sweating and gesticulating, and then from him to the compassionate priest at his side, watching and sanctioning Henry's crude, embryonic self-sacrifice. And just in case the reader is not aware of the shift away from talent and 'achieve', the last six lines are overt enough:

> Ah Nature, framed in fault,
> There's comfort then, there's salt;
> Nature, bad, base, and blind,
> Dearly thou canst be kind;
> There dearly thén, déarly,
> Dearly thou canst be kind.

In the early days of Hopkins's vocation, nature was a legitimate object of man's affection, and man only was to be suspected (Poem 34, 1877). Now all nature, both human and botanical, is indicted, for both may draw the mind away from eternal things. Only with the priest by his side is human love and admiration safe for Henry, and only then because it is totally disinterested. But except for such rare glimpses of benevolent human love, all nature is 'framed in fault'. It is clear that the boy on stage is an unhallowed example of 'Nature, bad, base, and blind', whereas Henry and his handsome gentlemanly heart exemplify the nobility possible in natural creatures under the protection of grace and humility.

'On the Portrait of Two Beautiful Young People: A Brother and Sister' (Poem 157, 1886) is another 'professional' poem about the dangers of beauty and talent. It also displays some of the 'supermorality of the nerves and the senses, of bodily repulsion and social alarm' that G. M. Young thought peculiar to the Victorians.[64] Hopkins called this poem an 'Elegy', and he complained to Dixon that he was having trouble with it: 'I cannot get my Elegy finished, but I hope in a few days to see the hero and heroine of it, which may enable me (or quite the reverse; perhaps that: it is not well to come too near things)' (CD, 154, 1887). The 'things' that Hopkins feared to approach were beauties of mind and body, and by now, it seemed, the more he admired them, the more he feared them. The conflict must have been severe, for the Elegy was never finished.

This poem is a Pre-Raphaelite portrait within a portrait. One Christmas day Hopkins was taken to see a portrait of the handsome, well-bred son and daughter of a country squire who lived in County Kildare. The opening stanza sets the mood of fear and grief:

> O I admire and sorrow! The heart's eye grieves
> Discovering you, dark tramplers, tyrant years.
> A juice rides rich through bluebells, in vine leaves,
> And beauty's dearest veriest vein is tears.

Stanzas IV to VI of Hopkins's Elegy treat the hierarchy of value quite explicitly. Beautiful things are beautiful things; a gentleman cannot deny that, but only Christian good earns eternal salvation, and beauty *may* lead to damnation:[65]

> She leans on him with such contentment fond
> As well the sister sits, would well the wife;
> His looks, the soul's own letters, see beyond,
> Gaze on, and fall directly forth on life.

> But ah, bright forelock, cluster that you are
> Of favoured make and mind and health and youth,
> Where lies your landmark, seamark, or soul's star?
> There's none but truth can stead you. Christ is truth.

These three 'professional' poems, 'The Handsome Heart', 'Brothers', and 'On the Portrait of Two Beautiful Young People', are more interesting on the whole as fairly crude glosses for 'The Windhover' and 'St. Alphonsus Rodriguez' than they are in themselves. But Sonnet 74 is not professional and not didactic. Hopkins wrote to Bridges that one of his earlier sonnets in this vein was 'written in blood' (*LB*, 219, 1885). Sonnet 74 'goes to the point of the terrible: the terrible crystal' (*CD*, 80, 1881), as Dixon said of earlier poems.

This sonnet is a grim record of the breakdown of a relationship between two Victorian gentlemen.[66] For Hopkins, of course, Christ is the Hero, the Arnoldian Gentleman Schoolmaster Who 'is interested in our undertakings', Who 'loved to praise' and Who 'loved to reward':

Love of God means the preferring his will to our own: it is the love of a subject for his ruler. By this we shall be saved, but this is a cold sort of love. Love for Christ is enthusiasm for a leader, a hero, love for a bosom friend, love for a lover.   (*S*, 38, 49, 48, 1879)

The sonnet contains unmistakable echoes of Hopkins's scholastic past. Part of its poignancy lies in the anthropomorphic nature of the silent God, to whom Hopkins twice addresses the schoolboy's deferential 'Sir':

> Thou art indeed just, Lord, if I contend
> With thee; but, sir, so what I plead is just.
> Why do sinners' ways prosper? and why must
> Disappointment all I endeavour end?
>
> Wert thou my enemy, O thou my friend,
> How wouldst thou worse, I wonder, than thou dost
> Defeat, thwart me? Oh, the sots and thralls of lust
> Do in spare hours more thrive than I that spend,
>
> Sir, life upon thy cause. See, banks and brakes
> Now, leavèd how thick! lacèd they are again
> With fretty chervil, look, and fresh wind shakes
>
> Them; birds build—but not I build; no, but strain,
> Time's eunuch, and not breed one work that wakes.
> Mine, O thou lord of life, send my roots rain.

It is often said that the burden of this sonnet is spiritual impotence; and impotence there clearly was until the moment the sonnet was undertaken, for the sonnet itself is a brilliant act of creation, and as such, holds impotence momentarily at bay. But the anguish is that of betrayal, not simple creative dryness. Hopkins is asking himself a very ancient question, as pertinent to classical man as to the Christian gentleman. Why do the petty men so often succeed and enjoy apparent favour; and why do they appear to be crowned with success at the moment of their most flagrant disobedience to divine commands? Hopkins is crying for an answer with the voice of Job. His meditations for the last five years of his life contain 'unnerving' evidences of moral and spiritual breakdown. There were some grim periods of 'Helpless loathing', of 'loathing and hopelessness', and ever 'more loathing'.[67] Christopher Devlin, the editor of Hopkins's sermons and spiritual notes, says that these moments of 'mental darkness and confusion were even occasionally accompanied by 'ugly forms of threatened self-destruction' (*S*, 218, 1884–5?). Although Father Devlin's discussion of Hopkins's torment is inclusive, yet cautious and fair,[68] he attributes the 'Manichean' or 'Jansenistic spirit' in Hopkins more to the spirit of 'Carlyle's Heroes, and the Victorian code of ethics' than to St Ignatius or to any required Jesuit reading in which a 'stark contrast is drawn between nature and grace', or recommended texts suggesting that 'all creatures have to be denied' (*S*, 120).

Without denying more than a touch of 'the Jansenistic spirit' in the code of ethics prevailing among the gentleman prophets, one should consider again the special tensions in the Victorian gentleman's code, tensions between antique classical values of harmonious self-fulfilment and antique medieval values of renunciation. These tensions would have been perfectly familiar to St Ignatius, himself a Renaissance figure who came from the luxurious and gracious courts of Spain to purify European Catholicism with the quiet force of his personal sacrifices. And he, too, like the gently bred university men of Victorian England, undertook arduous missionary tasks for which his upbringing had not prepared him.

Sonnet 74, then, is the record of moral and spiritual bankruptcy. Nothing else can explain the implied criticism of Christ, and the sense of barely controlled outrage. Something had gone quite wrong in the covert pact between Christ, the gentleman Don, and Hopkins, his willing student. Dr Arnold was haunted for years by a student of modest attainments who faced the frowning headmaster with the plea: 'Why do you speak angrily sir?—indeed I am doing the best that I can.'[69] This is the spirit in which Hopkins wrote his sonnet. The pain of disloyalty to the Hero he had trusted is compounded by the very bitterness at the betrayal; and the bitterness is exacerbated by the source of the betrayal, for Christ the Hero should be above the reproach of injustice.

So unstrung is Hopkins by his sufferings[70] that he forgets the dangers of 'Brute beauty', and once again turns his face toward nature, now no longer 'framed in fault'. By one of those paradoxical inversions that Hopkins often used when he was most committed to the poem in the making, Hopkins now sees Christ, the erstwhile friend, almost as a present enemy, while he now looks upon the fresh, teeming world before him as a vision of innocent joy from which he is shut out. The Ruskinian passages that follow the abrupt caesura in the ninth line are intensely moving because they are so unexpected. Hopkins has been delivering nothing but condemnations of nature for some while, and one suspects Sonnet 74 to be one of the poems that came to him, as he said of others, 'like inspiration unbidden and against my will' (*LB*, 221, 1885). Although he had deserted nature and condemned her, she is still there before him, lovely and offering comfort as always; but now her presence does not heal him, for her own gracious fertility seems to mock his desolation.

If the tension in the sonnet echoes the tensions under which the Victorian gentleman often found himself, and if the same loss of vitality had afflicted every one of the gentleman prophets at one time or another, with greater or lesser severity, Hopkins's solutions were common to them all: one does the job at hand; and Hopkins returned to his work with 'a barren submission to God's will' (*S*, 262, 1889) seeking what meagre and fleeting joys were to be found in his profession. The sonnet expresses a resolution rather than a successful solution. The tension between tenderness and loyalty for Christ and the muffled sense of outrage were both too fierce for easy solutions, and the conflict continues to be fought out all through the sonnet. In an act of incredible and redeeming humility in the last line, Hopkins turned to his 'enemy', his 'friend', and acknowledging eternal submission under all adversities, cries,

> Mine, O thou lord of life, send my roots rain.

The sonnet 'In honour of St. Alphonsus Rodriguez' (Poem 73, 1888) was one of the few successful poems Hopkins wrote to order or to satisfy his conscience as to what poetry was proper for a Jesuit priest. It is also autobiographical,[71] and it paints a familiar picture of the Victorian gentleman's code. St Alphonsus, Jesuit lay brother and hall porter of the Jesuit College of Palma in Majorca for forty years, would have been very pleasing to Jowett, who comforted a disconsolate farmer, late of Oxford University and Balliol, with the comment that he should be proud that he was now 'doing the one duty tolerably plain'.[72] St Alphonsus is a Carlylian Hero-Worker, and he would have been equally familiar to readers of Tennyson's *Idylls of the King*. In the second Idyll, high-born Gareth earned his right to squirehood by anonymous manual labour and by deference to his superiors.

Hopkins has not shunned didacticism in his sonnet to St Alphonsus, but his tact is almost without fault. The didacticism is unobtrusively carried out by a double series of images, one series harsh or dazzling in both sound and meaning, the other series soft or long drawn-out in sound, and submissive in meaning. In the first quatrain of the octave the imagery is brilliant; it is a celebration of the chivalric past and an extended metaphor for public careers and public struggle:

> Honour is flashed off exploit, so we say;
> And those strokes once that gashed flesh or galled shield
> Should tongue that time now, trumpet now that field,
> And, on the fighter, forge his glorious day.

Seldom has the 'romance of antiquity' been so passionately summarized in so small a space. The heroic traditions of the middle ages rise up before the reader's eyes in splendid technicolour. The second quatrain is brilliantly done; the imagery is turned inward in response to the process the poet priest is describing:

> On Christ they do and on the martyr may;
> But be the war within, the brand we wield
> Unseen, the heroic breast not outward-steeled,
> Earth hears no hurtle then from fiercest fray.

In the first quatrain Hopkins has produced the sound of battle in short, sharp sounds that alternately hiss and clang. Two lines of explosive terms like 'flashed', 'gashed', 'strokes', 'exploits', are succeeded by one line of humming sounds—'tongue that time now, trumpet now that field', as though Hopkins were attempting to reproduce first the clash of steel on steel and then the subsequent ringing hum that follows after the clash. The second quatrain, while still employing military imagery, is somewhat quieter. Hopkins has marvellously combined the sense of inner 'fray' with the gentleman sufferer's attempts to appear outwardly serene. He introduces many long vowel sounds such as 'may', 'do', 'Unseen', while reminding us that however serene and uneventful the life of self-sacrifice may seem from the outside, inside the struggle to achieve it demands constant private heroism. Inside 'the heroic breast not outward-steeled' a 'hurtle' is going on, the 'fiercest fray' possible.

The sestet develops even further the slower pace of the second quatrain. There is only a hint now of public battles in the phrase 'crowd career with conquest'. Like the vowel sounds in the second quatrain, the long, drawn-out vowels in the sestet are both descriptive and discreetly didactic; they demonstrate the state of mind that contented self-sacrifice is designed to produce:

> Yet God (that hews mountain and continent,
> Earth, all, out; who, with trickling increment,
> Veins violets and tall trees makes more and more)
> Could crowd career with conquest while there went

Those years and years by of world without event
That in Majorca Alfonso watched the door.

This sonnet is Hopkins's answer to his predicament of the final
years. It is also an elliptic recommendation of the Victorian hierarchy
of virtues. The first quatrain describes the gallant aspect of breeding
and talent when they are legitimately exercised in public. The second
quatrain describes the archetypal process of renunciation and its cost.
The sestet encompasses 'that chastity of mind which seems to live at
the very heart and be the parent of all other good'. Hopkins meant the
chastity of Christian purpose, more lofty than all other purposes,
however legitimate, because it receives very little public acclaim. In
this sestet Hopkins quietly reassigns to God the role of artist; it is God
Who brings beauty to the world, Who 'hews mountain and continent',
and 'Veins violets and tall trees makes more and more', and Who does
so with a sure splendour no mere human artist could achieve. And so in
this sonnet, the breach between nature and grace is healed, for the
Author of nature is also the Author of grace.

One may mourn that so many vigorous and talented Victorians
paid so highly for their diversity in excellence. But the dignity of their
purposes stifles criticism, and the sheer quantity of the talents they
could not hide under bushels—to say nothing of sustained quality—
suggests that in some benevolent way their sacrifices preserved them
better than they knew. As Christ said, a city that is set on a hill cannot
be hid. The Victorian prophet was determined to fashion himself
upon Spenser's 'gentleman or noble person in vertuous and gentle
discipline', and he largely succeeded. But he also took upon himself
burdens and responsibilities not shared by his Elizabethan counterparts. He was haunted by spectacles of mass suffering and mass intellectual and spiritual poverty, and he was equally determined to speak
out, at all costs to his art, his health and energies, and even his reputation for gentlemanly poise, so that he might perform the mission of the
authentic nobleman, and in small ways leave his troubled country
better than he found her.

At one time or another the social upheavals distressed the gentleman
prophets so severely that their voices took on the stridency of apocalyptic seers; and even the normally urbane Matthew Arnold upon
occasion gloomily predicted the downfall of England as a civilized
power if the reign of money-grasping mediocrity prevailed. At one
time or another the interior distress of these men who had made themselves England's barometers seemed to match the national chaos with-

out, and they all delivered themselves of Hopkins's complaints, that they were ill and mentally dry, that they could build nothing, nor 'breed one work that wakes'. Perhaps we are better judges of them than they were of themselves, for we can truly say of them exactly what Claude Colleer Abbott said of the Elizabethans: 'It is, indeed, with some difficulty that we look before and after the Victorians to find other mirrors of chivalry and courtesy, so enamoured are we of the energy abounding in that pregnant age.'*

* Abbott, of course, says that we have a difficult time looking 'before and after the *Elizabethans* to find other mirrors of chivalry and courtesy' typical of Spenser's *Faerie Queene*. But Abbott goes on to say that the Victorians cultivated their own examples of the 'noble heart' (*LB*, xv) and that Hopkins is clearly 'an Englishman and a Victorian. . . . No other moment could have produced him' (*LB*, xxi). Abbott is not contradicting himself; he is saying that the Victorian gentleman had the Renaissance gentleman for one of his models, and that he made the most of this model, but that after all, a Victorian gentleman is not precisely a Renaissance gentleman.

4

'The Horror and the Havoc and the Glory of it':
The Wreck of the Deutschland and the Calamitarian Mood

Hopkins 1889   The shepherd's brow, fronting forked lightning,
                                                              owns
            The horror and the havoc and the glory
            Of it.   (Poem 75, 1889)

Coleridge 1817[1]   For these noisy and calumnious zealots whom . . . St. John beheld in the Apocalyptic vision as a compound of locust and scorpion, are not of one place or of one season. They are the perennials of history; and though they may disappear for a time, they exist always in the egg and need only a distempered atmosphere and an accidental ferment to start up into life and activity.

Kingsley 1855[2]   I cannot escape that wretched fear of a national catastrophe which haunts me night and day.

Morley 1874[3]   Those who dwell in the tower of ancient faith look about them in constant apprehension, misgivings, and wonder, with the hurried uneasy mien of people living amid earthquakes. The ear seems to their alarms to be full of missiles, and all is doubt, hesitation, and shivering expectancy.

When Hopkins began working on *The Wreck of the Deutschland* after the seven-year silence, he adopted as his blueprint an archetypal model that would permit him to encompass many things he wanted to say about the troubled times he lived in. He wanted to talk about joy and suffering, salvation and damnation, guilt and innocence, God's mastery and God's mercy. He wanted to shock his countrymen with a comparison between Victorian England's Catholic past and her godless present, and to urge them to see that her future, even her very survival, lay in their hands. Nothing served his purposes so well as St John's Apocalypse.

The Wreck of the Deutschland is a complete Apocalypse rather than a work using scenes and images from the Apocalypse or other pre-Johannine writers, as some of Hopkins's lyrics do. It completes the apocalyptic[4] rhythm from horror and carnage to joy in the expectation of the second coming, and does so with St John's Apocalypse as the model, just as the *Divine Comedy* moves from hell to purgatory to heaven, and as *Paradise Lost* is followed by *Paradise Regained*. Once Hopkins had finished his great ode to the doomed and glorious *Deutschland*, he never completed another Apocalypse, although 'The Loss of the Eurydice' is a foiled attempt to duplicate the grand design of Revelation and of *The Wreck of the Deutschland*. But Hopkins's poems are full of echoes of St John's vision, now joyous, now gloomy, as most versions of the Apocalypse are; and in using the matter of the Apocalypse, Hopkins not only reveals his debt to St John and St John's predecessors, but to many later apocalyptic models, and to his own immediate Romantic and Victorian predecessors.[5] And so one finds him searching classical, medieval, Renaissance, and Romantic sources for his apocalyptic models, as well as contemporary writers; and from the pithy comments he made upon the great Victorian poets, essayists, and novelists, we know that he had read them often and with discrimination.

The apocalyptic mood, as revealed in Victorian writers, does not differ drastically from the mood of the Romantic poets who base their prophecies on the visions of St John's Apocalypse. Yet any writer who adapts these visions to his own ethical and social purposes is bound to use examples of chaos and upheaval not available to his predecessors. For example, the Romantic writers had not lived through the worst horrors of the industrial revolution as the late Victorians had, nor could they have foreseen the Tractarian wars, University reform, franchise reforms, the re-establishment of the Roman Catholic hierarchy in England, or the appearance of Continental communism in England. So that although the tone may be the same, and the ancient archetypal furniture will reappear in every generation, the specific local and contemporary furniture will shift from generation to generation and from country to country. This local apocalyptic furniture, as it appears, for example, in such classic examples as Morris's *News from Nowhere*, or Tennyson's *Idylls of the King*, and of course

Hopkins's *The Wreck of the Deutschland,* is as much a part of the Victorian temper as the perennial furniture Coleridge spoke of, and therefore as much a part of Hopkins's poetry, which itself displays that temper so openly.

In his provocative study of Victorian concepts of time, Jerome Hamilton Buckley described the anxiety with which innumerable Victorians, and Hopkins among them, approached the future:[6]

> It was in the nineteenth century, especially in Victorian England, that many modern attitudes toward the whole temporal process first emerged. The Victorians, at least as their verse and prose reveal them, were preoccupied almost obsessively with time and all the devices that measure time's flight.

Professor Buckley's adverb 'obsessively' is an interesting one, especially in view of his suggestion that neither the Romantics nor the Victorians were particularly anxious about the end of time:

> According to the traditional time-scheme of Christian orthodoxy, the Past was the period of the world's creation; the Present, the here and now of this mortal life; and the Future, the day of the Second Coming and apocalypse; Eternity entered human time at a precise juncture of history, the death and resurrection of Christ. Such a view seldom appears in Romantic or Victorian poetry, but it receives at least one striking expression, Hopkins's powerful lyric 'That Nature is a Heraclitean Fire and of the Comfort of the Resurrection.'

If Professor Buckley means that Christ's death, resurrection, and second coming and their effects upon human concepts of time were not vastly popular subjects with Romantic and Victorian lay writers, one can hardly argue. But a haunting anxiety about 'the Future, the day of the Second Coming and the apocalypse' was a topic for sermons all over England, even in sophisticated centres like Oxford and Cambridge, from the time when William Wilberforce first published his *Practical View of Christianity* in 1797. This anxiety was a commonplace among Tractarian and Evangelical priests and in Dissenting households. Its reappearance, either as a literal prophecy or as a half-believed metaphor for present and approaching calamities, is one of the distinguishing features of the nineteenth century; and one can hear the Romantic writers, one after the other voicing the apocalyptic cadence, both in joy and anguish, long before it swelled into a full-throated Victorian chorus. In fact, the Romantics, and to an even greater extent, the Victorians, exhibited an intensely apocalyptic view of history, and many of them feared national and international catastrophes not only as present dangers, but as semi-divine premonitions of more upheavals to come. Men of this temperament scanned the skies, the newspapers, and their favourite authors or sermon writers for auguries of some cosmic horror whose source they variously interpreted according to their social and religious affiliations. The calamitarian mood of the turn of the century became more and more marked, as Victoria's reign wore on, and the mood itself was one of the ways the Victorians demonstrated their obsessive preoccupation 'with time and all the devices that measure time's flight'.

It is true that the vision of divine retribution in the Apocalypse touched many Victorian writers more profoundly than visions of the resurrection or of the Heavenly City on earth. To these men, warnings of doom and destruction, it seemed, came more naturally, since doom and destruction seemed far more probable than any future joy or justice, divine or earthly, that they could imagine. And Hopkins, who accepted the joyous news of God contained in Revelation, as any Christian would, was still infinitely more haunted by the incipient 'horror and the havoc' in the second coming than he was exhilarated by the coming 'glory of it'. 'The night has got on, the day is nearer. This is, my brethren, always true and always getting truer. Mark these two things'; so Hopkins once warned his parishioners (*S*, 41, 1879):

> for it is at any minute true ... that the world has gone on some time since Christ's first coming and made some approach to his second; and also every minute truer for every minute we and the world are older, every minute our death and the world's end are nearer than before. For life and time are always losing, always spending, always running down and running out, therefore every hour that strikes is a warning of our end and the world's end, for both these things are an hour nearer than before.

Certainly the intellectual and religious life of the Victorians often aped the signs of decadence in the doomed Biblical cities, as Carlyle and Ruskin never tired of telling their readers. And furthermore, 'Darwin's *Origin of Species* had come into the theological world like a plough into an ant hill';[7] and to the Evangelicals and the Dissenters, as to the Tractarians and the conservative Anglicans, Darwin and all his works and all his followers appeared as engines of the devil, and the new sciences were looked upon as devices to destroy the national faith already weakened by Jowett's brand of Platonism at Oxford and by

Biblical criticism from abroad. Canon Liddon's ingenious description of man's progenitor would be laughable if one were unable to recognize the shattering blow that *The Origin of Species* must have dealt him. When geologists, said Liddon,

> come to us with their hands full of what they tell us are human bones, which judging from the strata in which they are found, must have belonged to an age prior to any that, with the utmost chronological literality, can be assigned to the Adam of Genesis, and then argue that death—human death, must have been much older than Adam, and that St. Paul is mistaken in tracing the origin of its empire to him—

the man of faith, Liddon preached, may justly argue that the bones are not human; they are the remains of pre-men, possibly even 'rational, responsible' creatures 'on their probation'. These pre-humans, like their descendants, must 'have failed in that probation and fallen under the law of death, and, finally, have disappeared at the terrible summons of some vast catastrophe which prepared the earth for their successors'.[8]

The ancient social hierarchies, so closely related to Christian belief and practice in the minds of the conservative religious parties, were themselves dissolving, as one franchise reform succeeded another throughout the century. And for all this social upheaval, the French Revolution was the model, ghastly or joyous in its outcome, but in any case, the signal for a new reign of horror upon earth from which Carlyle and his disciples, at least, expected no surcease.

But for Liddon the Tractarian, the French Revolution and the social and religious upheavals at home meant both horror and joy in the making, and for him, the joy was finally to prevail. True, as Liddon reminded his listeners, the French Revolution was the precursor of the day of judgment, a day that 'will come home to every one of us directly, as closely as anything can'. That calamitous event 'closed one period in the history of Europe and it opened another': now, for those who had eyes to see and ears to hear, it heralded a 'supernatural event yet to come, I say, yet to come'. The supernatural event that St John had prophesied, that Hopkins largely feared, and looked forward to only in his rare moments of hope for mankind, Liddon awaited with the quiet and incandescent happiness of a trusting child. For 'the true and highest work of great public calamities, of famines and revolutions as well as private sufferings, disease and death' is to represent 'God's judgments . . . abroad'[9] and thus to teach righteousness before it was too late for sinning mankind. And with the coming of righteousness in the hearts of men, 'Our Lord might become again' to His Church and His people 'what He was to His Apostle, a Living Being, Walking amidst the golden candlesticks'.[10]

But the 'workings of one mind, the features'

> Of the same face, blossoms upon one tree;
> Characters of the great Apocalypse,
> The types and symbols of Eternity,
> Of first, and last, and midst, and without end—

that Wordsworth had celebrated in Book VI of *The Prelude* and elsewhere, that Coleridge had described in his second Lay Sermon, and that Blake had made the burden of many of his prophetic writings, loomed with more terror before the Victorians than before their Romantic forebears, for the world at large gave little countenance to suppositions of future felicity. Affairs at home and abroad were like one vast heaving and menacing sea; one social, religious, or political upheaval might die down only to have another or several at a time take its place. First Carlyle and the Tractarians lifted their voices to counteract the joy in the apocalyptic utterances of Blake, Wordsworth, Coleridge, and the Evangelicals, only to be joined in turn by Carlyle's disciples and the Christian Socialists who preached reform and anticipated revolution. And the pleadings of all these men of such varied persuasions often sounded like the desolate calls of sea gulls, tossed about by hurricane winds, their shrill cries now waxing, now waning in the nautical tumult.

At the turn of the century William Wilberforce, lay leader of the Evangelical Protestants known as the Clapham Sect, pleaded feverishly with his large reading public[11] to watch and pray, for signs abounded that the second coming was at hand. His cries were heeded: 'Evangelical morality was the single most widespread influence in Victorian England', Noel Annan maintains,[12] and Elie Halévy tells us:[13]

> The belief was beginning to spread in British Protestant circles that the second advent of Jesus to judge the living and the dead must be preceded by a return of the Jews to Jerusalem, and the rebuilding of Solomon's temple that on the very spot where the Saviour had been crucified they might be confuted, converted and pardoned.

According to Halévy,[14] these nineteenth-century Protestants, at least, were haunted by the vision of time's end, and since there was room for differences of opinion as to the date, more or less close, of that event, an entire press and an entire body of literature came into existence to interpret on this point the Old Testament prophecies.

By the eighteen-thirties the Oxford temper was violently apocalyptic, and it continued to be so for four decades, despite everything Jowett and his disciples could later do to dispel morbid anxiety. Pusey and Newman both preached that the time when Christ would come to judge both the quick and the dead was near, and in the 'sixties, when Hopkins was in residence at Oxford, the quarrels between the scientists and the churchmen and between the radicals and the conservatives in the Church of England filled the air with shrill apocalyptic din. Liddon once told his parishioners that the second coming of the Lord would be anticipated by 'widespread intellectual confusion, political and social perplexity, material ruin', and a noticeable 'falling off from the Faith', and that a 'personage' would arrive on the national scene who would 'embody all the hostilities towards God that are scattered throughout human nature and history'.[15]

Hopkins himself was no doubt indebted to all three of these priests for his own apocalyptic alarms, Pusey and Liddon by personal example, and Newman by the heroic story of his conversion and its attendant sufferings. Apocalyptic alarm was always the more terrible because one never knew where the spirit of the Antichrist might be lodged, in the revolutionaries at large, or in the bosom of one's closest friend. After Newman's conversion to Roman Catholicism, Pusey and Newman each treated the other with the exquisite tact of implacable enemies combined with the compassion of old friends, as though each, by looking elsewhere, might escape the sight of the Antichrist in the other. And Hopkins's fears for his friends' spiritual state was not only on their account, but that in their ghastly plight their proud and blind ignorance might drag others down with them.

Innumerable contemporaries of Hopkins, who did not necessarily share his belief in the second coming, nonetheless used the scenes or the language of St John's Apocalypse[16] to express their moral and social anxieties. In 1858, Richard Watson Dixon, Hopkins's friend, offered a brilliant study of the tenth century for the Arnold history prize at Oxford. Dixon's thesis, 'that the Tenth Century was greatly obsessed by the dread of the millennium' and the end of all things, may be 'historically unsound', as Dixon's biographer has suggested, but the prize essay is a remarkable work, and one that played its part in shaping

Hopkins's apocalyptic temper. It is imbued with a curious dry melancholy that is far more compelling, in some ways, than the hoarse prophecies of Tennyson or of Carlyle and his disciples. The subject of Dixon's essay suggests the pervasiveness of the calamitarian mood, since so many writers, from the Poet Laureate to undergraduates at Oxford, were expressing the Victorian form of alienation rather than the joyful anticipation of Blake, Coleridge, and Wordsworth.

Dixon's essay described an 'anarchical doubt-ridden world' that permitted the youthful historian ample opportunities for indirect 'comments on the predicament of modern man, whom he sees as the bewildered victim of circumstances, hurled to and fro by fortune in a decaying and disintegrating society'. Dixon's bitterness against his own 'complacent and unjust society motivated', as he felt it was, 'by shallow intellectual philosophies',[17] shapes the entire essay. The opening pages state Dixon's apocalyptic thesis in the form of a question: 'What did this point of time receive from the past, which rendered it a crisis of development for the future?' In the tenth century of the Christian era Dixon had seen a 'practical credulity expressed by blood and rapine'. Like most writers who use the Apocalypse as a full or partial model for their prophetic utterances, Dixon expressed himself both openly and covertly. His open thesis, that Rome, Greece, and Byzantium had disappeared as important sovereign powers, partly concealed, as it partly disclosed, his prophecy: that such a fate was awaiting industrial England.

Dixon's essay is full of the familiar apocalyptic machinery; there are descriptions of suffering, famines, pestilence, deliberate starvation of the poor by rapacious and idolatrous upper classes, and several dread catastrophes on land and sea. With his eyes apparently fixed on the century he was describing, Dixon uttered comments that applied full well to his own: 'the social disorders had accumulated into an unendurable agony and wrong. The mass of mankind were fixed upon the globe in a servitude complete and hopeless.'[18]

When Hopkins was at Oxford, he came upon *Christ's Company*, Dixon's collection of poems; he unearthed the Arnold prize essay as well, and, as he wrote Dixon years later, he copied out parts of all these works, to keep by him (*CD*, 1, 1878). In many ways Dixon was a far more congenial friend to Hopkins than was Bridges, as one can see from the two correspondences. With Dixon Hopkins could pour out his fears about the last judgment. Yet even here Hopkins was careful, feeling his way delicately, probing Dixon step by step as to his actual beliefs on the second coming.

By the late eighteen-fifties, when Hopkins was still a schoolboy at

Highgate, and Dixon was at Oxford writing his threnodic essay on tenth-century Christianity, the outburst of apocalyptic warnings had become a torrent, issuing from prophets of every religious and professional persuasion. A new reading public had emerged, frightened by Tractarian and Evangelical warnings of perdition, both personal and cosmic. These readers knew their Bible as they knew no other literature; by now they were afflicted with a pervasive anxiety that craved to be stimulated as it yearned to be assuaged. Any writer who called upon readers' memories of the sufferings in Revelation was sure of a response from a large portion of his public. If he could also suggest a definite cure for public and private woes, a cure that would usher in the day of the City on the Hill, either in literal or metaphoric terms, he was all the more popular and comforting. Re-establish the aristocracy in all its old pomp and responsibility, abolish the aristocracy, excommunicate Darwin, enthrone Darwin, enfranchise the disenfranchised, enslave them further, turn Roman Catholic, curse the Pope—wherever one looked, exact prescriptions for salvation were on hand, together with exact methods to avoid the national doom.

The new reading classes might naively assume that their rise in the world, their thrift and their industry would automatically bring the New Jerusalem for all classes in good time; after all, they had plenty of examples of complacency before them in the classes they hoped to join. Yet they suffered themselves to buy and to read just those sermons, poems, and novels whose writers warned them, in gentle allegory or in angry outbursts, that in the past many a gracious merchant city had fallen at the height of her affluence, and all her princes and her captains of industry with her. The catastrophes prophesied in Revelation *had* happened in ancient times as in the immediate past. Indeed, these writers warned their readers, at the moment a man put down his novel or volume of poetry, essays, or sermons in favour of a comfortable sleep, another holocaust might be at hand.

Two years before Hopkins began to work on his ode to the *Deutschland,* the 'Storm Cloud'[19] of Revelation's warnings lay so low and so heavily upon the Victorians that John Morley felt compelled to comment on this phenomenon and to try to account for it. Morley attributed the calamitarian mood to 'the immense decline in sincerity of spiritual interest'. The 'flood tide of high profits' deplored by Morley in 1874, as it had been in and out of season by Carlyle, Ruskin, Morris, and Tennyson, the 'roaring trade', customarily 'engendering latitudinarians' and 'slackening moral vigour' were reminiscent of the luxury and infidelity in Babylon the Great and all the cities of the plains before their extinction. The 'root of the matter' was the 'slow transformation now at work of the whole spiritual basis of thought'. Admittedly, every 'age is in some sort an age of transition', but Morley thought his age was 'characteristically and cardinally an epoch of transitions in the very foundations of belief and conduct'.[20]

Morley's comments are all the more penetrating because he surveyed the contemporary scene with the detachment of a social scientist; he was not crying out in the prophetic cadences of Carlyle, Ruskin, or Morris. While these men, and others committed to every variety of religious and political parties, were preaching that England was risking God's wrath and subsequent physical or spiritual extinction, Morley saw the calamitarian mood to be a feature of the times, and not an accurate prediction of things to come:[21]

> The work of destruction is all the more perturbing to timorous spirits, and more harassing even to doughtier spirits, for being done impalpably, indirectly, almost silently and as if by unseen hands. Those who dwell in the tower of ancient faiths look about them in constant apprehension, misgivings, and wonder, with the hurried mien of people living amid earthquakes. The air seems to their alarms to be full of missiles, and all is doubt, hesitation, and shivering expectancy.

By the last four decades of the century, Darwin's spectacle of animal species in lethal competition for food and living space suggested a slower, but equally inevitable doom for man, and for the Englishman in particular. But even before 1859, the rumblings of the geologists had shaken the poise, if not the faith, of many a committed Christian. And the pangs of apocalyptic dismay occasionally gripped even the evolutionists themselves. As staunch a champion of Darwin as the zoologist George Romanes could not overcome the grief that his acceptance of the new scientific disciplines had created in him.[22] As an impartial scientist he had to accept the facts, but they seemed to him no blessing, but a universal horror:

> Never in the history of man has so terrific a calamity befallen the race as that which all who look may now behold advancing as a deluge, black with destruction, resistless in might, uprooting our most cherished hopes, engulfing our most precious creed, and burying our highest life in mindless desolation.

His own discipline had become for Romanes 'a meditation, not merely of death, but of annihilation'; science, whom erstwhile we thought a very angel of God, pointing to that great barrier of Law, and proclaiming to the restless sea of changing doubt, 'Hitherto shall thou come, but no further, and here shall thy proud waves be stayed—' even science has now herself thrown down this trusted barrier; the floodgates of infidelity are open, and atheism overwhelming is upon us.

Such cries from Romanes, the disciple of Darwin, sound at one time like the angry exhortations of priests and pastors and at others like Sartre's bleak comments upon the fate of modern man, alone upon a parched earth, his head tilted toward an empty sky, in the posture of unbearable memory. At other times, Romanes echoes the bleak sense of illimitable and indifferent space that appears in *In Memoriam*. Man, Romanes said mournfully,

has truly become in a new sense the measure of the universe, and in this the latest and most appalling of his soundings, indications are returned of the infinite voids of space and time by which he is surrounded, that his intelligence, with all its noble capacities for love and adoration, is yet alone, destitute of kith or kin in all this universe of being.

For Romanes, 'the universe' had 'lost its soul of loveliness' with man's 'virtual negation of God':

and although from henceforth the precept to 'work while it is yet day' will doubtless but gain an intensified force for the terribly intensified meaning of the words 'the night cometh when no man can work,' yet when at times I think, as think I must, of the appalling contrast between the hallowed glory of that creed which once was mine, and the lonely mystery of existence as I now find it,—at such times I shall ever feel it impossible to avoid the sharpest pang of which my nature is susceptible.

Charles Kingsley, liberal priest and amateur scientist, was also a victim of desolate anxieties. In 1855 he deplored the 'popular war' going on between the 'reason of a generation and its theology', and in the same lecture he complained 'that the religious temper of England for the last two or three generations has been unfavourable to a sound and scientific development of natural theology'.[23] Yet the same 'popular war' between reason and theology seemed to be taking place within Kingsley himself. While disapproving of 'that midcentury melancholy which produced *Maud* and the Spasmodics', he admitted to a friend that he was afflicted with the same disease:[24]

And when my trust in the Bible as a whole seems falling to pieces it is—you must feel it is—terrible work for a poor soul to know where the destructive process must stop; and one feels alone in the universe, at least alone among mankind, on a cliff which is crumbling beneath one, and falling piecemeal into the dark sea. . . . I cannot escape that wretched fear of a national catastrophe which haunts me night and day.

As a young man at Oxford, Hopkins himself was almost deafened by the prophetic cacophony. But the nineteenth-century Jesuits' predictions of doom for heretical England were as vehement as the Tractarians' or the Fundamentalist Dissenters'. If Hopkins had hoped for silence in the order of St Ignatius, he would have been doomed to disappointment, but one suspects that he joined the order partly because it offered him so legitimate a pulpit for his own apocalyptic sermons, and because Catholic permanence was in direct contrast to Victorian chaos, and Catholic beauty to Victorian ugliness. Matthew Arnold had called his times 'the iron age',[25] and as the consolidation of the iron age went on apace, it was accompanied by a callous destruction of 'the earth's sweet being' (Poem 33, 1877) that seemed to Hopkins, as it had to Ruskin, to be the visible and brutal token of some deep satanic force eroding the nation's conscience. Hopkins called the decades of his priesthood a 'sordid turbid time', and the towns in which most men were condemned to live were 'shallow and frail' (Poem 35, 1877), their growth invariably 'graceless'; even Oxford, once one of the loveliest towns in England, was now soured with commercial scum and had 'a base and brickish skirt'.

Hopkins feared more than the loss of pastoral beauty, a terrible enough punishment for national sins that had 'confounded' all 'rural keeping—folks, flocks, and flowers' (Poem 44, 1879).[26] The entire nation was contaminated with greed. 'All is from wreck':

> The times are nightfall, look, their light grows less;
> The times are winter, watch, a world undone:
> They waste, they wither worse; they as they run
> Or bring more or more blazon man's distress.
>
> (Poem 150, n.d.)

The men who were ravishing the earth were to their 'own selfbent so bound' (Poem 58) that they were willing to 'waste' and 'wither' whole cities and their populations and to 'Hack and rack the growing green' (Poem 43) without the slightest 'reck of world after' (Poem 58, 1882), either the temporal world they had despoiled or the divine world from which their conduct would debar them.

Like all apocalyptic writers, Hopkins preached not only for the sake of the individual sinner but for the sake of the community. The more lax the community was, the more it worshipped money rather than God, the greater and more imminent was the risk of the last days. No one could decide how many greedy and idolatrous sinners comprised a modern Babylon, or how much public and private sin would bring the community under the wrathful eye of God for the last time. But so much was clear: each violation of God's laws on the part of each sinner made the individual's damnation that much surer; it also brought the end of the world that much nearer. So the individual risked not only his own damnation with every fresh sin; he risked the end of days for mankind as well. Hopkins thought he saw a decay in the minds and the bodies of the English people that might prefigure the human extinction, as St John had prophesied.

But a nation so heretical, and so careless of God's bounty, might not even be given time to slither, eon by eon, into a retrogressive evolution, like a mud-covered amphibian, draining 'fast towards man's first slime'. God can punish all or some; he can do so with lightning, or man can bring about his own slow extinction in the shape of befouled cities, exhausted labourers, and scarred countryside. And Hopkins was only one of hundreds of social critics who prophesied that the industrial revolution's 'make and making' was almost totally destructive; it was 'breaking, down/To man's last dust' (Poem 35, 1877).

'Man's smudge' and 'man's smell' were fit corollaries to the contemporary scene, 'seared with trade; bleared, smeared with toil'; and the grandeur of God would 'flame out, like shining from shook foil' (Poem 31, 1877), not only as a comforting reminder of His presence even in the midst of filth, but as a warning to money worshippers of the future holocaust awaiting them. Hopkins was merely adapting the classical terminology of St John and his predecessors to Victorian problems. He maintained that poverty and plunder were all part of a sinful conspiracy, that the captains of industry and the princes of the state were as indifferent to the welfare of those who created their wealth as they were to the hideous disfigurement they visited upon the earth. No possessing classes had ever treated the classes in their power with more wanton and vicious disregard; one contemporary after the other turned first from the spectacle of complacent greed to the even more terrifying spectacle of what it bred. The contempt of the possessing classes for the most elementary rights of the lower orders, Hopkins warned, was bound to spawn countercontempt and then violence:

> This, by Despair, bred Hangdog dull; by Rage,
> Manwolf, worse; and their packs infest the age.
>
> (Poem 70, 1887)

Hopkins followed the apocalyptic tradition in even more specific ways. Insurrection, St John had urged in his vision, is not only a crime against the public order and a sin against God; it is simultaneously an engine of divine retribution. And so it had proved during the French Revolution, and if the English classes in power did not heed the cries of pain from below, God would use the lower classes as scourges with which to chastise the upper classes. 'It is what Carlyle has long threatened and foretold', Hopkins wrote Bridges, adding that in his own opinion the 'too intelligent artisan' was already 'master of the situation' (*LB*, 27, 1871). Carlyle did indeed anticipate the coming of the 'frightful coughings of street musketry' unless all classes returned to a code of honour and mutual responsibility. The 'howlings and bellowings' of 'chartists, Repeal Agitators, Red Republics' and other scum were both retributive and admonitory. They were international warnings which 'all the populations of the world' should heed.[27]

With fine Carlylian bombast, and with reasoning perhaps borrowed from Dickens's *Hard Times* as well, Hopkins also took violent issue with 'Radical Levellers'; he thought they were opportunists battening on the sufferings of the lower classes, and he considered them as responsible for the 'Loafers, Tramps, Cornerboys, Roughs, and other pests of society' as the heartless conduct of the controlling classes.[28] Carlyle had looked at mid-Victorian society, particularly in *Latter-Day Pamphlets*, and he had cried out in paroxysms of fear and rage that large segments of all classes were conducting themselves as though preparing for their own damnation. The citizens' howls of rage and their acts of destruction all over the Continent may well have been partly justified, he had admitted in earlier works, but in the manner of the Apocalypse, Carlyle now saw insurrection as both sin deserving punishment and as a punitive warning to the insurgents' oppressors. The violent conduct of the lower classes, whether justified or not, was the modern equivalent of Apocalyptic retributions; for behind the human producers of these 'whirlwinds, conflagrations, earthquakes', Carlyle had glimpsed some unspecified divine agent. And one day, he chanted, 'the popular lightning, descending forked and horrible from the black air, will annihilate' the upper classes, whose decadence reminded him of 'some carcass of a drowned ass'.[29]

Hopkins may well have picked up Carlyle's image of the 'forked' lightning, since *forked* lightning does not appear in either Testament of the Bible. The sonnet in which it appears, written only a few weeks before Hopkins's final illness, is the only poem that offers no suggestion of salvation after death, or hope for a rational life on earth. In its almost unrelieved gloom, it echoes some of Carlyle's most hopeless moods:

> The shepherd's brow, fronting forked lightning, owns
> The horror and the havoc and the glory
> Of it. Angels fall, they are towers, from heaven—a story
> Of just, majestical, and giant groans.
> But man—we, scaffold of score brittle bones;
> Who breathe, from groundlong babyhood to hoary
> Age gasp; whose breath is our *memento mori*—
> What bass is *our* viol for tragic tones?

This is one of the rare poems in which Christ the Shepherd or Guardian of erring man appears in retributive mien. The phrase *'our* viol' refers once again to Isaiah xiv,[30] and Hopkins's predictions for man are as dismal as those of the apocalyptic prophet. The sonnet's octave contrasts Lucifer's proud fall with modern man's cosmic pettiness, for at least the divine prototype of pride and destruction, of which all subsequent sins and falls are mere pale copies, took place in a majestic setting; at least the issues, then, were monumental and the sinners had once possessed the awesome stature commensurate with their divine origin. But contemporary man, being only human, is without dignity, and his life, bereft of the faith and honour that could have been his in Eden, is simply one sordid function after the other. In the sestet, Hopkins answers his own rhetorical question—'What bass is *our* viol for tragic tones?'—with a sourly ironic look at himself and his neighbours:

> He! Hand to mouth he lives, and voids with shame;
> And, blazoned in however bold the name,
> Man Jack the man is, just; his mate a hussy.
> And I that die these deaths, that feed this flame,
> That . . . in smooth spoons spy life's masque mirrored: tame
> My tempests there, my fire and fever fussy.
>
> (Poem 75, 1889)

In his treatment of working men, Hopkins once again followed Carlyle, who had told his readers that 'the highest eye may look on' all products of honest workmanship 'without displeasure, nay, with a kind of satisfaction'.[31] Hopkins's poetic eye also looked with a kind of satisfaction upon honest labour and all its products. His 'Harry Ploughman', his 'Felix Randal', his hob-nailed 'Tom Navvy', and 'sturdy Dick' elicited a good deal of sentimental praise from him; and 'plough down sillion' shone with far more moral lustre than the gaudy and irresponsible windhover.[32] All these Victorian figures, from Carlyle's Gurth the Churl, Dickens's Stephen Blackpool, Kingsley's Alton Locke to Hopkins's humble workers and ploughmen, were to serve in the public's mind as wholesome foils for the decadent aristocrats and brutal industrialists; as such they have some of the charming simplicity of characters in a morality play.

Pastoral scenes and pastoral characters are not invariably part of the apocalyptic furniture, either in the Old Testament or the New. That they appear so frequently both in Romantic and Victorian literature, sometimes in the same works containing apocalyptic material, suggests that these writers were instinctively drawing upon recurrent English themes as moral substitutes for corruption. On the one hand, nineteenth-century readers were offered version after version of Hopkins's 'Sweet especial rural scene' (Poem 43, 1879), from the cleared tracts around Camelot to the wholesome countryside of *News from Nowhere*, and from the green haunts of the shy Scholar Gypsy to Ruskin's magnificent composite panorama of lakes, seas, skies, woods, and mountains. On the other hand, there was a resurgence of staple apocalyptic themes and metaphors, such as wrecks at sea, violent and flaming lightning, volcanoes, plagues, wars, and insurrections among the lower orders.

And so, pastoral themes in the nineteenth century took on a new didactic urgency, as writers and their readers attempted to come to terms with the insurrectionary mood of the age. Under these incendiary conditions the pastoral mode was used not only to evoke elegiac memory but horror over the radically shifting relationship between man and God and man and man. As the religious disputes went on and on during the century, as factories sprang up all over urban and rural England, vomiting smoke by day and searing the night skies with their tongues of fire, and as great sections of the cities became more and more like grave-sites for the abandoned poor, many men looked back to a semi-feudal past and forward to a future that would be controlled— they thought—by a faceless and illiterate mob.

Another familiar apocalyptic metaphor appeared with renewed force in nineteenth-century literature. Even more aptly than metaphors of wars, revolutions, natural or man-made devastations of the countryside, and other calamitous events, it could be used to express personal foreboding or to warn a heedless population. Acrophobia, or fear of precipitous rocks, peaks, cliffs, or desolate mountain ranges is also a staple in apocalyptic works. The metaphor usually takes one of two forms: either the climber fears he is about to lose his precarious hold on some pinnacle, or the rock itself is cracking beneath his weight. In Kingsley's metaphor of the mountain climber, perched on a 'cliff which is crumbling beneath one, and falling piecemeal into the dark sea',[33] the mountain itself is the intended victim, and the mountain climber merely an innocent bystander. In Hopkins's metaphor of the 'frightful, sheer, no-man-fathomed' mountains of the mind, man himself is the intended victim. In Ruskin's passages on mountain gloom in the fourth volume of *Modern Painters,* man, beast, and rocks are all menaced by some malign force, a force itself in the grip of some nameless cosmic sadness.

Hopkins could hardly have come upon Kingsley's letter containing the acrophobic metaphor. He probably drew his own metaphor from *Modern Painters,* from a trip to the Alps, or from reading Romantic poetry. Hopkins, dutifully following Wordsworth, Ruskin, and many another university graduate, in a conventional post-graduate trip to the Alps, had at first merely felt the obligatory awe, until suddenly his own private vision of mountain gloom had gripped him, 'and after that it was strange', he confided in his journal, 'for Nature became Nemesis' (*JP*, 177, 1868).

Wordsworth had helped to reintroduce apocalyptic sensibilities to nineteenth-century moralists. Turner's awesome Alpine scenes and the fourth book of *The Prelude,*[34] with the descriptions of narrow chasms, gloomy straits, and

> The immeasurable height
> Of woods decaying, never to be decayed,
> The stationary blasts of waterfalls,
> And in the narrow rent at every turn
> Winds thwarting winds, bewildered and forlorn,
> The torrents shooting from the clear blue sky,
> The rocks that muttered close upon our ears,
> Black drizzling crags that spake by the way-side
> As if a voice were in them, the sick sight
> And giddy prospect of the raving stream,
> The unfettered clouds and region of the Heavens,
> Tumult and peace, the darkness and the light—

all these scenes of gloom and desolation, whether they come from the hand of God or the hand of man the artist, Wordsworth himself had recognized as 'Characters of the great Apocalypse'.[35]

Wordsworth was not the only Romantic artist and moralist to become conscious that after the Enlightenment had come the deluge. Coleridge was deeply disturbed by what he called 'the distempered atmosphere' of the French Revolution, much as he had hoped from it at first, and its aftermath had indeed stirred into 'activity' these apocalyptic 'perennials of history'.[36] Revelation had warned that the second angel, with a mere trumpet call, would dislodge a 'great mountain burning with fire' and send it hurtling into the sea to bloody the waters, and that 'the third part of the creatures that were in the sea and had life' and 'the third part of the ships' at sea would be destroyed.[37]

Tarpeian imagery of this sort undoubtedly had historical origins in the Roman custom of executing criminals by throwing them off the Tarpeian rock on to the jagged stones below. As a Roman subject, St John would have been well aware of the ugly scenes that took place on the Capitoline hill, and the custom must have been known to university men and classical scholars. Tarpeian imagery is associated not only with fear and doom, but with sensations of guilt, either covertly or openly recognized. Hopkins unmistakably guides us to the historical association in *The Wreck of the Deutschland* (Poem 28, 1876). The tall nun, whose death in the 'white-fiery' waters of the Thames serves, in part, as expiation for humanity's sins, is compared both to Simon Peter[38] and to a Roman criminal awaiting execution:[39]

> The Simon Peter of a soul! to the blast
> Tarpeian-fast, but a blown beacon of light.
>
> (Poem 28, Stanza 29)

Some of the most impressive passages of Tarpeian imagery that must have rung in Hopkins's ears[40] occur in the fourth volume of *Modern Painters*. Ruskin's terrifying samples haunt the mind because Ruskin treats the mountain peaks even more anthropomorphically than Wordsworth, or Dante, or St John, yet he is faithful to the apocalyptic tradition. His peaks serve the same function as St John's fiery mountain, as Hopkins's 'no-man-fathomed cliffs of fall', and as the raging river mouth in *The Wreck of the Deutschland*. Nature is both sinner and sinned against, both the destructive agent and the symbolic victim of the doom she precipitated. Ruskin's passages on mountain gloom are worth studying, not only in their own right, and not only because they are typical, in an intensified way, of the apocalyptic cadences all around Hopkins, but because more than any other samples of Victorian writing, they show us a great deal about Hopkins's elliptical techniques—how he was able to compress into a fourteen-line sonnet, or a few stanzas, a mounting mood of fear and horror, for which Ruskin perfectly legitimately allowed himself almost a hundred pages.

Ruskin's treatment of precipitous peaks is deliberately modelled upon Revelation. The peaks are described as both proud and corruptible, like the doomed cities of the plains, and when they crack, the din is as loud as the clamour in ruined Babylon:

> Where the soil is rich and the climate soft, the hills are low and safe; as the ground becomes poorer and the air keener, they rise in forms of more peril and pride; and their utmost terror is shown only where their fragments fall on trackless ice, and the thunder of their ruin can be heard but by the ibex and the eagle.
>
> (VI, 279, 199)

The most 'frightful' of these precipitous mountains, 'the most impressive as well as the most dangerous of mountain ranges' beyond the endurance of the human imagination were

> dark in colour, robed in everlasting mourning for ever tottering like a great fortress shaken by war, fearful as much in their weakness as in their strength, yet gathered after every fall into darker frowns and unhumiliated threatening; for ever incapable of comfort or of healing of the herb flower, nourishing no root in the crevices, touched by no hue of life on buttress or ledge, but to the utmost, desolate.
>
> (VI, 295-6)

Each of these Tarpeian passages is longer and more full of terror than the last, until finally Ruskin bursts out into an awed peroration of one sentence lasting half a page of *Modern Painters*. At the peak of peaks, the climber, if he could ever crawl gasping to its top and cling to its pinnacle, would find there no leaves, no grass,

> no motion but their own mortal shivering, the dreadful crumbling of atom from atom in the corrupting stones; knowing no sound of living voice or living tread, cheered neither by the kid's bleat nor the marmot's cry; haunted only by uninterrupted echoes from far off, wandering hither and thither, among their walls, unable to escape, and by the hiss of angry torrents, and sometimes, when the echo has fainted and the wind has carried the sound of the torrent away, and the bird has vanished, and the mouldering stones are still for a

little time,—a brown moth, opening and shutting its wings upon a grain of dust, may be the only thing that moves or feels, in all the waste of weary precipice, darkening five thousand feet of the blue depth of heaven. (VI, 296)

In each of these mournful passages, the threatening, crumbling cliffs seem to serve as interchangeable images for the helpless human victims clinging to them. But this confusion, or fusion, between the victim and the sinner is apocalyptic and is particularly strong in Revelation. In Ruskin's passages, the climber's mounting anguish, rising and falling and rising to greater heights than before, paragraph by paragraph, page by page, resembles the awe and the terror of Hopkins's penitent in Part The First of *The Wreck of the Deutschland*, swooning 'with a horror of height', his heart now numbed, now on fire, now quiescent again and now bursting out in stunned praise of the Lord's magnificence as he struggles to keep his footing on the towers of grace (stanza 2).

Hopkins devotes one of his last sonnets to moral suffering of the kind that Ruskin described in his passages on mountain gloom. In this sonnet Hopkins appears to link the imagery of childbirth with Tarpeian metaphors, as he struggles to express both personal and cosmic doom:

> No worst, there is none. Pitched past pitch of grief,
> More pangs will, schooled at forepangs, wilder wring.
> Comforter, where, where is your comforting?
> Mary, mother of us, where is your relief?
> My cries heave, herds-long; huddle in a main, a chief-
> woe, world-sorrow; on an age-old anvil wince and sing—
> Then lull, then leave off. Fury had shrieked 'No ling-
> ering! Let me be fell: force I must be brief'.
> O the mind, mind has mountains; cliffs of fall
> Frightful, sheer, no-man-fathomed. Hold them cheap
> May who ne'er hung there. Nor does long our small
> Durance deal with that steep or deep. Here! creep,
> Wretch, under a comfort serves in a whirlwind: all
> Life death does end and each day dies with sleep.
>
> (Poem 65)

Just as Ruskin's passages imitate both the mounting fear of the climber and the mounting torture of a woman in prolonged and difficult labour, in the sonnet's octave, the accelerating rhythm of childbirth is compared to the sterile throes of a human being in utmost desolation, and in the

177

sestet, the moral suffering is linked by metaphor to the terrors of mountain climbing. The whole tone of this sonnet is mountain gloom revisited.[41] In the first quatrain Hopkins begs for comfort; Ruskin's peaks are 'desolate' and 'forever incapable of comfort'. Ruskin's peaks are 'frightful'; Hopkins's 'cliffs of fall' are equally 'Frightful'. Ruskin's are 'wholly inaccessible either from below or above'; Hopkins's are 'no-man-fathomed' in 'steep or deep'.

For the Victorians, fear, awe, or suffering of this kind was supposed to issue in moral improvement; the same could be said of any intense emotion that directed the mass of men back to the eternal heart of things.[42] As an earnest Victorian and a post-Romantic, Hopkins accepted moral suffering; as a Catholic priest and a Jesuit missionary, he preached literally what Ruskin and Carlyle had preached metaphorically. He wanted to teach his contemporaries of man's first disobedience and the fruit of the forbidden tree; and suffering was part of that fruit. But man's end was even more important to Hopkins than his beginning. Hopkins's most compelling mission was to teach men of the end of time and what they might do to earn eternal life in the City of God when the end of temporal things arrived.

But Hopkins was a man speaking under the handicap of partial self-censorship. Time and again he started to speak openly in his poems of the 'glory' that might be England's if one by one, or all in a body, her citizens returned to Roman Catholicism before the second coming, and the 'horror and the havoc' awaiting her if she did not.[43] But if she *should* return to the Roman fold, if the spirit of the Holy Ghost brooding over England could bring this about, then all her people, and Hopkins too, could await the second coming with far more equanimity than was now possible. As it was, only converts could hope for a seat close to the throne of God, and not all of them. What awaited the others, including his entire family and most of his friends, Hopkins could not always bear to think. For the unconverted ones, 'hell knows' no 'redeeming'; though Hopkins hoped against hope that he might be wrong, he feared that for non-Catholics who came before the judgment seat 'at the awful overtaking' when 'doomfire' was to 'burn all', even his most anguished prayers might not 'fetch pity eternal' (Poem 41, 1878).

This, then, was the nature of Hopkins's obsession with the future, an obsession that we know he shared with many of his contemporaries. Before we turn to his one complete Apocalypse in *The Wreck of the Deutschland,* we ought to look at his elliptical treatment of the second Advent in his lyrics. Some of them, hitherto obscure, seem to explode with significance, when one accepts them as the record of Hopkins's desperate concern for the eternal preservation of 'dear and dogged man' (Poem 58, 1882).

Like many of Hopkins's poems, 'That Nature is a Heraclitean Fire and of the Comfort of the Resurrection' is a study in the Christian riddle of mutability and eternity. Heraclitus was himself known as a 'riddler': he was said to have written the book on nature attributed to him in a deliberately obscure style 'so that only those of rank and influence should have access to it, and it should not be easily despised by the populace'. In any case, 'his pronouncements were undeniably often cryptic, probably intentionally so', and it was therefore an easy matter for the Stoics to attribute to him 'the idea of *ecpyrosis*, the periodical consumption of the whole world by fire'. He did believe fire to be an 'archetypal form of matter', and, as such divine and 'on a par with . . . water in general'. He also believed that the 'world order as a whole' could be 'described as a fire of which measures are being extinguished, and corresponding measures being re-kindled; not all of it is burning at the same time. It always has been, and always will be in this condition.'[44]

Hopkins's Heraclitean poem is also 'undeniably cryptic': he is wrestling with the problem of what remains (immortal diamond) if, as Heraclitus says, 'the soul itself is made of fire'[45] and is therefore partially extinguishable.

The first octave describes the Heraclitean change, decay, and flux as 'Million-fuelèd, nature's bonfire burns on'. But man, being part of nature, as the second octave says, is also ephemeral, 'his mark on mind' easily extinguished, destroyed in the archetypal elements (fire or water).[46] But the 'trumpet crash'[47] ends mortal time and begins immortal timelessness. For the last judgment will carbonize all the saved souls into jewels, just as the earth will be transported into heaven where flux and change are done away with (Poem 72, 1888).

Usually the concept of passing time and the mutability of all earthly things distressed Hopkins so that he could not comfort himself with the thought of the resurrection:

> The times are nightfall, look, their light grows less;
> The times are winter, watch, a world undone:
> They waste, they wither worse; they as they run
> Or bring more or more blazon man's distress.
> And I not help. Nor word now of success:—
> All is from wreck, here, there, to rescue one—

Work which to see scarce so much as begun
Makes welcome death, does dear forgetfulness.

(Poem 150, n.d.)

Sometimes Hopkins could persuade himself that nature herself seemed indestructible, whatever could be said for man, and that her very fluctuations and returns argued perdurability:

On ear and ear two noises too old to end
Trench—right, the tide that ramps against the shore;
With a flood or a fall, low lull-off or all roar,
Frequenting there while moon shall wear and wend.

(Poem 35, 1877)

But sometimes nature herself and all her fluctuations became models for human decay and death and these, in turn, prefigurations for the end of time. And *this* is 'the blight man was born for'; *this* is the secret that 'heart heard of' and 'ghost guessed': the 'worlds of wanwood' now decaying in 'leafmeal' are merely rehearsals for the final day of days. Margaret's sins, like those of all mankind, may bring about suffering to her and to the world compared with which the dying year should evoke no mourning at all (Poem 55, 1880).

Sometimes Hopkins speaks tentatively about the second coming. ' "Were I to come o'er again" cries Christ', men should be as soldiers under his banner (Poem 63, 1885). Sometimes he appeared to hope that the day of judgment following the second coming could be postponed, or possibly averted altogether; 'the last lights off the black West' may go out, but the Holy Ghost may save mankind, coming as a light from the east, or as a mother hen who broods over her eggs until they are hatched (Poem 31, 1877). And sometimes it seemed to this tortured poet who watched over the Catholic Church—'Time's Andromeda on this rock rude'—as though 'the wilder beast from West than all were' would devour her before Christ (Perseus) could come again and rescue her (Poem 50, 1879). Like the groaning martyrs crying out to the Lord of Hosts, 'How long, oh Lord, how long', Hopkins begged in 'cries countless, cries like dead letters sent/To dearest him that lives alas! away', that the spirit of the Holy Ghost would melt the hearts of all Englishmen and set his countrymen free (Poem 67, 1885?).

At other times the suffering going on all over England, and the even greater suffering to come under God's judgment, froze the marrow in Hopkins's bones and his apocalyptic utterances became almost incoherent. The imagery in 'Spelt from Sibyl's Leaves' is that of a man coming out of shock and moaning to himself in disconnected fragments. The leaves that the poet interprets from the Sibylline oracles are of unrelieved gloom. As evening gives way to night, Hopkins undergoes a ghastly fantasy that this is the last evening of the world and the oncoming night is to be the 'hearse-of-all' things as it is to be the 'womb-of-all' new life. Man, for the most part, is done for— 'páshed' (destroyed) in the Heraclitean element of 'Fire-féaturing heaven'; the firmament is to become 'earthless', her being 'unbound; her dapple' will come to 'an end'. 'Óur évening is over us; óur night whélms, whélms, ánd will end us.'

No wonder that with nights like these to endure, Hopkins's 'thóughts agáinst thoughts ín groans grínd' (Poem 61, 1885?). Some of the 'world-woe' in the terrible sonnets now becomes clear. How was Hopkins to save himself, his friends and relatives, to say nothing of all England, or all mankind, from the wrath of judgment following the second coming? How much did he dare speak out? Who would believe him? Was he, who felt he faced damnation himself, in a position to save anyone else? 'Only what word', Hopkins asks himself,

> Wisest my heart breeds dark heaven's baffling ban
> Bars or hell's spell thwarts. This to hoard unheard,
> Heard unheeded, leaves me a lonely began.
>
> (Poem 66, 1885?)

Four years before writing this sonnet, Hopkins had informed Bridges that he was awaiting a supernatural sign of England's preparation for the second Advent. He was evidently preparing himself for it, for he was planning to take the final vows of his tertianship[48] and he 'wanted to get some things done' before that date. He told Bridges that one of the tasks he had set himself was

> a great ode on Edmund Campion S. J. For the 1st of December is the 300th anniversary of his, Sherwin's and Bryant's martyrdom, from which I expect of heaven, some I cannot guess what, great conversion or other blessing to the Church in England (*LB*, 135–6, 1881).

In a sermon for the first day of Advent, Hopkins used linked images of dark and light to describe a world bereft of Catholic truth and daily drawing upon itself greater and greater wrath against the time of judgment. That world, Hopkins said, is dark: it is night and night is dark at best. And this night is not of so many hours, a number known beforehand; it is of quite uncertain length; and there is no dawn, no dayspring, to tell of the day coming, no morning twilight, sunrise will be sudden, will be lightning, we are told, will overtake us without warning, will entrap us, will come as a snare upon all that are on the face of the earth.

Before his parishioners, who did not need the shock of conversion to be saved, but only to be led to sinless lives, Hopkins could speak quite openly of the second coming:

There are indeed signs, but none but believers will heed them, and these signs will still leave the time uncertain though they will shew that it is near. So when Christ comes his coming will still surprise, men will be unaware and will be overtaken.

Like all orthodox Christians, Hopkins made a distinction between the individual judgment that awaits every man at his death, and the physical extinction of the globe and of all things upon it, as prophesied in Revelation. 'It may not be in our time', Hopkins preached in a sermon on the Apocalypse:

none of us may live to see it. But if our judge does not come to us we shall go to him: we shall die and after death is the judgment. For every man is judged once at death though at the Last Day all men are to be judged together: those that are judged already, their judgment will not be set aside; it will be confirmed with all the world to hear it.   (*S*, 40–1, 1879)

In a remarkable article, '*The Wreck of the Deutschland:* a New Reading',[49] the author makes the startling suggestion that Hopkins's tall nun actually 'saw Christ', or so Hopkins believed; 'and it seems . . . equally clear that what is implied is a supernatural event, not an ambiguous "vision" or a hallucination.' Professor Schneider clearly believes that for Hopkins, a physical 'miracle had occurred' and 'that during the night of terror at sea Christ had appeared to the nun, not in a subjective or imagined vision but as a real miraculous presence and that this, once acknowledged and published to the world, might become the needed signal, the turning point for the conversion of English Christians'.

As an Oxford Tractarian, Hopkins had ample opportunity to hear some of Liddon's or Pusey's sermons on the imminence of the second coming; the Tractarians believed that Christ would soon arrive to claim and judge the souls of all men and abolish the globe; they also believed that He would signal His return by appearing here and there to ready souls all over the world. And certainly, as Professor Schneider declares, Hopkins 'was not among the Victorian Christians who found' miracles in any form 'a stumbling block in the way of belief':[50]

> On the contrary, not only did biblical and the early saints' miracles move him deeply, but he also sought reasons to believe any accounts of contemporary miraculous healing or other miraculous signs of grace, and these appear often to have been associated in his mind with the conversion of England. Miracles enter prominently into the *Deutschland*, and the whole poem really turns on the hinge of a miraculous presence through which the wreck and the conversion are brought within a single focus.

Professor Schneider's interpretation explains many of Hopkins's sly little asides on the nature of art and its double role of concealing yet revealing Catholic truth. But Hopkins wanted to make one thing unmistakably clear, Professor Schneider reminds us: he went out of his way to inform Bridges that his description of his own experience 'is all strictly and literally true and did all occur; nothing is added for poetic padding'. And when we remember that Hopkins once begged Bridges to read *The Wreck of the Deutschland* again, and that in doing so he used the fevered language he typically employed when he was covertly discussing the future of the human race, we suspect that Hopkins hoped that the miraculous presence would move from himself to his agnostic friend, just as it had moved from the nun to himself. It is no wonder that Hopkins implored Bridges to reread at least 'the best and most intelligible stanzas, as the two last of each part and the narrative of the wreck' (*LB*, 47, 46). As Professor Schneider says 'the autobiographical first part' is deliberately designed to serve 'as microcosm, prelude, and in a sense pattern to Part The Second, with the implication that what has happened in one soul may happen to all',[51] In this letter to Bridges, Hopkins twice used the word 'convert'; presumably Bridges was to be converted to Hopkins's prosodic methods: 'I think if you will study what I have said here you will be much more pleased with it and may I say? converted to it?' And in the disingenuous remark 'You are my public and I hope to convert you' (*LB*, 46, 1878), Hopkins was obviously playing upon the meaning of the word 'convert'.

If we accept Part The First of *The Wreck of the Deutschland* as both an architectural and moral microcosm of Part The Second, we ought to

take quite literally another obscure little aside that Hopkins made to
Bridges:

> I cannot in conscience spend time on poetry, neither have I the
> inducements and inspirations that make others compose. Feeling,
> love in particular, is the great moving power and spring of verse and
> the only person that I am in love with seldom, especially now, stirs
> my heart sensibly and when he does I cannot always 'make capital'
> of it, it would be a sacrilege to do so.   (*LB*, 66, 1879)

I believe that Hopkins meant to hint, without openly saying so, that
Christ had appeared to him at one time or another, just as He had
appeared to the tall nun. If so, Christ's apparent desertion of him must
have added immeasurably to his 'world woe'. And if he believed that
Christ had come to him and then disappeared, he would have to
believe that the end of the world was indeed on its way, for sudden
apparitions, in imitation of the vision of St John, were perennially
awaited by men of the apocalyptic temper.

If Professor Schneider had needed further justification for her thesis,
which she did not, she might have offered Hopkins's strange letter to
Dixon on the nature of miraculous visitations. Hopkins used the
cryptic language deriving, as scholars of allegory say, 'from the
dedicated experience, isolated vision, and judgment of the solitary man,
the seer, the unlicensed and obscure sage'.[52] In praising Wordsworth's
'Intimations of Immortality', Hopkins pointedly alluded to visionaries,
both Christian and pagan:

> There have been in all history a few men, whom common repute,
> even where it did not trust them, has treated as having had some-
> thing happen to them that does not happen to other men, as having
> *seen something*, whatever that really was. (*CD*, 147, 1886; his italics)

Plato, Hopkins thought, was the most famous example of these men
whose 'human nature . . . saw something, got a shock; wavers in
opinion, looking back, whether there was anything in it or not, but is
in a tremble ever since'. Hopkins's comments on the nature of the
'shock' were enigmatic, as usual, but he left little doubt that he too had
'*seen something*' and that although the exact nature of his vision was a
private matter, its source was divine and its significance for foundering
man was incalculable. Hopkins also hinted that both Wordsworth and
Blake had been the recipients of the same visions, but that neither they
nor the rest of Protestant England had correctly acknowledged the
origins or the purpose of them:

Now what Wordsworthians mean is, what would seem to be the growing mind of the English speaking world and may perhaps come to be that of the world at large is that in Wordsworth when he wrote that ode human nature got another of these shocks, and the tremble of it is spreading. That opinion I do strongly share; I am, ever since I knew the ode, in that tremble.

Whatever it was that made Wordsworth 'tremble like a guilty thing surprised' had also put Blake 'in that tremble', almost, Hopkins said, to the point of hysteria:[53]

You know what happened to crazy Blake, himself a most poetically electric subject both active and passive, at his first hearing: when the reader came to 'The pansy at my feet' he fell into a hysterical excitement. Now common sense forbid we should take on like these unstrung creatures: still it was proof of the power of the shock.

(CD, 147–8)

Calamitarians like Hopkins could not understand how men could pick and choose those portions of scripture they wished to accept, and reject anything that made them uncomfortable. Those who believe literally in Revelation all see man's expulsion from his first home, his nostalgia for it, his continual falling away from grace, his sufferings, and the end of time, as following inevitably, one might say even organically, upon his first act of disobedience. Only faith and grace interrupt the organic continuum of sin and its consequences, more sinning, more sufferings, and the end of time. Wordsworth said he had received a vision of man's lost home and that this vision had filled him with nostalgic grief. Hopkins would naturally assume that Wordsworth's vision had taken in the whole spectrum of man's time on earth, from his delightful beginnings in Edenic felicity to his end as a creature. Wordsworth's grief would have been incomprehensible to Hopkins otherwise.

When Hopkins sat down to write his ode on the *Deutschland*, these were the portents that he wanted to reveal to men who had ears to hear and eyes to see. Professor Schneider noticed that the ode possesses 'the organic symmetry of a living form', and that none of Hopkins's other poems exhibits 'a more carefully wrought structure than the *Wreck*'. She also noticed that the 'primary outline is simple but the detail of the design is complex'.[54] Professor Schneider has put her finger on one of the characteristics of works modelled on the Apocalypse; they are designed with some of the purity of effect we associate with allegory, since everything must be 'subordinated to the announcement of the End. Everything leads up to Judgment and the New Age that follows it.'[55]

In *The Wreck of the Deutschland*, Hopkins subordinated all the apocalyptic scenes and metaphors to the triumphant ending. The typical scenes and metaphors that Northrop Frye calls apocalyptic— 'ordeals of water and fire', the images of the 'garden and the sheepfold', of 'sun, moon and stars', the collusive bestiality of men and nature operating according to God's blueprint[56]—all this apocalyptic furniture appears in full both in Revelation and in Hopkins's ode, and it all leads inevitably to the promise of the new age, when Christ will reign again over His English people before the end of days. Hopkins has infused his own Victorian Apocalypse with 'the rhythm of the total cyclical *mythos*' characterizing complete apocalypses. According to Frye, the total cycle includes both 'the epic of wrath and the epic of return as disaster is followed by restoration, humiliation by prosperity'.[57]

The Wreck of the Deutschland bears the marks both of its Biblical and its contemporary origins. From the newspaper reports of the *Deutschland*'s misadventure, Hopkins incorporated many factual details of the shipwreck, such as the weather conditions, the number of passengers on board, various nautical phenomena, and the time-scheme, from the first hint of danger to the final swamping of the *Deutschland* in the wind-whipped seas.[58] But Hopkins's purposes were clearly allegorical from the first stanza; and as the ode proceeds, his concatenation of reds, whites, and golds emerges as a carefully designed symbolic colour pageantry. The sun piercing the drifting snowflakes and lighting up the grim events of the shipwreck with its 'all-fire glances' and 'fall-gold mercies' (stanza 23) is an emblem both of the admonitory wrath and the benevolence of God.*

* One wonders how familiar Hopkins was with Ruskin's famous passage on Turner's painting called 'Slave Ship' (*Modern Painters*, 1, 571-3). All three works, Turner's 'Slave Ship', Ruskin's description of it, and *The Wreck of the Deutschland* treat factual contemporary events as modern analogues of the Apocalypse; all three emphasize the apocalyptic colours of red, white, and gold. Like most Turner critics, Ruskin was deter-mined to link much of Turner's work, particularly 'Slave Ship', with Revelation. Turner's painting shows a capsizing ship expelling her cargo of chained slaves into the water, as they had first been forcibly expelled from their African homeland. Just so, Hopkins's equally guilty and equally doomed ship spills its nuns into the Thames after their expulsion from their Rhineland home. All three works make full use of apocalyptic themes and imagery, such as fire and flood, wrath, guilt, and suffering, fear and the sudden destruction of the just and unjust alike.

The sea dragon in Revelation, who fascinated Hopkins (*S*, 198–9), turns up in Turner's painting as a predatory sea beast; he appears by inference in *The Wreck of the Deutschland* as 'the wind's burly and beat of endragonèd seas' (stanza 27). Ruskin does not mention

The three emblematic colours most often described in the Apocalypse are red, white, and gold. Whenever an angel appears before St John in his dream, to announce destruction at sea, the prophecy is accompanied by the fire-blood-water imagery of red and white. When gold is combined with the red and white, St John is indicating the divine element present in the destructive plan. The first time St John saw Christ in his vision, the Saviour and Avenger emerged out of the mist of dreams, an apparition of wonder and terror, surrounded by seven golden candlesticks. He wore a golden girdle and His hair had turned 'white like wool, as white as snow; and his eyes *were* as a flame of fire'. His feet were burnished like brass, 'as if they burned in a furnace; and his voice', to the frightened prophet, was 'as the sound of many waters'.[60] The flames and the waters signify the natural agents of destruction; but St John saw Christ's aspect as a manifestation of divine concern somewhat removed from single revenge. Christ's thunder and lightning were supposed to be didactic: 'As many as I love I rebuke and chasten: be zealous therefore and repent', said the Lord of St John's vision.[61] This was the way Hopkins interpreted the *Deutschland*'s ordeal, as an opportunity for the confessed souls on board to show their spiritual mettle and to reap thereby eternal glory and eternal bliss. The comprehensive Christ of *The Wreck of the Deutschland* is the Christ of Revelation, a didactic Avenger of sin, the Son of man, the slain Lamb, and the Bridegroom of the new Jerusalem,[62] awaiting the Church and her zealous penitents as His bride.

The same sense of wonder and terror that overcame the waiting victims of God's wrath in the Apocalypse surrounded the foundering *Deutschland*. The Apocalyptic menace is there in the 'black-about air', the 'sea flint-flake, black-backed in the regular blow', and the relentlessness of the 'unkind' and 'infinite air' (stanzas 24, 13). The adjective 'infinite' is there to prompt the reader to look for the source of the menace; it is not finite, or purely natural, but 'infinite'. Hopkins's colour scheme is another strong hint of the catastrophe's source. The

---

the dragon but his 'fiery-flying' whitecaps become 'Wiry and white-fiery and whirlwind-swivellèd snow' in Hopkins's ode (stanza 13); Ruskin's 'flakes of crimson and scarlet' are symbolized in the ode as 'the ruddying of the rose-flake' snowdrops (stanza 22). Hopkins's nuns are bathed in 'fall-gold mercies' (stanza 23), while Ruskin's heaving seas, with their burden of drowning slaves, are, like Turner's, dyed with 'an awful but glorious light, the intense and lurid splendour which burns like gold, and bathes like blood'. The macabre 'shadow of death', 'the guilty ship . . . its thin masts written upon the sky in lines of blood', the 'horror', the mixture of 'flaming flood' and 'sunlight'—all these apocalyptic images frame Turner's 'Slave Ship', just as they are organic symbols throughout *The Wreck of the Deutschland*.[59]

'wiry and white-fiery and whirlwind-swivellèd snow' is emblematically paired with the 'ruddying of the rose-flake', the 'token' for the 'lettering of the lamb's fleece' (stanza 22).

In interpreting contemporary events as prophetic signals, Hopkins followed the apocalyptic tradition from the Old Testament onwards, and his ode, despite its obvious topical origins,[63] combines violence with a mythical, dreamlike quality characteristic of Revelation. The death of the nuns was a contemporary copy of a sacred epic. It was a divine repetition of the death of the Apocalyptic martyrs, and the death of the unconfessed passengers and crew was a copy of the deaths of the careless sinners in Revelation who would not hear the wrathful warnings. The Apocalyptic martyrs were comforted by the memory of Christ's crucifixion and the consequent gift of eternal life to man, and so the nuns were bathed in the all-fire glances of the Lord because they were undergoing a 'Lovescape crucified' (stanza 23); their martyrdom was to free them from all temporal bondage for service at the throne of God.

Like the Apocalyptic martyrs, whose sturdy faith under adversity entitles them to the seal of Christ upon their brow and a place near the throne when their martyrdom is over,[64] the five nuns bear the 'seal of his seraph-arrival' and are 'sisterly sealed in wild waters' (stanza 23). The 'seraph-arrival' serves notice upon Hopkins's readers that he intends not only to be faithful to the factual phenomena and the time-scheme of the *Deutschland*'s destruction but to symbolize part of the divine time-scheme revealed to St John in his vision as well. The Biblical scholar Austin Farrer,[65] urges that readers of Revelation keep in mind 'one fixed rule and guide', and that is

> the sequence in climax of the seals, trumpets, vials, and last things. The woes of the seals destroy a quarter, the woes of the trumpets a third, the woes of the vials destroy all. These judgments are all of them ministered by angels and belong to this world. The last things are effected by direct intervention of Christ and introduce the world to come.

Hopkins's 'woe of the trumpets'—the storms that 'bugle' Christ's 'fame' (stanza 11)—occurs before his 'woe of the seals', and his 'woe of the trumpets' destroys a quarter of the company rather than a third of them:

> On Saturday sailed from Bremen,
> American-outward-bound,

Take settler and seamen, tell men with women,
   Two hundred souls in the round—
O Father, not under thy feathers nor ever as guessing
The goal was a shoal, of a fourth the doom to be drowned;

                                                   (stanza 12)

and the bugle or trumpet accomplishes this prophecy rather than the
seals. But Hopkins did copy Revelation's tradition that angels or
'seraphs' precede the intervention of Christ and the last things. The
poet-prophet's wringing cry '*Ipse*' (stanza 28), announcing the arrival
of Christ on the waters, does not take place until almost the end of the
ode, and the last things are announced in the last two stanzas, after
Christ has made His appearance on the waters and takes over the shires
to accomplish the 'epic of return'.[66]

Hopkins did not say which newspaper story of the wreck of the
Deutschland he had read; he simply said that he had been 'affected by
the account of it' (*CD*, 14, 1878), but he combined details from more
than one account and used the details from the account most closely
resembling St John's vision. *The Times* story carried a description of
the tall sister, one of five 'German nuns whose bodies are now in the
dead house here'. These five women had 'clasped hands and were
drowned together, the chief sister, a gaunt woman 6 ft. high, calling
loudly and often, "O Christ, come quickly!"' Another account
described the gaunt nun as a woman

> noted for her extreme tallness . . . who at midnight on Monday, by
> standing on a table in the saloon, was able to thrust her head
> through the skylight, and kept exclaiming in a voice heard by those
> in the rigging above the roar of the storm, 'My God, my God, make
> haste, make haste!'   (*FL*, 443, n. 2; 1875)

Either of these two cries, 'My God, make haste!' or 'Christ, come
quickly!' is dogmatically ambiguous. Either cry could mean 'Come
and get us, come and take us to death!' or 'Come and save us our
lives!' Hopkins interpreted the nun's cry as a desire for death, for
escape from temporal horror into the bliss of eternal life. Christ is to
'despatch and have done with his doom there' (stanza 28). Accordingly
Hopkins chose for his ode the cry 'O Christ, Christ, come quickly!'
(stanza 24), for this cry resembles Christ's loving admonitions to the
suffering martyrs in Revelation, who are urged to be 'faithful unto
death' that they might earn the martyr's crown at the conclusion of
their ordeals. 'Behold', Christ promised the martyrs, 'I come quickly:

hold fast that which thou hast, that no man take thy crown.' In the last chapter of Revelation, as the martyrdom of all the faithful is nearing its end and they can expect shortly to join the heavenly hosts, Christ repeats this cry three times. In the next to last verse Christ makes the reassuring pronouncement for the last time: 'He that testifieth these things saith, Surely I come quickly: Amen.' And St John, the witness of these strange things, replies antiphonally: 'Even so, come Lord Jesus.'[67]

Hopkins's tall nun played as comprehensive a role as his Apocalyptic Christ. She was first a modern St John, a 'prophetess' anticipating the second coming and the day of judgment. When she 'cried for the crown then' (stanzas 17, 25), in her longing for the accomplishment of her martyrdom, she became the body of the Church under persecution and the Virgin Mary—the woman with the crown of twelve stars in Revelation, who 'being with child, cried, travailing in birth and pained to be delivered'. The woman in childbirth is attended by a dragon who awaits the delivery 'for to devour her child as soon as it was born. And she brought forth a man child, who was to rule all nations with a rod of iron: and her child was caught up into God and *to* his throne.'[68]

Hopkins was fascinated by the woman in childbirth. He mused often on her mystical significance to St John, to the Church, and to modern man,[69] and he comforted himself with her triple role of martyr, prophet, and bride of the Lamb of Revelation, and with the sacramental paradox of birth, and death, the Christian rebirth. In her ecstasy of her terror and her love of Christ, the nun 'conceives' the *Logos*, the word of God. By a series of linked metaphors, Hopkins suggests a divine analogy between three archetypal scenes of suffering, the birth of the Christ Child, the agony on Calvary, and the nun's death as a symbol of God's wrath and man's martyrdom. Stanzas six to eight discuss the crucifixion and its implications for man. There is a mounting rhythm of pain and terror; these stanzas are filled with metaphors applicable both to maternal labour and delivery and to the crucifixion: 'the dense and the driven Passion, and frightful sweat', the 'discharge of it' and 'its swelling to be' refer not only to Part The First, and to Hopkins's own knowledge of the spiritual exercises of St Ignatius, but to separate divine events portrayed in Part The Second, the Nativity and childhood of Christ—'Manger, maiden's knee'—to the crucifixion—'hero of Calvary'—and to the Christian paradox of life, death, and rebirth. Hopkins even suggests a further paradox: 'Warm-laid grave of a womb-life grey' indicates that in being born to a human as humans are, Christ metaphorically, if not dogmatically, died, for the time being, to His own divinity, at least to all outward appearances of divinity (stanzas 6–8).

In stanzas twenty-four to thirty, a similar mounting rhythm takes place, followed, as in stanzas six to eight, by a sudden drop into ruminative quietness. In these later stanzas the analogies between conception, birth, martyrdom, and death, are absolutely clear. The 'heaven of desire' the nun felt was the 'love in her of the being as her lover had been'; her lover, the 'body of lovely Death', is the agent by which she conceives the *Logos*:

> For so conceivèd, so to conceive thee is done;
> But here was heart-throe, birth of a brain,
> Word, that heard and kept thee and uttered thee outright.

The tall nun is even more concretely the 'bride of Christ':

> Jesu, heart's light,
> Jesu, maid's son,
> What was the feast followed the night
> Thou hadst glory of this nun?

(stanzas 26, 25, 30)

The paradoxes with which Hopkins is dealing in his gnarled yet sensual metaphors become even more paradoxical when one realizes that Hopkins is also celebrating the Feast of the Immaculate Conception, which took place on 8 December 1875, the day after the nun's martyrdom.[70]

The analogous metaphors of conception, birth, martyrdom, death, and rebirth are not mere poetic decorations. They are there so that the reader 'that *hath* an ear, let him hear what the Spirit saith'[71] would be frightened by the similarity between St John's vision and the *Deutschland*'s disaster. In Revelation, the marriage feast of the Lamb and His Bride is followed by the appearance of Christ in yet another role, that of the Dispenser of the *Logos* (Word) of God: 'His eyes *were* as a flame of fire and on his head were many crowns'; and this awesome figure '*was* clothed in a vesture dipped in blood; and his name is called the Word of God.'[72] The nun's martyrdom had stirred in the heart of at least one English priest the hope that England herself might become a haven of the 'Word' and a 'holy city', a new Jerusalem 'coming down from God out of heaven, prepared as a bride adorned for her husband'.[73]

Hopkins not only translates the factual outlines of the *Deutschland*'s ordeal into apocalyptic language, but he superimposes the whole rhythm of the Apocalypse upon the events he describes. Both the

Apocalypse and *The Wreck of the Deutschland* move from terror to joy, and from a private vision to the public catastrophe that was prophesied in the vision, and finally to a harvest of souls raising their voices in adoration of the 'Lord of living and dead' (stanza 1). Like the Apocalypse, *The Wreck of the Deutschland* is divided into two parts: a short prologue embodying the private vision of one of God's seers, full of swooning terror and comfort;[74] and a long section to follow, in which the series of ghastly punishments and warnings function as analogues for the potential fate of all mankind.[75]

Part The First of Hopkins's ode corresponds in several precise ways to the first three chapters of Revelation. In the middle of his vision St John faints with awe at Christ's feet.[76] The postulant in Part The First of the ode, who is undergoing the rigours of the Ignatian exercises, also acknowledges

> The swoon of a heart that the sweep and the hurl of thee trod
>   Hard down with a horror of height:
> And the midriff astrain with leaning of, laced with fire of stress.
>
> (stanza 2)

After St John's swoon, Christ places a soothing hand upon the terrified dreamer 'saying . . . Fear not; I am the first and last; I am he that liveth and was dead; and behold, I am alive for evermore, Amen; and have the keys of hell and death.'[77] In the ode, the postulant priest determines to wring comfort from the very source of the terror itself, as the nun was to do—as all men should do:

> Hither then, last or first,
>   To hero of Calvary, Christ,'s feet—
> Never ask if meaning it, wanting it, warned of it—men go.
>
> (stanza 8)

For Hopkins, as for St John, Christ, the 'hero of Calvary', carries a 'Double-naturèd name' (stanza 34): He is implacable with sinners who will not be swayed to faith, and He permits a violent death to be visited upon the faithful even while He comforts them. The poet-prophet in the ode worships both natures of God—the 'Christ of the Father compassionate' (stanza 33) and the rebel-wringer who checks humanity's 'malice, with wrecking and storm' (stanza 9), lashing at sinners with Apocalyptic upheavals of 'Surf, snow, river and earth' (stanza 21). In the midst of his devotions Hopkins's terrified prophet sees the 'frown' of God's face before him, 'the hurtle of hell/Behind', even as he is momentarily soothed by a 'fling of the heart to the heart

of the Host' (stanza 3). This paradox, at least, he could trust: God
could be simultaneously

> lightning and love, I found it, a winter and warm;
> Father and fondler of heart thou has wrung:
> Hast thy dark descending and most art merciful then.
>
> (stanza 9)

Stanza eleven,[78] which opens Part The Second of Hopkins's ode,
clearly announces its kinship with Revelation:

> 'Some find me a sword; some
> The flange and the rail; flame,
> Fang, or flood' goes Death on drum,
> And storms bugle his fame.
> But wé dream we are rooted in earth—Dust!
> Flesh falls within sight of us, we, though our flower the same,
> Wave with the meadow, forget that there must
> The sour scythe cringe, and the blear share come.

The imagery is particularly dense, even for Hopkins, but he is trying
to encompass events that take place over several chapters in Revelation.
In this stanza a drum and a bugle proclaim the usual apocalyptic[79]
catalogue of deaths, death by sword, flame, animal ravage, flood, and
storm. In Revelation the harvest of souls is accomplished verse by
verse, chapter by chapter, to the accompaniment of trumpeting angels.
In *The Wreck of the Deutschland* also, the Son of man reaps a harvest
of death with the 'sour scythe' (stanza 11); in both works of prophecy
'the shipwreck' or the destruction becomes a 'harvest' of saved souls
as well as a pile of bodies awaiting damnation: the 'tempest' carries the
'grain' for Christ (stanza 31).

The Apocalyptic rhythm is most obvious in Hopkins's treatment
of the harvest of souls. What is a harvest of carnage in stanza eleven
has become a harvest of hope by the last stanza. But the Apocalyptic
rejoicing has begun to triumph over the sense of doom long before the
end of the ode. In a delightful metamorphosis Hopkins even manages
to convert the nun's 'tears' and her shrieks of supplication into a
'melting, a madrigal start', a 'glee' song, which finds its answer in his
own heart. The two of them, the priest 'under a roof . . . at rest', and
the nun, 'the prey of the gales', imitate the music and the songs of
praise that rise from the faithful martyrs at Revelation's end (stanzas
18, 24).[80]

As the mood of *The Wreck of the Deutschland* shifts, in order to accommodate itself to the final ecstatic cadences of the Apocalypse, Hopkins's language undergoes a transformation similar to that in Revelation. Hopkins carries out the Apocalyptic progress from terror and destruction to joy and salvation by modulating the imagery from punitive metaphors of violence to metaphors of joy and happiness, sometimes symbolized by the garden and floral imagery of Revelation. The 'storm flakes' of the 'white-fiery and whirlwind-swivellèd snow' (stanza 13) are now no more malevolent than 'scroll-leaved flowers, lily showers', and by now 'sweet heaven' is 'astrew in them' (stanza 21). The 'lightning and lashed rod' (stanza 2) and the 'stroke and a stress that stars and storms deliver' (stanza 6) are no longer interpreted as a 'dooms-day dazzle' (stanza 34) but as the 'dayspring to the dimness of us'. Hopkins is eager to describe how benevolent Christ's sway would be upon English souls, and he can afford gentler imagery. As Christ's 'reign rolls' (stanza 35), He will be 'Kind, but royally reclaiming his own': His coming will be announced by a 'released shower, let flash to the shire, not a lightning of fire hard-hurled' (stanza 34).

By means of prophecy, Hopkins has translated a contemporary 'ordeal of the waters', which took place on 7 December 1875, into a mystical event; as in Revelation, death has become life, anguish has become joy and hope. For Hopkins's 'released shower' functions both as a life-giving fire and life-giving water. It will 'flash to the shire' like a river in a parched country, bringing the good news of God. Its power, suitably subdued to ordinary human use, is to kindle a homely and receptive answer in the ordinary Englishman's 'heart's charity's hearth's fire' (stanza 35).

The Wreck of the Deutschland is a pivotal work in Victorian literature because it is the only major Victorian work in a distinctively aesthetic form—as opposed to a sermon—that treats the Apocalypse as indisputable prophecy. The Tractarian priests who believed in the second coming galvanized a nation with their apocalyptic sermons; their names as preachers of the new pure dogma were on as many tongues as the dread name of Wilberforce before them, and they even rivalled the famous lay poets, essayists, and novelists, in securing the public's attention for their apocalyptic warnings. But they achieved this fame and this power in sermons only; the poetry of such apocalyptic prophets as Keble and Newman was minor compared to the grandeur of their sermons.

Lay writers like Tennyson or Morris, on the other hand, placed no comprehensive dogma before the public. They did not take the prospect of the second coming literally, although they took England's corruption and the apocalyptic mood seriously enough to embrace the Apocalypse as a vehicle for their anxieties.

And so, because *The Wreck of the Deutschland* is the only major Victorian work in a lay form that presents the matter and the symbols of the Apocalypse to the public as absolute dogma, it is also the only one that is totally shaped by the Apocalypse. For works of equivalent dogma coupled with the power of passionate belief, one must turn to some of the great Victorian sermons; for other aesthetic models of the Apocalypse, comparable in scope and design to *The Wreck of the Deutschland*, one has to turn to lay writers. And these laymen use the model and the matter of the Apocalypse only as persuasive allegory, deeply felt, but not dogmatically conceived, and thus the apocalyptic urgency of their works differs radically from that of Hopkins's ode, both in kind and in degree.

The ode thus fills a void in Victorian poetry and it preserves a specific and most important current of Victorian history in a lay form that has survived time. *The Wreck of the Deutschland* like most of Hopkins's mature poetry is available in almost any respectable library where English is spoken, whereas some of the most impressive Victorian sermons are hard to come by, even for scholars. Many of the most impressive lay Apocalypses are accessible to us, and they do preserve for us much of the contemporary anxiety and the apocalyptic terminology, both local and Biblical, but not the hard, precise dogma that shapes *The Wreck of the Deutschland* and the most electrifying Victorian sermons.

Hopkins adapted the materials of Victorian England and of Europe's past wherever he found them pertinent, and used them effectively wherever he could, in and out of the pulpit. *The Wreck of the Deutschland* may be a maverick poem and Hopkins a maverick poet. If so, he is one simply because he succeeded, against heartbreaking odds, in doing exactly what he set out to do, and it was a rare and a magnificent achievement. He elected to try to enchant us and to move us, in order that he might warn us and persuade us, not only from the pulpit, as a priest should, but as a poet should—from the pages of his slim volume of poems.

Appendix A

Chronology for Oxford and the Tractarian Wars
In italic: chronology for Hopkins

14 July 1833	John Keble's sermon on 'National Apostasy'.
September 1833	Newman's 'Tract 1' of the 'Oxford Tracts' ('Tracts for the Times').
1834	Edward Bouverie Pusey joins Tractarian movement (Oxford movement).
1838	Benjamin Jowett made Fellow of Balliol while still an undergraduate.
1841	Newman's 'Tract 90'; Oxford Tracts suppressed.
11 June 1844	*Birth of Gerard Manley Hopkins.*
1845	Newman ordained and receives Doctor of Divinity in Rome.
1847	Newman founds English Order of Oratorians and Catholic boys' school at Birmingham.
1850	'Papal Aggression'; Papal Bull declaring re-establishment of the Roman Catholic hierarchy in England.
1854	Jowett loses election to Mastership of Balliol for his unorthodox religious views and for his part in university reform.
1854	Jowett appointed Regius Professor of Greek at Oxford— salary, forty pounds a year.
1854 63	*Hopkins boarding and day pupil at Sir Robert Cholmondeley's Grammar School at Highgate.*
1857–62	Matthew Arnold elected as first lay professor to Poetry Chair at Oxford, for five-year term; he offers four lectures annually, for the first time in English.
1859	*Hopkins wins school prize at age of 15 for his poem 'The Escorial'. First allusion to Ruskin (see 'The Escorial', Poem 1, stanzas 6 and 7).*

1859	Mill's *On Liberty*; Darwin's *Origin of Species*. The Rev. Henry Parry Liddon, Hopkins's probable first Tractarian confessor, joins Pusey at Christ Church, Oxford.
1860	The year of 'the grand assault' upon the Tractarian movement (Young, *Daylight and Champaign*, 254).
February 1860	*Essays and Reviews* published.
June 1860	Huxley–Wilberforce debate before the British Association at Oxford.
June 1861	The seven *Essays and Reviews* cited for probable heresy before the Lower (synodical) House.
October 1861	Bishop John Colenso of Natal publishes his *Commentary on the Epistle to the Romans*. Bishop Gray of Cape Town initiates unilateral action against Colenso.
December 1861	The Rev. Henry Bristow Wilson, editor, and the Rev. Rowland Williams, two contributors to *Essays and Reviews*, summoned for trial before Court of Arches (see of Canterbury). The two priests suspended for a year. Case appealed.
1862	Matthew Arnold elected for second five-year term to Poetry Chair. Last lecture in the Chair: 'Culture and its Enemies'.
1862	*Hopkins wins second Highgate prize for 'A Vision of Mermaids'.*
1862–3	Colenso publishes first three volumes of his seven-volume work disputing historicity of the Pentateuch and the Book of Joshua.
1863	The Jowett party still in a minority at Balliol.
February 1863	Jowett summoned before Vice-Chancellor at Oxford for his contribution to *Essays and Reviews*. Jowett refuses to acknowledge the authority of Pusey *et al.* Charges dismissed.
April 1863	*Hopkins matriculates at Balliol; calls on Jowett, his tutor, and receives advice on how to succeed at Oxford (FL, 73).*
May 1863	*Hopkins starts going to Liddon's weekly series of Tractarian lectures (FL, 77).*
May 1863	Legal capitulation of Pusey party against Jowett.
November 1863	Bishop Gray summoned Bishop Colenso from Natal to Cape Town for judgment. Colenso denies Gray's authority; appeals to the Queen's Council.
1864	Newman publishes *Apologia pro Vita Sua;* book enormously popular at Oxford, as elsewhere.
1864	Walter Pater, one of Hopkins's tutors, unable to find fellowship because of heretical views, finally appointed to rare non-clerical fellowship at Brasenose College.

1864   Reads his first essay, 'Diaphaneité', before 'Old Mortality' Society.

February 1864   Wilson and Williams case heard again; judgments against them overturned.

March 1864   Attempts to double Jowett's salary for his duties as Regius Professor of Greek defeated in public debate at Oxford. Students hissing and cheering in the gallery.

June 1864   *Essays and Reviews* again condemned, this time by a majority of both synodical Houses.

July 1864   'Oxford Declaration', condemning heresy, and suggesting it might be punished by eternal damnation, signed by over eleven thousand priests.

October 1864   Height of the scandal over Jowett's salary. Second attempt in Convocation to raise salary from forty pounds voted down.

November 1864   *Hopkins possibly in confession with Liddon* (see confused text and footnotes in *JP*, 54, and 322, note 54:2).

1865   Courtenay Ilbert, Hopkins's friend, achieves status as voting Fellow at Balliol; thanks to Ilbert, the Jowett men at Balliol now in a majority (see Abbott and Campbell, *Life and Letters of Jowett*, I, 376, and *JP*, 347, note 134:2).

January 1865   Legal proof offered to *The Times* that Christ Church alone was responsible for Jowett's salary.

February 1865   Christ Church denies all legal and historical responsibility for Jowett's salary, but consents to raise it to five hundred pounds per annum.

February 1865   *Hopkins urging himself to read* Essays and Reviews *and 'Matthew Arnold's Essays'* (*JP*, 56).

March 1865   Bishop Colenso's case upheld by the Queen's Council.

November 1865   Colenso returns to Natal; excommunicated by Gray, refuses Gray's judgment, and continues episcopal functions.

December 1865   *Hopkins now in confession with Dr Pusey* (*JP*, 71).

May 1866   'Matthew Arnold lectured on the Celtic element in English poetry' (*JP*, 137 and 351, note 137:6).

May 1866   *Hopkins 'Coaching [for examinations] with W. H. Pater this term'* (*JP*, 133).

June 1866   *Hopkins and Addis, fellow convert, go to Benedictine Monastery at Belmont; talk with Dom Paul Raynal about the 'doubtful validity' of Anglican orders* (*JP*, 141 and 358, note 141:4).

16 October 1866   *Hopkins writes to his father: 'the Tractarian ground I have seen broken to pieces under my feet', and admits that when Pusey's and Liddon's 'influence gave way everything was gone' (FL, 92 and 94).*

21 October 1866   *Hopkins received into the Roman Catholic Church by Dr (afterwards Cardinal) Newman at the Birmingham Oratory.*

Spring 1867   *Hopkins awarded a double first in classics.*

September 1867   *Teaching under Newman at the Oratory School.*

7 September 1868   *Hopkins enters Jesuit Novitiate at Roehampton, near London* (source on chronology for Hopkins as a Jesuit largely Lahey's biography).

1870   Jowett made Master of Balliol until his death in 1893.

1870   *Hopkins taking course in philosophy at St Mary's Hall, Stonyhurst, Lancashire.*

1873   *Teaching classics at Manresa House, Roehampton.*

1874   *Reading theology, St Beuno's College, North Wales.*

1876   The Wreck of the Deutschland, *Hopkin's first serious poem as a priest.*

1877   *Ordination.*
Preacher, Farm Street Church, London. Subminister, Mount St Mary's College, Chesterfield.

1878   *Back at Oxford; Preacher, St Aloysius Presbytery.*

1879   *Preacher, St Francis Xavier Church, Liverpool.*

1881   *Supply priest, St Joseph's, Glasgow. Roehampton: tertianship (third probationary period in the Jesuit Order).*

1882   *Teaching classics at Stonyhurst.*

1884   *Nominated to Chair of Greek at the Royal University of Ireland in Dublin (later the National University).*

April 1889   *Falls ill of typhoid fever.*

8 June 1889   *Death of Gerard Manley Hopkins.*

Appendix B

Brief History of the Tractarian Wars

'The Tractarian wars' is a term describing the intense theological quarrels between the 'Tractarians' (the neo-Catholic High Church party of the Anglican Establishment), and the liberal, or Broad Church party (as they gradually came to be called), a group of men loosely associating with one another because of the flexible way they permitted interpretations of scripture. The Tractarians derived their popular name from their habit of writing 'Tracts for the Times' (often called 'The Oxford Tracts'), which periodically issued out of Oxford from 1833 to 1841.[1]

The Oxford movement was, in part, a medievalizing spirit that was to find its aesthetic counterpart in Ruskin, in the Pre-Raphaelites, and in Hopkins's own poetry. Victorian scholars rightly suggested that these medievalizing movements were radical in the Latin sense of the word. They represented searches for spiritual roots in a society undergoing enormous changes, and they expressed a national desire for some continuity between past and present.

The earliest representatives of the Oxford movement included such Oxonians as Richard Hurrel Froude, William George Ward, John Keble, and John Henry Newman. In 1834 Dr Edward Bouverie Pusey of Christ Church joined the movement, and he became its master logician within the Oxford colleges, thus conferring upon it another of its Oxonian nicknames— 'Puseyism'.

After Newman, Ward, and their disciples had been converted to Roman Catholicism, and after Keble had left Oxford, Pusey was bereft of close Tractarian companionship within the Oxford colleges, until his old pupil, Henry Parry Liddon, arrived in Oxford (1859) to take up a post as Vice-Principal of St Edmund's Hall.

The Broad Church movement was also, in its way, a radical movement. It was animated not only by the new scientific spirit, characterized by disciplines that examined the past, and thus man's evolution—disciplines such as paleontology, geology, and animal and human biology. But the Broad Church party was quite conscious that in many ways it was animated by a spirit as fresh and as invigorating as that which produced the new classical learning in early sixteenth-century England; Oxonian Broad Churchmen shared with Broad Churchmen elsewhere an enthusiasm for the new Biblical scholarship emanating from Germany, which subjected both Testaments to retranslation and to rigorous historical and linguistical analysis. The Broad Church party may have been more congenial to the rational spirit of Cambridge; but just as the Oxford movement was not confined to Oxford, 'Cambridge' rationalism was not confined to Cambridge. And the Broad Church party included such famous Oxonian figures as Benjamin Jowett, Dr Thomas Arnold of Rugby, Arthur Penrhyn Stanley, later Dean of Westminster, and Mark Pattison. Jowett had introduced Hegel and Plato to his students as soon as he became tutor at Balliol in 1842; and his translations and commentaries of scripture, particularly of the Pauline Epistles, marked him as typical of the new breed of inquiring scholar priest, who believed reverently in the symbols of Christ's life, but not necessarily in the literal truth of each and every word in scripture.

These two parties and their various adherents attacked one another in and out of Oxford and in and out of law courts from 1833 to 1865.[2] When Benjamin Jowett was finally made Master of Balliol in 1870, after losing the Mastership in 1854 for his Broad Church views, the power of the Tractarians over affairs at Oxford and opinions at large was publicly crushed in symbol, as time and again, to the distress of hopeful young Tractarians such as Hopkins, it had been denied in heresy trials.

The Tractarian wars may be divided into three distinct campaigns: 1833–41; 1842–59; 1860–70. Since the last phase was naturally the one in which Hopkins was most interested, it is discussed in chapter 1 rather than here. The first phase (1833–41) may be very precisely dated from John Keble's Oxford Assize sermon, 'National Apostasy', in which Keble launched an attack upon the Whigs, who were attempting to disestablish ten Anglican bishoprics in Ireland. This sermon took place in July 1833. In September, Newman hurried to Keble's assistance with 'Tract 1' of the 'Tracts for the Times'.

The conclusion of the first phase may be equally precisely dated from the publication, early in 1841, of Newman's notorious 'Tract 90', in which Newman suggested that the Thirty-Nine Articles that had precariously buttressed the Anglican faith since the Reformation were susceptible to Roman Catholic interpretation. Public anger, both lay and clerical, had been gathering force since Newman's first tract was issued from Oxford eight years earlier. In 1841 the rage was powerful enough to suppress the tracts altogether and eventually to exile Newman from Oxford. Newman's conversion to Roman Catholicism (1845) along with a considerable number of his disciples, appeared to exemplify to the anti-Tractarian Anglicans just that sort of non-

English mischief and betrayal of which they had accused the Tractarians all along.

During the second phase of the Tractarian wars (1841–59), both parties were relatively quiescent, except for sporadic attacks and counterattacks. For one thing, there was an exodus of Anglican Tractarians from Oxford, many of them quite rightly fearing the sort of university reprisals of which they were frequent victims wherever they lacked power, and the engineers wherever they were in positions of power. Others frankly hoped to work with less strain, and therefore with more quiet effectiveness in less public vineyards. But there was another spectre haunting the entire Anglican community, and that was 'Papal Aggression'. The Pope had created Newman a Doctor of Divinity at the time of his ordination; in 1847 Dr Newman opened an English branch of the order of Oratorians in Birmingham, and founded there a Catholic school for boys. In 1850 a Papal Bull re-established the Catholic hierarchy in England, and Cardinal Wiseman was enthroned at St George's Cathedral, Southwark, as the first English Catholic Primate since the reign of Henry VIII. And so the Tractarians found themselves attacked on both flanks, and they were forced to pause and consider how they should resist not only the heresy of liberalism on the left, but of Roman Catholicism on the right.

The third phase of the Tractarian wars (1860–70) began as it ended, with an *annus mirabile* for the Broad Church forces, in 1860, the publication of the Broad Church work *Essays and Reviews*, and in 1870, Jowett's accession to the Mastership of Balliol. During this decade, the Tractarians risked and lost almost all power in official places; they also lost many Tractarian converts, some to the Broad Church party, some to outright agnosticism, and some to Roman Catholicism.

Notes

Abbreviations used for Hopkins's own works are listed on p. xiii.

Introduction

1 See George Levine's discriminating collection of Victorian essays called *The Emergence of Victorian Consciousness: The Spirit of the Age*, 41.

2 On the complexity of mood and the 'nervous self-examination' that we now see as paradigmatic of the Victorian temper, see Wendell Stacy Johnson, *Gerard Manley Hopkins: The Poet as Victorian*, chap. i, especially 18–29. See also Humbert Wolfe's essay, 'Arthur Hugh Clough', in *The Eighteen-Sixties*, John Drinkwater, ed.; Wolfe's comments on Clough might almost describe Hopkins: 'But this holy simplicity was not in the Victorian character. Action was always the result of introspection so intense that the observer appeared always to see right through himself and out at the other side—with no very noticeable intensification of vision' (*The Eighteen-Sixties*, 22). With his conversion to Roman Catholicism, and even before, Hopkins's dogma became much sharper and more constant than that of most non-Catholic Victorians who suffered from anxiety. But dogma tells a man what he ought to do or to believe or to feel; and though Hopkins never doubted his dogma, he did not always do or feel as he thought he ought. In fact, he seemed to be practising a very Victorian Catholicism, spontaneous and intensely introspective, full of joy and guilt.

3 Levine, 70–1. The term 'sociology' comes into the language in the eighteen-forties through Auguste Comte. If Hazlitt was the first social critic to make the phrase 'the spirit of the age' a fashionable one, then Mill was exploiting novel and popular terminology to express his sense of extraordinary times, and to analyse precisely what he found extraordinary

about them. Mill's essay, 'The Spirit of the Age', published in 1831, follows Hazlitt's *The Spirit of the Age: Contemporary Portraits* by a bare six years. But Hazlitt rarely examines what he means by 'the spirit of the age' in his contemporary portraits, as he was later to do more frequently in his four-volume life of Napoleon: apparently he was not at this time as consumed by the 'dominant idea' of his age as Mill was, or as Hazlitt's very title, *The Spirit of the Age*, suggests that he was.

4 All these articles are conveniently collected in Levine's anthology of early nineteenth-century essays.

Chapter 1 'The Sense of Gentle Fellowship' and 'The Spy in the Wilderness': the Years at Oxford

1 See Appendix A for the chronology of the Tractarian wars, and see also Appendix B for a description of such terms as 'the Tractarian movement' ('the Oxford movement'), the 'Tracts for the Times' (the 'Oxford Tracts for the Times'), and the 'Broad Church movement', etc.

2 Charles P. S. Clarke, *The Oxford Movement and After*, vii.

3 George Malcolm Young, *Daylight and Champaign*, 107.

4 Geoffrey Faber, *Jowett, a Portrait with Background*, 314, 25. I am incalculably indebted to Faber, not only for the account of Jowett's sufferings at Oxford, but for the chronology of the Tractarian wars (Appendices A and B).

5 George R. Parkin, *The Life, Diary and Letters of Edward Thring*, 300–1.

6 Geoffrey Faber, *Jowett, a Portrait with Background*, 23, 346.

7 G. M. Young, *Daylight and Champaign*, 173.

8 See for example the hilarious description of the proceedings of the British Association, in Leonard Huxley's life and letters of his father, 1, 193ff, and William Irvine's *Apes, Angels, and Victorians*, 1–8.

9 Young, *Daylight and Champaign*, 254.

10 'Puseyism' and 'Puseyite' were popular terms for Tractarian practices during the 'sixties. See for example, *LB*, 39 and 58.

11 See *Pusey and Others v. Jowett: The Argument and Decisions as to the Jurisdiction of the Chancellor's Court at Oxford*, frontispiece of charges.

12 Abbott & Campbell, *Life and Letters of Jowett*, 1, 313.

13 Besides Faber's indispensable portrait of Jowett, esp. 266–72, see Abbott and Campbell, 1, the letters and descriptions 1860–5. See also H. W. C. Davis, *Oxford University College Histories: Balliol College*, 213–14, and *passim*.

14 Faber, 339.

15 I am indebted for this suggestion to Dr Carol Silver of Stern College, New York City.

16 See *JP*, 141, and 357–8, notes 141: 2–4 (1866).
17 For some of the accounts of the Christ Church gatherings of young Tractarians, see *JP*, 16, 299; *FL*, 76–7; and Henry Parry Liddon's *The Life of Edward Bouverie Pusey*, IV, 75.
18 See 'To Oxford', Poem 12 (1865); and 'Fragments of *Richard*', Poem 107 (1865).
19 On the missionary ethos of friendship at Oxford see, for example, *Henry Parry Liddon: A Centenary Memoir*, 1; J. O. Johnston, *Life and Letters of Henry Parry Liddon*, 51–2; Mark Pattison, *Memoirs*, 220–2; Noel Annan, *Leslie Stephen: His Thought and Character in Relation to his Time*, 132–3.
20 William S. Knickerbocker, *Creative Oxford: Its Influence in Victorian Literature*, 48 and *passim*.
21 The list of letters, memoirs, lives, and diaries that artlessly reveal the Oxonian passion for missionary friendships is too long to cite fully, but for Hopkins's own zealous attitude toward his friends, see *FL*, 16–17, 19–20, 40–1; *LB*, 95; for other versions of Oxonian missionary zeal, see Stephen Paget, *Henry Scott Holland: Memoirs and Letters, passim;* Holland was a friend of Hopkins before Hopkins's conversion to Catholicism. See also John Henry Newman's letters to Thomas Mozley, Matthew Arnold's letters to Clough, Dr Arnold's letters to his pupils in Stanley's *Life and Correspondence of Dr. Arnold.*
22 Annan, *Leslie Stephen*, 139.
23 *Ibid.*, 132.
24 Leslie Stephen, *Studies of a Biographer*, II, 124–7.
25 Annan, *Leslie Stephen*, 132.
26 See Stephen Paget's biography, *Henry Scott Holland*, 51–2 (1870), v (1921), 29–30 (1868).
27 Liddon, *Life of Pusey*, IV, 74.
28 Stephen, *Studies of a Biographer*, II, 124, 78.
29 Talbott and Stone, *Liddon: A Centenary Memoir*, 3.
30 Josephine Miles, 'The Sweet and Lovely Language', *Gerard Manley Hopkins by the Kenyon Critics*, 57, 58, 71. Arthur Henry Hallam, Tennyson's dead friend for whom he mourned in *In Memoriam*, was in many ways more typical of Oxford than he was of Cambridge, where he matriculated.
31 See particularly Hopkins's sermon on the character and person of Christ in *S*, 34–8 (1879).
32 Paget, *Henry Scott Holland*, 94–5 (1878).
33 *Cornhill Magazine*, x (Sept. 1864), 299, 300.
34 Matthew Arnold, *Essays in Criticism*, First Series, x–xi.
35 *Cornhill Magazine*, xiv (July 1866), 120.
36 Walter Houghton, *The Victorian Frame of Mind: 1830–1870*, chap. 11.
37 *Cornhill Magazine*, xiv (July 1866), 128.

38 *Essays in Criticism,* First Series, vii.

39 *Cornhill Magazine,* xiv (July 1866), 128.

40 Thomas Wright, *The Life of Walter Pater,* I, 150, 173 and n. 3.

41 Max Müller, *My Autobiography: A Fragment,* 283.

42 Stephen, *Studies of a Biographer,* II, 109.

43 Faber, *Jowett, a Portrait,* 39.

44 Nitram Tradleg [Edmund Martin Geldart], *A Son of Belial,* 155–6. Geldart barely bothered to disguise names in his sour but amusing *roman à clef.*

45 Stephen, *Studies of a Biographer,* II, 133, 154.

46 But as all Jowett's biographers report, there was never a hint of favouritism; Jowett was as glad to coach men from other colleges as from his own; to be sure it may have been part of his unappeasable pedagogical itch, but when one considers how dear Balliol was to him, his kindness to other students is very appealing.

47 Jowett's respect for Hopkins is part of the Jesuit lore about Hopkins that emerged after his death. See *A Page of Irish History: Story of University College, Dublin, 1883–1909* (compiled by Fathers of the Society of Jesus), 1930, 104–5. A fragment of this *Page of Irish History* occurs in *LB,* 216, 319–20, note v. Part of the fragment is interesting not only for what it tells us about Hopkins's posthumous reputation among his fellow Jesuits, for example that 'to those who knew' him 'his career will always suggest the idea of tragedy', but for what it tells us about Jowett's reputation among the Jesuits: 'The genius of Hopkins was indeed remarkable, nor was it confined to one branch of mental excellence. As a Greek scholar, had he fully utilized his talents, he could have stood in the first rank; in fact, at Balliol College, Oxford, the celebrated master, Dr. Jowett, had declared that he never met a more promising pupil' (*LB,* 319). Father Lahey's biography of Hopkins informs us that Jowett had called Hopkins 'the star of Balliol'; but Lahey rather spoils matters by his statement that Pusey 'respected Hopkins greatly, and is said to have styled him "The Star of Balliol" ' (Lahey, 139, 43). But it is highly unlikely that Pusey would have praised any student of Jowett's for demonstrating Balliol excellences.

48 Davis, *Oxford Histories: Balliol College,* 215.

49 Abbott & Campbell, *Jowett, Life and Letters,* I, 416.

50 Jowett may well have practised humility in a Jesuitical spirit, so that he might chasten pride in the enormous amount of covert power he exercised. Long before he became actual Master of Balliol, Jowett was the adviser to prime ministers, the Foreign Office, and cabinet members, often recommending successful young Balliol graduates who might be of service to the Crown. It is one of the paradoxes about this fascinating, yet enigmatic man that he would be accused of wielding great power openly and secretly, fairly and unfairly, and that other charges such as

snobbery and humility, kindness and fierceness, intellectual integrity and intellectual casuistry should all be laid at his door.

51 Davis, *Balliol College*, 219–21.
52 Faber, *Jowett, a Portrait*, 407–8.
53 Davis, *Balliol College*, 198.
54 Richard L. Nettleship, *Memoir of Thomas Hill Green*, 90.
55 Stephen, *Studies of a Biographer*, II, 153.
56 Paget, *Henry Scott Holland*, 19 (1866).
57 See also Abbott & Campbell, *Jowett, Life and Letters*, I, 376, and Faber, *Jowett, a Portrait*, 346.
58 See *FL*, 68, 71, 75; *JP*, 311.
59 Herbert Arthur Morrah, *The Oxford Union: 1823–1923*, 215.
60 Morrah, *The Oxford Union*, 61–2.
61 *Ibid.*, 226–7.
62 *Ibid.*, 215; John Buchan, *Pilgrim's Way*, 76.
63 Johnston, *Life of Liddon*, 8.
64 For photographs of Balliol men, see the snapshot of the Balliol crew of 1869 in Paget, *Henry Scott Holland*, facing p. 25. Several of these men were friends of Hopkins. See also *FL*, facing p. 20.
65 Davis, *Oxford Histories: Balliol College*, 222.
66 Abbott & Campbell, *Jowett, Life and Letters*, I, 390.
67 Davis, *Oxford Histories: Balliol College*, 221.
68 And see Hopkins's graceful bow to *Stones of Venice*, II, in his schoolboy poem 'The Escorial'. Here Hopkins devotes two stanzas (6 and 7) to an elliptic discussion of the Doric, Corinthian, and Gothic principles, with obvious Ruskinian bias in favour of the Gothic.
69 See especially Hopkins's undergraduate essays 'On the Signs of Health and Decay in the Arts' (1864), and 'On the Origin of Beauty' (1865), in *JP*.
70 On the prevalence of the Oxford cult, see Knickerbocker, *Creative Oxford*, chap. i and *passim*.
71 Wright, *Pater*, I, 12.
72 Will Rothenstein, *Oxford Characters: Twenty-four Lithographs* (London, 1896), no pagination.
73 Wright, *Pater*, I, 192.
74 *Ibid.*, 236–9; 192–3.
75 *Ibid.*, 109, 136–7.
76 *Ibid.*, 169–70, 200–4.
77 *Ibid.*, 217.
78 *Ibid.*, II, 277.
79 *Ibid.*, I, 218.
80 John Buchan, *University of Oxford College Histories: Brasenose College*, 140, 139.
81 Arthur Benson, *Walter Pater* (English Men of Letters), 17, 19.

82 See *FL*, 151 and n. 2 (1879); see also *FL* 246 (1880).
83 Walter Pater, 'Diaphaneité', *Miscellaneous Studies*, 248.
84 *Ibid.*, 254, 253.
85 *Ibid.*, 248.
86 *Ibid.*, 254, 248.
87 In the Hopkins canon that has been rescued from oblivion so far, the terms 'inscape' and 'instress' do not turn up in his prose until just after he left Oxford (see his essay on Parmenides, *JP*, 127, which was presumably written in February 1868); but he was already experimenting with the term 'stress' in his undergraduate poetry of 1865. By 'stress' Hopkins meant some quality in objects outside the self that aided— or did not aid—the self to respond to them. See Poems 107 (iv) and 117.
88 Pater, *Miscellaneous Studies*, 249, 252, 254.
89 *Ibid.*, 254, 249.
90 'The Two Voices'.
91 *In Memoriam*, VII, 10.
92 See *JP*, 325–6.
93 James J. Moore, *The Historical Handbook and Guide to Oxford*, especially 153 and 256; H. J. L. Masse, *Oxford*, 54, 110–11; A. J. Kersting, *Portrait of Oxford*, 20; Edmund Alden, *Alden's Oxford Guide*, 100–1. See also *FL*, 100–1; *JP*, 21, 136, 310, 350.
94 Kersting, 20; Moore, 256.
95 *The Poems of Digby Mackworth Dolben*, ed. Robert Bridges, lxviii.
96 *Ibid.*, lxxxvi.
97 See *JP*, 325–6; see also the notes to Hopkins's Poems, 249–50, the note to Poem 13.
98 *FL*, 407, Letter C10 (1867); *LB* 7 (1866), 17 (1867).
99 *Poems of Dolben*, vii-ix, xii, xiv, xcvi.
100 *Ibid.*, poems 1–3, 18, 28, 48, 53.
101 *Ibid.*, poem 43.
102 *Ibid.*, lxxxvi.
103 See *LB*, 16. For some mysterious reason, Bridges omitted this translated poem from his posthumous edition of Dolben's poems. In his collection of Hopkins's letters (*LB*), he also omitted that part of Hopkins's letter to him that contains this translated poem, along with Hopkins's comments on it. The poem and the comments appear only in Lahey's biography of Hopkins (*Gerard Manley Hopkins*, 30).
104 Lahey, 30–1; also omitted in Bridges's 1918 edition of Hopkins's poems and all subsequent editions of the poems.
105 Keith Feiling, *In Christ Church Hall*, 131.
106 Liddon, *Life of Pusey*, IV, 118.
107 Feiling, 131.
108 Liddon, *Life of Pusey*, IV, 77.

109 For reports of Hopkins's four close friends who converted at that time, see *FL*, 30, 401; *JP*, 311, 352, 378.
110 Feiling, 130–1.
111 J. O. Johnston, *Life and Letters of Henry Parry Liddon*, 37, 45–6.
112 See the photographic frontispiece taken by Lewis Carroll in *Henry Parry Liddon: A Centenary Memoir*.
113 *Liddon: A Centenary Memoir*, 23, 3–4.
114 Johnston, 51.
115 *Ibid.*, 77ff.
116 *Apologia pro Vita Sua*, 99.
117 *Loss and Gain: The Story of a Convert*, 354–5.

Chapter 2 *'Heaven's Sweet Gift': Hopkins, Ruskin, and the Plenitude of God*

1 St Ignatius Loyola, *Manresa: Or the Spiritual Exercises of Ignatius Loyola for General Use*, 22.
2 See Amy Cruse, *The Victorians and Their Reading*, 364–5, 369.
3 *Westminster Review*, 65 (April 1856), 626; quoted in Gordon Haight, *The George Eliot Letters*, II, 228n.
4 Frederic Harrison, *John Ruskin* (English Men of Letters), 44.
5 J. H. Hobson, *John Ruskin, Social Reformer*, 37.
6 Leslie Stephen, *Studies of a Biographer*, III, 86.
7 Hallam Tennyson, *Alfred Lord Tennyson: A Memoir by his Son*, I, 223.
8 *The Life of William Wordsworth*, ii (*Works of Wordsworth*, X), ed. William Knight, 334.
9 Cruse, *Victorians and Their Reading*, 364–8.
10 Abbott & Campbell, *Life and Letters of Jowett*, I, 144.
11 Cruse, *Victorians and Their Reading*, 369.
12 John Rosenberg, *The Darkening Glass: A Portrait of Ruskin's Genius*, 6.
13 *The George Eliot Letters*, II, 228.
14 J. W. MacKail, *The Life of William Morris*, I, 45, 46.
15 See Ruskin, xx, xviii–xix; xiv, 483; and XVI, 449–54.
16 Title of chap.i, *Modern Painters*, v (*Works*, VII).
17 Alan Heuser, *The Shaping Vision of Gerard Manley Hopkins*, 50.
18 It will help us if we remember that in the word 'praise' Ruskin and Hopkins usually included all three steps in the artist's creative process; 'praise' encompasses both the mimetic and the laudatory function of art.
19 Ruskin's term for the sacrament of energy in nature is 'vital beauty'; see chapter heading 'Of Vital Beauty', chap. xii, *Modern Painters*, ii (*Works*, IV).
20 Rosenberg, *The Darkening Glass*, 95.
21 Neither Ruskin nor Hopkins resorted to terms such as 'paradox' or

'dualism'. We may clear up some of the confusion they themselves discovered in all these 'contrasts and disparities' if we distinguish, as they did, between mere Platonic *antonyms* such as hot and cold, or *paradoxes* such as the mercy to be found at the heart of God's mastery, or the violence to be found at the heart of nature's benevolence, and *dualism,* where two unalterably opposed forces, such as good and evil, confront each other. Where dualisms appear, they are all types of good and evil, and man must choose between them. He may see some good within evil men and institutions, and some evil within the good—that is one of the characteristics of the universal paradoxes; but Ruskin and Hopkins are most careful not to say that good itself lies at the heart of evil, or evil itself lies at the heart of good. Yet their metaphysics allow frank admissions that good and evil are often factually mixed, though morally distinct.

22 Rosenberg, *The Darkening Glass*, 95, 96.

23 See especially chap. v, 'Of Turnerian Mystery:—Secondly, Wilful' in *Modern Painters*, iv (*Works*, VI).

24 Christopher Devlin, S. J., the editor of Hopkins's sermons, describes Hopkins's discrimination between good spirits and spirits dangerous to man in this fashion. Ruskin had once said, while urging the principle of submission to authority, that 'the Society of Jesus is a splendid proof of the power of obedience' (*Letters*, II, XXXVII, 207).

25 The correct pronunciation of 'windhover', as one hears it in northern England, in Ireland, Scotland, and in parts of northern New England, suggests this interpretation. The 'hover' in 'windhover' is pronounced to rhyme with 'cover' or 'lover'. There is no such bird as a 'windhover' pronounced to rhyme with 'rover' or 'clover'.

26 Isaiah xiv.12–14. 'How art thou fallen from heaven, O Lucifer, son of the morning! how art thou cut down to the ground which didst weaken the nations.' Lucifer was using his art to 'ascend above the heights of the clouds' and 'be like the most high'. See also Hopkins's spiritual writings for the second week of retreat (*S*, 179–80, 1881), where Hopkins described Lucifer as a chorister, 'required to adore God', who then 'learns by the use in the church itself the strength and beauty of his voice'.

27 See for example chap. II in *Stones of Venice*, iii (XI), especially the sections on 'Pride of Science', 'Pride of State', and 'Pride of System'. But these proud, often admirable figures are typical of all three volumes of *Stones of Venice.*

28 This generosity toward beautiful and talented creatures is not only consistent with Ruskinian principles, and with a certain kind of honest Victorian aesthetic, but with Ignatian principles as well. Hopkins does not say that Lucifer became physically ugly during the process of spiritual disintegration; Lucifer's tragedy, for himself, as well as for his onlooker, was that he remained beautiful, and therefore he was a trap for others—that at the moment when he was lifting his own glorious voice

in adoration of God, 'he became aware ... of the riches in his nature'; and so, 'ravished by his own sweetness and dazzled by his beauty', Lucifer 'prolonged the first note'. After that he 'was involved in spiritual sloth', and perhaps even worse, 'spiritual luxury and spiritual vainglory'. But he was still talented, still dazzling; Hopkins refused to deny him his virtues (S, 180, 1881).

This Ignatian generosity is not without psychological soundness. Souls undergoing the rigour of St Ignatius's spiritual exercises during a retreat are unusually sensitive to the influence of all spirits, both diabolic and angelic. They must therefore remember just how attractive diabolic figures can be, and they must put their admiration in perspective. This process is known as 'discernment of spirits', and it results in 'The Great Election' between diabolic spirits and angelic spirits. Nobody asks the retreatants to deny the attraction of diabolic spirits. In fact it was wise to dwell momentarily upon those very attractions, for just so did Satan and all his hosts once appear to the angels wondering which side to take in the heavenly quarrel. See the translation of *The Spiritual Exercises of St. Ignatius Loyola*, by Thomas Corbishley, S.J., 15, 34, 52, 56, 12. See also *Manresa*, xxii–xxiii, 10, 44–5, 58–9, and 166. Hopkins's poems are full of the great election and the inevitable difficulties humans experience in making it. See 'The Leaden Echo and the Golden Echo', 'Morning, Midday and Evening Sacrifice', 'On a Piece of Music', 'To what serves Mortal Beauty?', 'St. Alphonsus Rodriguez', and 'Brothers'. All these poems treat the Ignatian and Ruskinian problem of natural beauty and achievement and its foil, 'God's better beauty, grace'.

29 See Eugene August, 'Hopkins' Dangerous Fire', *Victorian Poetry*, I, i, 72–4.
30 See William Templeman, 'Ruskin's Ploughshare and Hopkins' "Windhover"', *English Studies*, xliii, 103–6.
31 Epistle to the Ephesians ii.2–5.
32 'Sillion' is Hopkins's version of the French word *sillon*, meaning the furrow made by a plough.

Chapter 3 'New Na͡areths in Us': the Making of a Victorian Gentleman

1 Houghton, *The Victorian Frame of Mind*, 282, 288.
2 But see Jerome Buckley's *The Victorian Temper*, 11, G. M. Young's *Victorian England, Portrait of an Age*, 237–8, and Frances M. Brookfield, *The Cambridge 'Apostles'*, 4–5, 14. Cambridge by no means lacked appreciation for 'diversity in excellence': in the eighteen-twenties, a group of delightful and extravagant virtuosos founded 'The Cambridge *Conversa͡ione* Society'; henceforth the group was known as 'The Apostles', not for excessive or exclusive piety, but on the contrary because

the membership was always confined to twelve of the most brilliant as well as the most attractive and the most virtuous men in Cambridge.

3 'Pathos' was one of Hopkins's favourite words. He was very conscious of its abuse in Tennyson and Dickens, for instance, but as a Ruskinian disciple he would call no painter or poet or novelist an artist who was without the capacity for pathos. Perhaps this emphasis upon pathos is where the Victorians part company with the Elizabethans.

4 Maurice Valency, *In Praise of Love: An Introduction to the Love Poetry of the Renaissance*, 42–4. See Hopkins's Poem 47, 'The Handsome Heart: at a Gracious Answer'.

5 John Holloway has pointed out the classic process of becoming a true gentleman as opposed to a mere hereditary rich man, in two of Disraeli's heroes. Coningsby is not worthy of the rank he will some day inherit until he feels a heroic stirring of the heart; though a man may be born with this feeling, he does not inherit it. He has to discover it in himself by practising sympathy for others. And the father of Coningsby's friend Oswald, Mr Millbank, the *nouveau riche* mill-owner, successfully grafts upon his own vigorous personality not only the deportment and graces of a country squire, but all the benevolence toward his workers that the upper classes so often lacked. Millbank would have won Carlyle's allegiance as a type of hero-capitalist, if he had existed in the flesh (see John Holloway, *The Victorian Sage: Studies in Argument*, 96, 106).

6 This seems to be another moment when Hopkins is admiring the way of the windhover, a type of creature whose 'Honour is flashed off exploit, so we say' (see Poem 73, 1888), while frankly pointing out that the way of the ploughman may be safer. He also says in this letter to Bridges: 'I say it deliberately and before God, I would have you and Canon Dixon and all true poets remember that fame, the being known, though in itself one of the most dangerous things to man, is nevertheless the true and appointed air, element and setting of genius and its works.' The word 'necessary' is crossed out and the word 'true' is substituted.

7 Ruskin frankly admitted his descent from the ranks of humble people such as bakers, tanners, and sailors. His mother 'felt the defects of her education in cultivated society, and so always visited in a familiar way only those whom she thought inferior' (see *Fors Clavigera*, iv, 147–8, and v, 387, in *Works*, XXVIII).

8 James Laver, *Manners and Morals in the Age of Optimism: 1848–1914*, 44–5.

9 See *Queen of the Air* (*Works*, XIX), 298 and note; *Fors Clavigera*, v (*Works*, XXVIII), 448; and *St. Mark's Rest* (*Works*, XXIV), 375. Esmé Wingfield-Stratford attributes some of the 'colour and sweetness' of Victorian England to the Romantic movement and to the romantic strains absorbed by the most interesting Victorians, despite the watchful apprehension of the 'hard-headed Benthamites and Puritan Killjoys':

No doubt Puritan discipline, . . . fostered the concentration that is the element most needful to any work of permanent value. The utilitarians may have played a part in stimulating the aggressive individualism that renders the Victorians, with all their faults, so intensely interesting. But for the colour and sweetness of that age we are indebted neither to its philosophy nor its religion, but to that deliberate stimulation of the emotion that is summed up in the term 'romance' (*Those Earnest Victorians*, 87).

But the Romantic movement itself was a synthesizing one, combining fresh treatments of classical and medieval themes with revolutionary ardour from the Continent. And it is quite typical of a variety of Victorians to absorb all sorts of influences into their work and their personalities, even though their work appears to us quite Victorian.

Nonetheless I believe that the 'romance' in the Victorian period may be fully as much intellectual and classical as spiritual, medieval, or post-Romantic; it is the combination of all these strands in so many vigorous Victorians, of whom Hopkins is a prototype, that makes them, as Wingfield-Stratford said, 'so intensely interesting'.

10 John Stuart Mill implicitly describes the same kind of model citizen, although his language is less effusive than the Oxonians. But Mill's model Englishman is tough-minded about himself and his own intellectuality, yet very generous toward others.

11 And at Cambridge also; as always, Leslie Stephen came forward with a saving touch of mockery when Victorian thirst for piety and pathos went to the lengths of the absurd:

The very tone of voice of a true Rugbeian implied, modestly, but firmly, that he was endowed with a 'moral consciousness.' He had a quasi-official right to share the lofty view which he had imbibed at the feet of the master. He always seemed to be radiating virtuous influences (*Studies of a Biographer*, II, 128)

Although only one side of Hopkins's correspondence with Bridges remains, one suspects that Hopkins himself had the same chilling effect upon Bridges, if Hopkins's feints, retreats, apologies, and resumption of the attacks upon Bridges's life and practices indicate anything.

12 E. D. H. Johnson believes this discomfort in the prophetic role is a common affliction of the more impressive Victorian poets. See *The Alien Vision of Victorian Poetry*, especially Johnson's preface.

13 Tennyson, Newman, the Arnolds, Jowett, Disraeli, Carlyle, and Ruskin. I am not arguing that these nine men formed a cohesive movement, but that they responded to many of the same problems of caste and class responsibilities as though they were all members of a tight little club, constantly arguing or agreeing with one another. They used the same rhetoric and they frequently resorted to some of the same metaphors and

archetypes, such as the gentleman ploughman, or the soldier of the plough, the admirable churl (Gurth the churl or Harry Ploughman), the well-educated public-school type whose heart is full of pity for the lesser breeds without the law, and so forth. William Monypenny, Disraeli's first biographer, said that 'Newman, Carlyle, and Disraeli were far different figures; but little as they may have known it, they were . . . spiritual brethren, engaged in a desperate fight against a common enemy, working in their several ways with a common purpose'. Monypenny sees them as sharing a romantic and an artistic temperament and also 'that historical sentiment which is the fatal enemy of Benthamism, as of every kind of system-mongering' (*The Life of Benjamin Disraeli, Earl of Beaconsfield,* 1, 297). And Hopkins placed Ruskin and Carlyle with ' "the true men" as agst. the Sophistik . . . Philistine, Doctrinaire, Utilitarian, Positive, and on the whole Negative (as Carlyle wd. put it) side' (*FL*, 231, 1868). And on the relationship of Tractarianism, the Gothic revival, and other sorts of 'romantic Toryism' to the Young England movement, see Robert Blake, *Disraeli,* 170–2.

14 Rupert Wilkinson, *Gentlemanly Power: British Leadership and the Public School Tradition,* 40. These nine men, Carlyle, Ruskin, Newman, the Arnolds, Jowett, Disraeli, Tennyson and Hopkins frequently mentioned 'the question of gentility'; it was almost an obsession with all of them. And of the nine, Tennyson was the only one whose family had legitimate pretensions to membership in the landed gentry, but his father had been disinherited and had apparently been prostrated by the shock. Tennyson's rage on the subject of wealthy snobs and parasites may spring as much from the painful ambiguity of his reduced rank as from the injustice and the deprivation inflicted on his family and himself.

But none of the other nine would have been considered a gentleman born. For example, Ruskin, Hopkins, and the Arnolds were all matriculated at Oxford with the ambiguous title of '*arm*', (*armiger*, or armourbearer to a knight-gentleman), or yeoman, meaning that their fathers were not 'bart.', or noble, nor yet 'gent.', nor so low in the social scale as 'pleb.'.

Hopkins's father was a mercantile Consul-General to the Hawaiian Islands in the British Isles. As a servant of the Queen he was required to call himself 'Esquire', but his association with trade and his lowly position as 'Home Civil Servant' rather than a member of the more aristocratic Foreign Service would hardly have entitled his son to an ﹍utomatic berth at Eton, Harrow, or Winchester. Instead, he sent his son to a minor day-boarding school.

Carlyle's father was a stonemason, and a Scottish one at that, thus compounding his social ignominy; Newman's was a banker, Ruskin's a sherry merchant, and Jowett's an impoverished drifter, and his preoccupation with national power and public conduct may have stemmed in part from his miserable origins. He came up to Oxford in a threadbare condition, forced to support his family, and too poor, therefore, to buy new clothing or to entertain in his room. He remained in this condition for twenty years or more, while the Tractarian dons withheld his salary. Disraeli's position was the most painful of all. He could be Prime Minister of England and still an outsider, barred from most clubs; and even today his biographers spend time and energy deciding whether he was a gentleman or a howling Jewish cad. Nor did Dr Thomas Arnold of Rugby escape the iron social laws: his father was a mere tax collector on the Isle of Wight.

It would seem that all these Victorian gentlemen in the making cherished what Gladstone once called a 'sneaking kindness for a lord' (G. M. Young, *Victorian England,* 128). Hopkins once wrote to his mother during his novitiate that he had come across the Hopkins arms and crest on 'the tomb of William Mansel Phillips of Coedair in Carmarthenshire, second son of Sr. Wm. Mansel, baronet of Iscoed in the same county, and of Caroline his wife only child of Benjamin Bod Hopkins Esq.' Hopkins remarked to his mother that 'it looks very much as if the Hopkinses had an old connection with Wimbledon. I shd. like to hear about this anything you know' (*FL,* 109, 1869). One wonders whether the connection Hopkins hoped for was with Sir Wm. Mansel, the baronet rather than with the town of Wimbledon. (On the parentage and social standing of boys who went to minor public schools or grammar schools, such as Hopkins's Highgate, see Wilkinson, *Gentlemanly Power,* 23. See Burke's *Peerage* on the titles of Home Civil Servants, and in the *Dictionary of National Biography,* see the biography of Sir Roger Cholmley, the Elizabethan founder of Highgate School. On the career of Hopkins's father, see *British Authors of the Nineteenth Century,* eds Stanley Kunitz and Howard Haycroft. See *Alumni Oxoniensis: 1715–1886,* for rank, parentage, and birthplace of Oxford students.)

15 Frederick Temple, later Archbishop of Canterbury, was one of the 'seven against Christ' who had written an article in *Essays and Reviews.*

16 Charles Kingsley once begged Victorian parents to sense when their offspring were going through religious crises and to sympathize with them (*Yeast: A Problem,* xix). Amy Cruse suggests that the typical family pattern, where religious differences existed, would contain a Calvinistic mother, horrified by the Tractarians, and a more easy-going Anglican father, mediating with as much good humour as possible between the mother and any fledgling Tractarians in the family (*The Victorians and Their Reading,* 16–20).

17 Thomas Carlyle, *Past and Present,* 10.

18 For convenience sake we might describe more fully the eight men whom I have chosen to place along with Hopkins in the company of the

'gentleman prophets'. Of the nine, seven of them, Hopkins, Ruskin, Newman, Tennyson, Jowett, and the Arnolds, were trained at one of the two great universities; Disraeli received a solid classical education at home, and Carlyle attended Edinburgh University. Of the seven men trained at English universities, six were Oxonian; Tennyson was at Cambridge. Of the six Oxford men, four of them, Hopkins, Jowett, and the Arnolds, were either Balliol men, or, like Dr Arnold, closely associated with Jowett's work at Balliol.

With the exception of Carlyle, all of these men became, or had been at one time or another, either nominal or practising Anglicans. Four of them were priests, two of them in the Church of England and two converts to Rome. In all cases except Disraeli's and Dr Arnold's there had been an evangelizing parent or relative in the immediate background. In Tennyson and the six Oxonians, there was an equally strong Platonic strain, picked up at school or in the universities, which they never entirely lost.

Obviously these nine 'gentleman prophets' have a good deal in common with John Holloway's 'Victorian sages', Carlyle, Disraeli, George Eliot, Newman, Matthew Arnold, and Hardy, who 'all knew that what they had to offer was special in kind', and who took pains 'to show how it is confirmed and given meaning in its own way, or how to grasp it properly, the reader requires a special insight or sense' (*The Victorian Sage*, 4). Certainly George Eliot and Hardy implicitly talked about gentlemen and non-gentlemen in their novels, but by substituting Dr Arnold, Tennyson, Jowett, and Hopkins, for George Eliot and Hardy, I am including those who explicitly discussed the making of a gentleman, who had an overwhelming sense of the romance of the past, and with the exception of Carlyle, a sense of the classical past as well as the medieval past. I am excluding those writers like John Morley, George Eliot, John Stuart Mill, Hardy, Huxley, or Leslie Stephen, whose particular sense of the present and the future tinges much of what they said with a strong flavour of empiricism not typical of the gentleman prophets.

19 E. D. H. Johnson believes that this sense of alienation constitutes 'the dichotomy which emerges from any close analysis of the relations between the artist and society in the Victorian period. The hallmark of the literary personalities of Tennyson, Browning, and Arnold alike is a certain aristocratic aloofness, a stubborn intractability which is likely to manifest itself at just those points where the contemporary social order assumed automatic conformity with its dictates.'

On the other hand, 'Tennyson, Browning, and Arnold never went to the lengths of the poets who came after them in disassociating themselves from their audience'. To fail to see where and how these men compromised, and where they refused, Johnson says, is to miss 'that quality of double awareness which we are now to investigate as the crux of the

Victorian literary consciousness' (*The Alien Vision of Vict*
xv).

The 'double awareness' that Johnson speaks of is equall
understanding of Hopkins's moral and prosodic prol
Hopkins argued with Bridges in favour of his right to pro-
syncrasy, he was arguing for the integrity of the artist in Rus----
terms. When he indicated to his friends that henceforth his vocation
called for nothing more than presentation pieces of the occasional type,
he was arguing for the right of the poet's public, whoever that might be,
to dictate its terms; he was then responding to the social and religious
pressures that he did not wish to ignore.

Hopkins's miracle as a poet is that he achieved two quite diverse aims,
at whatever cost to his spiritual and physical health. Even in his finest
poetry he was giving the public what he thought it needed: he said that
goodness was finer than the finest and most exquisite manners and fine
manners finer than innate virtues like beauty and talent, but that all three
were important. He said that nature was God's handiwork and that response to nature—providing no sin or indulgence was involved—was
desirable. Yet he said all these Victorian commonplaces in a form that
challenges us today because of its radical techniques and vigorous spirit;
and so he has survived as a Victorian poet.

20 Houghton says that the 'central note' of this ubiquitous malaise was
'weakness and frustration' and that 'to some extent' it was experienced
'by nearly all educated Victorians' (*The Victorian Frame of Mind*, 64–5).

21 *The Works of Walter Bagehot*, I, 236.

22 Young, *Victorian England*, 153–4.

23 Benjamin Disraeli, Earl of Beaconsfield, *Sybil, or The Two Nations*, v.

24 Buckley, *The Victorian Temper*, 6.

25 On the spiritual distress of Hopkins and Matthew Arnold, see Miller,
The Disappearance of God.

26 See Wilkinson, *Gentlemanly Power*, especially 30–1, for an assessment of
the incredible burden these Sixth Form Prefects (called Praeposters at
Rugby) bore upon their shoulders, as counsellors, tutors, and disciplin-
arians to boys in the lower forms. The system, partly designed to prepare
men for public service, was not new, but Arnold put enormous stress
upon it because it entailed Christian self-sacrifice.

27 Arnold of Rugby is the one great public figure in this book whom
Hopkins never mentioned. Yet it would be ludicrous to describe the
making of Hopkins, an exemplar of the new Victorian gentleman, without
mentioning Arnold. In the first place, Arnold was to Rugby what Jowett
was to Balliol, and he was quite conscious of his role as maker of model
gentlemen. Hopkins was obviously not aware of it, but his own model
gentleman is as Arnoldian as he is Ignatian.

Arnold took over the Headmastership of Rugby in 1828, a year before the appearance of Carlyle's 'Signs of the Times'; by 1833 the Arnoldian ladder of virtues had begun to spread beyond the confines of Rugby. See for example the description by the Harrovian, Richard Trench, of a departing friend, whose loss Trench dreaded; this member of the Cambridge 'Apostles' was 'a *Christian*, a *scholar* and a *gentleman*' (Brookfield, *The Cambridge 'Apostles'*, 173). And see also Arthur Henry Hallam's warning to the despondent Tennyson against the pride of artistry, since God enabled a man to judge the difference between 'the Beautiful and the Good!' (*Tennyson*, by his Son, I, 81). And see Gladstone's comment upon the dead youth Hallam, that had he lived, he might well have righted this world because he meant 'to deal with it *comprehensively*'. Among Hallam's talents, which must indeed have been comprehensive in the sense both Arnolds admired, Gladstone enumerated 'a *mind* full of beauty and power', and this '*powerful intellect*' was 'joined to a *purer* and *holier heart*; and the whole illuminated with a richer *imagination*, with the most *sparkling*, yet the *kindest wit*' (Brookfield, 156–7). And see the letter from one of Hopkins's friends after his death, describing him as '*lovable*', '*singularly gifted*', and *saintly*. Hopkins was said to possess a 'beautifully *gentle* & *generous* nature', which enabled his friends to feel that their 'lives were better, & the world richer because of him' (*JP*, 301, 1889). And though the tale does not come from Jowett's pen, we should remember Hopkins's reputation among the Irish Jesuits as the intellectual 'Star of Balliol'.

28 Arthur Penrhyn Stanley, *The Life and Correspondence of Thomas Arnold*, I, 120, 114. Of course Lionel Trilling has already suggested the similarities of vision between father and son, in *Matthew Arnold*.

29 Stanley, *Arnold*, I, 130, 133–4.

30 See for example the passage where Dr Arnold is urging his Sixth Form boys to think of themselves as 'officers in the army or navy whose want of moral courage would, indeed, be thought cowardice' in *ibid.*, 121.

31 Thomas Arnold, *Christian Life, Its Hopes, Its Fears, Its Close*, III, 138.

32 See *DNB*. Arnold 'was the first to add mathematics, modern history, and modern languages to the ordinary school course'.

33 This is Arthur Henry Hallam's phrase describing the quality of Tennyson's genius. See *Tennyson*, by his Son, I, 81.

34 Thomas Arnold, *Christian Life*, II, 145.

35 *Ibid.*, III, 137.

36 Walter Houghton, *The Victorian Frame of Mind*, 277–8.

37 Stanley, *Arnold*, II, 170.

38 *Ibid.*, I, 159. Hopkins was no egalitarian either; none of the Victorian gentleman prophets tended to look kindly upon efforts of the lower classes to enfranchise themselves. But more than any of the gentleman prophets except Ruskin, Hopkins looked upon the sufferings of the

poor as personal wounds that would not heal. His vocation took him among them, as Dr Arnold's did not; and his distress for them constituted a considerable part of his 'chief-woe, world-sorrow' (Poem 65, 1885?).

39 Valency, *In Praise of Love*, 42, 43.

40 Wilkinson, *Gentlemanly Power*, 13.

41 Asa Briggs, *Victorian People: A Reassessment of Persons and Themes*, 144–5.

42 George Granville Bradley, *Recollections of Arthur Penrhyn Stanley*, 33.

43 Almost all editions of Stanley's *Arnold, Life and Correspondence* contain a reproduction of a portrait in the first volume.

44 See *DNB*; see also Holloway, *The Victorian Sage*, 4, 9. Holloway believes that the Victorian sage habitually sways his readers and his audience by the magic of his voice where he cannot persuade by reason alone, although he is not averse to reason. Holloway suggests that 'Coleridge might almost be called the founder in modern England of this kind of thought, and his influence on both Newman and Carlyle was very great'. Coleridge's influence on Dr Arnold was equally great, and Arnold's attempt to induce his pupils and masters to seek the invisible kingdom was in no way daunted by the fact that he was not always sure it was there. But the line from Coleridge to Hopkins, through Tennyson, the Arnolds, Newman and Carlyle, seems very clear, for this intense desire to make the invisible radiantly visible and the inaudible hauntingly audible was as typical of Hopkins as it was of these older gentleman prophets whom he often discussed (with the exception of Dr Arnold).

45 Matthew Arnold, 'Rugby Chapel'.

46 See 'An Eton Boy', *Essays in Criticism*, Third Series, 256, 296. Matthew Arnold, an erstwhile Rugbeian under his father's headmastership, wrote these words as a memorial essay to a young Etonian, Arthur Mynors, who died in his teens of fever during a campaign in South Africa. We might mourn the waste of a young life; the Victorian gentleman prophets would spend more time applauding the heroism. Mynors was apparently a 'comprehensive' boy of the Arnoldian stamp; he was not only a 'charming boy' but an industrious one in his slow way, just the sort of schoolboy hero, Matthew Arnold said, whom the best public schools were designed to produce, and whose modesty and self-sacrifice were 'part of the very tradition and life of England'.

47 Wilkinson, *Gentlemanly Power*, 10, 23; Howard Staunton, *The Great Schools of England: An Account of the Foundations, Endowments, and Discipline of the Chief Seminaries of Learning in England, including Eton, Winchester, Westminster, St. Paul's, Charter-House, Merchant Taylor's, Harrow, Rugby, Shrewsbury, Etc. Etc.* See also Edward Clarence Mack, *Public Schools and British Opinion, 1780–1860*. Staunton's account, published in 1865, does not even place Highgate among the etcetera etceteras, nor do Mack or Wilkinson mention it, so presumably it stood

very low, at that time, 'on a rigorous social hierarchy' of schools (Wilkinson, 9).

48 *CD*, 12 (1878). We know from sources other than Hopkins that his head-master was known as 'blustering Dyne'; such a nickname could hardly have lent Dyne 'magic', even if Highgate had possessed more lustre. See *FL*, 1–4, 15–16, 394–6.

49 Wilkinson, *Gentlemanly Power*, 29.

50 *FL*, 220 (1864); Hopkins was still referring to Anglo-Catholicism here.

51 *CD*, 75, 59 (1881).

52 Liddon was very well aware of Hopkins's capacity for hero-worship; he once warned that Hopkins's 'love & sympathy' for Hopkins's hero, William Addis, might be 'the strongest motive' urging Hopkins toward Roman Catholicism; while admitting that this prompting was 'natural enough toward such a man as' Addis was, Liddon felt it necessary to caution Hopkins how likely he was 'to be influenced by the example of friends' whom he loved as he loved Addis (*FL*, 401, 1866).

53 Wilkinson, *Gentlemanly Power*, 73. See also 6–7, 185, 202–4, and 215–17. Wilkinson never mentions Carlyle, but he describes how, in more urbane, more Arnoldian form, these same virtues were inculcated in the Victorian schools touched by the spirit of Dr Arnold. Wilkinson is the first con-firmation I have been able to find for my own theory that the Ignatian spirit has in it far more of the Arnoldian spirit of the whole than is usually assumed, zealously missionary as it may be.

54 The tendency to resort to military metaphors to describe a nation in peril was very common among the gentleman prophets. It was not perhaps typical of Matthew Arnold, except when he was thinking of his father. But we have only to think of the mid-century Laureate's ringing praise for a useless sacrifice—

> Theirs not to make reply,
> Theirs not to reason why,
> Theirs but to do and die

—or Ruskin's praise of St George, the travelling soldier, or Hopkins's fictive soldiers, heroic tars, and medieval knights, or the hymn 'Onward Christian Soldiers' to see the popularity of the military metaphor. In this hymn, written by a Tractarian priest, Sabine Baring-Gould, Christ is a 'Royal Master', leading the faithful, who are 'Marching as to war'. All these military metaphors echo Carlyle's call to the nation: 'Here on Earth we are as Soldiers fighting in a foreign land; that understand not the plan of campaign and have no need to understand it; seeing well what is at our hand to be done. Let us do it like Soldiers; with submission, with courage, with heroic joy' (see 'Characteristics', *Critical and Miscellaneous Essays*, III, 48).

55 Carlyle, *Past and Present*, 207–8; see also *Heroes and Hero-Worship*, 2.
56 Carlyle, 'Characteristics', *Critical and Miscellaneous Essays*, III, 42.
57 Carlyle, *Past and Present*, 233–4, 234–5.
58 Young, *Victorian England*, 43. It would be presumptuous for me to suggest that the celibacy of Ruskin, Jowett, Hopkins, and Newman was derived from 'animal sensibility of conscience' or 'bodily repulsion', but one senses a 'super-morality of the nerves' in all the gentleman prophets whom I associate with Hopkins's model gentleman, except perhaps in Disraeli; and in all cases, including Disraeli, there was extreme 'social alarm'.
59 To Catholics of the British Isles, a classical education acquired in Victorian England meant Oxford or Cambridge, both seats of the Church of England, the enemy of Roman Catholicism. They were also closed clubs for Anglicans; Hopkins was one of the first Catholics to be permitted to take a degree at Oxford (*FL*, 91, 1866), and matters were fully as difficult for members of the dissenting sects.
60 Newman, *Idea of a University*, 82, 102, 104–5.
61 *Ibid.*, xxxviii, 153; see also Edmund Burke, *Reflections on the Revolution in France and Other Essays*, 73, for the Burkeian model whom Newman condemned as a typical eighteenth-century 'howling cad'.
62 *Idea of a University*, 105.
63 Poems 46 and 75 (1879, 1889).
64 One of the most extreme examples of troubled morality occurs in one of Hopkins's letters to Bridges. Hopkins mentions his poem, 'The Bugler's First Communion', another Pre-Raphaelite morality play in poetry. The bugler boy comes to Father Hopkins, 'Breathing bloom of a chastity in mansex fine', and Hopkins is so distressed over the 'Disaster' he prophesies in the form of 'hell-rooks' waiting to molest the boy's chastity that the poet cries out, 'let me see no more of him', and Hopkins laconically writes to Bridges: 'I enclose the poem the Bugler. I am half inclined to hope the hero of it may be killed in Afghanistan' (*LB*, 92, 1879).
65 In all fairness to Hillis Miller, I ought to say that although he agrees with me that Hopkins came to distrust natural things, Miller does not agree that the windhover is a symbol of one of them. See the section on Hopkins in *The Disappearance of God*.
66 Hopkins was always quite frank (as most Victorians were) about the anthropomorphic nature of his love for Christ: 'Feeling, love in particular, is the great moving power and spring of verse and the only person I am in love with seldom, especially now, stirs my heart sensibly and when he does I cannot always "make capital" of it, it would be a sacrilege to do so' (*LB*, 66, 1879). If this ambiguous statement means that Hopkins had been granted visions of Christ, this deep personal love for Christ is even more understandable. In his sermons, Hopkins called Christ 'a thinker', 'an orator and a poet', 'a statesman', splendid and beautiful

in both 'mind and body', 'our noble lover, our prince, our champion', and 'the greatest genius that ever lived' (*S*, 15, 34–6, 1879).

67 *S*, 220, 263, 262; probably 1889, though Hopkins's date is 1888; see *FL*, 191, n. 3.

68 For example, Father Devlin says that there may have been severe extenuating circumstances, that for example, Father Purbrick, Hopkins's Provincial, might have dealt with him in a more sensitive manner (*S*, 214–15), and that there were 'Jesuits themselves among Hopkins' contemporaries who felt that he was being wasted and misused' (*S*, 219). With typical insight, Father Devlin suggests that Hopkins 'had, as one or two of his sermons show, a slight—*but fatal*—sympathy with the Pharisee rather than with the Publican' (*S*, 217). Devlin also hints, as all biographies of St Ignatius frankly admit, that in order to subdue his own proud spirit, Ignatius himself once undertook penances so severe that he never allowed his followers to adopt them (*S*, 119). Perhaps this 'slight—*but fatal*—sympathy with the Pharisee rather than with the Publican' overtook even St Ignatius himself at that time. Most of the gentleman prophets appeared to suffer from this sympathy now and again, especially when they forgot that without compensatory delight, virtue and morality can appear to those of unheroic stature as ugly as sin itself.

69 Stanley, *Arnold, Life and Correspondence*, I, 132.

70 This sonnet was written two months before Hopkins's final illness. After his death, a Catholic laywoman wrote to Hopkins's mother: 'My Husband was in Dublin for a few days before Easter, & saw Father Gerard once or twice; & they spent an Evening together. He thought him looking very ill then, & said that he was much depressed. . . . When my Husband came back he spoke of Father Gerard to others; & we had just managed that he should be sent for—back to England—when we heard of his illness' (*JP*, 301, 1889).

71 As a young priest, Hopkins wrote his mother with some pride that he had received the 'four minor orders . . . those of Doorkeepers, Readers, Exorcisists, and Acolytes'. Their use, he told her, was 'almost obsolete' (*FL*, 126, 1874), but the levitical sacrifice would therefore be all the greater, and tradition has it that 'Hopkins fulfilled the office of Porter with due credit' (*LB*, 26 note; n.d.).

72 Abbott & Campbell, *Life of Jowett*, I, 171.

Chapter 4 '*The Horror and the Havoc and the Glory of it*': The Wreck of the Deutschland *and the Calamitarian Mood*

1 Samuel Taylor Coleridge, *A Lay Sermon Addressed to the Higher and Middle Classes on the Existing Distresses and Discontents, Complete Works*, VI, 164.

2 Margaret Farrand Thorp, *Charles Kingsley: 1819–1875*, 125.
3 John Morley, *On Compromise*, 36–7.
4 When Apocalypse or Apocalyptic is spelt with a capital letter, it refers either to the Apocalypse, or Revelation of St John of Patmos, or to an almost complete Apocalypse, such as Hopkins's *Wreck of the Deutschland*. This Apocalypse is clearly and deliberately based on St John's, not only in symbolic details, in mood and tone, but in its progress from suffering, horror and fear, to joy and peace.

When apocalypse or apocalyptic is spelt with a small letter, it refers to works that have taken the Apocalypse—or other pre-Johannine apocalyptic material—only as a partial model, and not always literally at that, but sometimes merely as a symbol. Hopkins believed that what St John of Patmos had revealed might well be about to occur. Literal belief in the imminence of the second coming and the day of judgment was a conspicuous feature of Tractarian preaching, whereas many other nineteenth-century writers adapted the apocalyptic mood, or language, or some of the symbolic details of the Apocalypse, without accepting a literal belief in the second coming or the day of judgment.

5 Obviously each writer creates his own Apocalypse anew, as each age refashions the matter of the Apocalypse to its own ends. Hopkins did not use St John's Apocalypse and apocalyptic material in the manner of the Romantic poets, nor, for example, did he adapt Revelation to the more definitively secular purposes to which Carlyle, Ruskin, Tennyson, and William Morris usually subjected it. Hopkins believed that the day of divine judgment was at hand, and with it the end of the world, whereas in these other writers the apocalyptic material appears in a more purely archetypal guise as symbolic of contemporary corruption, both civil and moral.

Wordsworth, Coleridge, and Blake, at least in their earlier writings, saw the French Revolution as a joyful rebirth, despite its blood and terror, and so Morris interpreted all Victorian upheaval. Carlyle treated the French Revolution and all insurrections as warnings of the end of western civility, and so, on the whole did Ruskin. As everyone knows, Tennyson's feelings about the future were ambivalent; but for Hopkins, the issues were absolute. He feared the eternal damnation of all Protestant countries and all individual Protestants, including his friends and family, and sometimes he quite obviously feared his own. And yet, because he too was bitterly distressed by civil and moral corruption, and sick with anxiety for England, his apocalyptic voice is sometimes indistinguishable from that of other Victorian prophets.

I shall dispense with familiar apocalyptic utterances of the nineteenth century, except where they illuminate Hopkins's own. But there are some little-known calamitarian cries in writers like Liddon, Romanes, Huxley, Kingsley, and Dixon, which would interest us because two of these men served as schoolmasters for Hopkins and because their common distress suggests the ubiquity of the calamitarian mood and the manner in which it was clearly a seedbed for Hopkins's poetry. (It was here that I was particularly indebted to Walter Houghton's *Victorian Frame of Mind*; see also M. H. Abrams, 'English Romanticism: The Spirit of the Age', in *Romanticism Reconsidered*, ed. Northrop Frye, 26–72.)

6 Jerome Hamilton Buckley, *The Triumph of Time*, 1–2, 139.

7 James M. Kennedy, *Henry Drummond: An Anthology*, 223.

8 Henry Parry Liddon, *Advent in St. Pauls: Sermons Bearing Chiefly on the Two Comings of Our Lord* (London, 1892), 55–6.

9 Liddon, *Advent Sermons*, 23, 223, 14.

10 Liddon, *Sermons on Old Testament Subjects*, 330; and see Rev. ii.5. Liddon transmutes Christ's ominous warnings into a loving promise of felicity that does not come until much later in the Apocalypse.

11 Wilberforce's *Practical View of Christianity* went into edition after edition throughout the nineteenth century until almost the end of Queen Victoria's reign.

12 Annan, *Leslie Stephen*, 110.

13 Elie Halévy, *Victorian Years (1841–1895)*, vol. IV of Halévy's *History of the English People in the Nineteenth Century*, 62.

14 *Ibid.*, 349–50.

15 *Advent Sermons*, 277. See also Newman's electrifying sermon, famous in its day, called 'The Second Spring', in *Sermons Preached on Various Occasions*, new ed. (London, 1898); for Pusey's apocalyptic chants, see *Nine Sermons Preached Before the University at Oxford and Printed Chiefly Between A.D. 1843–1855*, especially 12–13, 4, and 26.

16 Throughout this chapter, the Apocalypse (or the Revelation) of St John of Patmos, as he is often called, will appear in the footnotes as Revelation, or Rev. followed by the chapter and verse. Modern Biblical scholarship distinguishes between St John of Patmos, the author of the Apocalypse, and St John the Gospeller, whose apocalyptic visions follow the synoptic gospels of Matthew, Mark, and Luke. These two Johns are also to be distinguished from John the Disciple of Christ, brother of James and son of Zebedee who was often called 'the beloved of Christ'. The Victorians, even fairly knowledgeable Bible scholars, did not always distinguish between these three Biblical Johns, but we are mostly concerned with St John of Patmos, the author of Revelation.

17 James Sambrook, *A Poet Hidden: The Life of Richard Watson Dixon, 1833–1890*, 79, 113.

18 Richard Watson Dixon, 'The Close of the Tenth Century of the Christian Era', The Arnold Prize Essay for 1858, 65. Dixon also won a prize for a long poem called *St. John of Patmos*.

19 Ruskin's pair of impassioned essays called *The Storm Cloud of the Nineteenth Century* is one of the most remarkable records of the calami-

tarian mood in Victorian England; it is part careful observation of cloud and smog formations, part incoherent ravings. As an example of pure terror it can hardly be matched.

20 Morley, *On Compromise*, 34, 35, 36.

21 *Ibid.*, 36-7.

22 George Romanes ('Physicus'), *A Candid Examination of Theism*, 51-2, 63, 114.

23 Charles Kingsley, *Scientific Lectures and Essays*, 315, 316.

24 Thorp, *Charles Kingsley*, 119, 124-5.

25 'Memorial Verses', April 1850.

26 Hopkins's apparent confusion between crime and punishment is part of the fabric of Revelation. Catastrophies and suffering perform several functions. They punish men for former sins, and thus mitigate eternal punishment. Punishments and suffering also warn men that as individuals or as a species, their occupation of the earth has a time limit to it, and that this time limit has been stressed in both Testaments. It is to be hoped that suffering of any kind turns men to the paths of righteousness, and their sufferings may also be a warning to others. In this whole matter of crime and suffering as both warning and deterrent, the nation is simply the macrocosm for the individual.

27 Thomas Carlyle, *Latter-Day Pamphlets*, in *The Works of Thomas Carlyle*, XX, 184, 40.

28 Notes to 'Tom's Garland', in *Poems*, 247.

29 *Latter-Day Pamphlets*, 3, 37.

30 'Thy pomp is brought down to the grave, *and* the noise of thy *viols*: the worm is spread under thee, and the worms cover thee.

How art thou fallen from heaven, O Lucifer, son of the morning! *how* art thou cut down to the ground, which didst weaken the nations' (Isaiah xiv.11–12).

31 *Latter-Day Pamphlets*, 290.

32 The model for the Victorian humble worker goes way back beyond Carlyle, or figures like Wordsworth's leech-gatherer. The Christian prototype is, of course, the patient shepherd.

33 Thorp, *Charles Kingsley*, 125.

34 *The Prelude*, book VI, 624-35. Turner's awesome alpine scenes are also a response to the same moral sensibility. Ruskin made it perfectly plain that he was as impressed with Turner's moral concerns as with his honest rendering of nature.

35 They are also staples of *The Inferno*.

36 'Second Lay Sermon' (*Complete Works*, VI), 164.

37 Rev. viii.8–9.

38 Lat. *petra*, rock—'thou art Peter, and upon this rock I build my church'—(Matt. xvi.18). The *Deutschland* was wrecked on a sandbar at the 'Kentish Knock' (see *FL*, 439–40), one of the outer shoals at the mouth of the

Thames. The wreck paradoxically turns into an apocalyptic 'beacon', or a warning to heretical England.

39 *The Wreck of the Deutschland.* Henceforth I will refer only to stanza numbers.

40 Hopkins was most obliging about leading future scholars to his sources. His frequent allusions to the synoptic Gospels, to St John's Apocalypse, and to *Paradise Lost* and *Paradise Regained* suggest that he was conscious of Tarpeian analogues such as Lucifer's fall from heaven into the fiery crags of hell, Christ's temptation upon the mountainside and on the pinnacle of the temple, and Milton's version of the expulsion from Eden. According to Milton, man's first parents were hustled out of Paradise 'and down the cliff as fast' (*Paradise Lost*, XII, 639)—or almost as precipitously as Lucifer had been hurled out of heaven. *Paradise Lost* is framed by the story of these expulsions, Lucifer's, and Adam's and Eve's, and in both scenes of expulsions, rocks, pits, crags, and flames figure prominently.

41 Another fascinating contemporary parallel can be found in Newman's 'Gerontius'; as the old man lies dying, he feels as though he were leaning over a 'dizzy brink' of a 'sheer infinite descent', or as though he were 'falling through' the reliable 'framework of created things' and would 'sink and sink' into a 'vast abyss' (lines 111–18).

42 No wonder the Victorians are sometimes called the post-Romantics; their respectability and their cosy family lives frequently belie their cosmic anxieties, as though they wanted to play the role of the Ancient Mariner and the Wedding Guest simultaneously.

43 We can only guess some of the reasons for his reticence. D. H. Lawrence insists that the language of the Apocalypse assumes the covert guises of the underdog (*Apocalypse* [New York, 1932], 10–18). Certainly Catholics did not want to appear to be on the prowl for converts the minute the hierarchy was re-established and a few Jesuit houses had opened on English soil. Northrop Frye suggests that apocalyptic language of all centuries is both obscure and revelatory: 'Apocalypse means revelation, and when art becomes apocalyptic it reveals. But it reveals only on its own terms and in its own forms' (*Anatomy of Criticism*, 125). Some of Hopkins's reticence may be attributed to his distrust of his own sinning heart; he frequently urged himself to clean his own house before he attempted to save his compatriots.

44 G. S. Kirk and J. E. Raven, *The PreSocratic Philosophers: A Critical History, with a Selection of Texts,* 184, and 195, n. 1.

45 *Ibid.,* 215.

46 St John also used the archetypal elements, fire and water, as part of his master plan for world extinction, and it was part of the machinery of apocalyptic prophets in both Old and New Testaments.

47 I think that Hopkins is alluding not only to the metaphoric trumpet crash

of Christ's resurrection, but to the various angelic trumpet crashes that were to precede the various plagues, wars, pestilences, signalling the coming of judgment day.

48 Hopkins described the 'tertianship' to Dixon as 'the third year of noviceship we make before taking our last vows' (*CD*, 52, 1881).

49 Elisabeth Schneider, '*The Wreck of the Deutschland*: a New Reading', *PMLA*, lxxxi, 1 (March 1966), 117, 116.

50 *Ibid.*, 113.

51 *Ibid.*

52 Edwin Honig, *Dark Conceit: The Making of Allegory* (New York, 1966), 107.

53 See Alexander Gilchrist, *The Life of William Blake*, 362, for a similar report of Blake's 'hysterical rapture'.

54 Schneider, 122, 120.

55 F. Crawford Burkitt, *Jewish and Christian Apocalypses: The Schweich Lectures*, 46–7.

56 Frye, *Anatomy of Criticism*, 125, 141, 145. I am by no means the first Hopkins scholar to suggest that *The Wreck of the Deutschland* contains a good deal of the matter of the Apocalypse; see, for example, John E. Keating, ' "*The Wreck of the Deutschland*": An Essay and Commentary', *Kent State University Bulletin*, vol. li, no. 1; John Wain, 'Gerard Manley Hopkins: An Idiom of Desperation', *Proceedings of the British Academy* (London, 1959), xlv, 173–97; and Sister Mary Adorita Hart, *The Christocentric Theme in Gerard Manley Hopkins' 'The Wreck of the Deutschland'*. I believe I am the first student of Hopkins to suggest that his ode is consciously based upon Revelation from beginning to end.

57 Frye, *Anatomy of Criticism*, 316, 217.

58 See the reports from *The Times* and the *Illustrated London News* in *FL*, 439ff, 442ff.

59 Turner's 'Slave Ship' now hangs in the Museum of Fine Arts, Boston, Mass.

60 Rev. i.12–15.

61 Rev. iii.19.

62 See Hopkins's meditations on Christ's role in the Apocalypse as 'the lamb of God, the victims', in *S*, 177, 1881.

63 See, for example, stanza 12, where Hopkins gets down to the burden of the narrative; although he reports matters in an almost journalistic style ('On Saturday sailed from Bremen,/American-outward bound') he then proceeds to use numerical facts, such as the number of souls on board, as part of a mythological symbolism, in imitation of the apocalyptic numerology.

64 Rev. vii.1–8; xix.1.

65 Austin Farrer, *A Rebirth of Images: The Making of St. John's Apocalypse*, 299.

66 Stanzas 28, 34, 35; Frye, *Anatomy of Criticism*, 217.
67 Rev. iii.11; xxii.7, 12, 20. Again I find I have an ally in Sister Mary
Adorita Hart, who sees the nun's cry, 'O Christ, come quickly', as a
yearning for the second coming as prophesied in Rev. xxii.12–21: 'This
call finds an echo and an answer in the Apocalypse' (*The Christocentric
Theme*, 127 and *passim*).
68 Rev. xii.1–5.
69 See, for example, *S*, 170–1; 177; 198–200.
70 Notes to stanza 30 in *Poems*, 262. See also Hopkins's dedicatory statement
under the title of this poem.
71 Rev. ii.17.
72 Rev. xix.12–13.
73 Rev. xxi.2.
74 Stanzas 1–10 (Part The First); Rev. i-iii.
75 Stanzas 11–35 (Part The Second); Rev. iv-xxii.
76 Rev. i.17.
77 Rev. i.17–18.
78 This stanza is an interesting example of Hopkins's elliptical techniques.
The coming of the railways to England brought as many horrors as
improvements, if one were to believe Carlyle or Ruskin. But the 'flange
and the rail' signify contemporary horrors, while the rest of the stanza
enumerates apocalyptic commonplaces about death and decay.
79 This catalogue occurs in several pre-Apocalyptic prophets, such as
Isaiah and Ezekiel.
80 See also Rev. xix.6.

Appendix B   Brief History of the Tractarian Wars

1 There are scholars, James F. White and David Newsome among them,
who believe that England at large, and especially Cambridge University,
came to be centres almost as important for the Oxford movement as
Oxford itself. Newsome remarks for example that 'the greatest deficiency
in Tractarian historiography has been the tendency to concentrate upon
the figures of Newman, Pusey, Keble and Froude, and to suppose that the
Oxford Movement can be fully understood by studying only the most
notable of its pioneers and leaders' (Newsome, *The Wilberforces and
Henry Manning*, 372–3). The claims of these scholars are just; but the
popular terms, 'The Oxford Movement' (more often 'Oxford movement'),
'The Oxford Tracts', 'The Tracts for the Times', etc., do suggest how
largely the Oxonian 'figures of Newman, Pusey, Keble and Froude . . .
the most notable' of the Oxford movement's 'pioneers and leaders'
loomed in the public's imagination. It may have been an Oxonian stereo-
type that lured pious young Tractarians like Hopkins and Digby Dolben

to Oxford, rather than to Cambridge. But Oxford, rather than Cambridge, is where they went, and so for our purposes, it is Oxford, rather than Cambridge, that should interest us particularly.

2 In the eighteen-seventies, priests were occasionally tried for 'ritualism', a mid- and late-nineteenth-century sobriquet for 'Tractarianism', and there was at least one prison sentence for an intransigent 'ritualist' priest. But the constant scrutiny priests had to endure as to the degree of their ritualism, and even the savagery of a prison sentence for genuflecting too many times in the wrong direction, or wearing a cassock, indicate how thoroughly routed the Tractarians were by then, and how frightened the English public had become by what they considered dangerous ultramontane excesses.

Selected Bibliography

Abbott, Evelyn, & Campbell, Lewis, *The Life and Letters of Benjamin Jowett, M. A.* 2 vols, London: John Murray, 1897.

Alden, Edmund, *Alden's Oxford Guide.* 7th ed., Oxford: E. C. Alden, 1881.

Alumni Oxoniensis: The Members of the University of Oxford, 1715–1886, their Parentage, Birthplace, and Year of Birth, with a Record of their Degrees: being the Matriculation Register of the University, Alphabetically Arranged, Revised and Annotated (ed. Joseph Foster). London: Oxford University Press, 1888.

Annan, Noel, *Leslie Stephen: His Thought and Character in Relation to his Time.* Cambridge, Mass.: Harvard University Press, 1952.

Arnold, Matthew, *Essays in Criticism,* First Series. New York: Macmillan, 1883.

> 'An Eton Boy', *Essays in Criticism,* Third Series, with an introduction by Edward J. O'Brien. Boston: Ball Publishing Co., 1910.
>
> *A French Eton: or Middle Class Education and the State.* London: Macmillan, 1864.
>
> *Letters of Matthew Arnold,* collected and arranged by George E. Russell. 2 vols, New York: Macmillan, 1895.
>
> 'Literature and Science', *Discourses in America.* London: Macmillan, 1885.
>
> 'A Speech at Eton', *Irish Essays and Others.* London: Smith & Elder, 1882.
>
> 'The Study of Celtic Literature', part iv, *Cornhill Magazine,* xiv (July 1866).

Arnold, Thomas, *Christian Life, Its Hopes, Its Fears and Its Close: Sermons Preached Mostly in the Chapel at Rugby School, 1841–1842.* New ed. in 6 vols, revised by his daughter, Mrs William E. Forster, London: Longmans, Green, 1878.

August, Eugene R., 'The Growth of "The Windhover"', *PMLA*, lxxxii, 5 (October 1967), 465–8.

'Hopkins' Dangerous Fire', *Victorian Poetry*, i, i (January 1963), 72–4.

Bagehot, Walter, *The Works of Walter Bagehot*, with the Memoir by R. H. Hutton, ed. Forrest Morgan, vol. i. Hartford, Conn.: Travelers Insurance Co., 1891.

Baker, Joseph, *The Reinterpretation of Victorian Literature*, ed. Joseph Baker for the Victorian Group of the Modern Language Association of America. New York: Russell & Russell, 1962.

Baker, Joseph Ellis, 'The Novel and the Oxford Movement', *Princeton University Studies in English*, no. 8: Princeton University Press, 1932.

Balleine, G. R., *A History of the Evangelical Party and the Church of England*. London: Longmans, Green, 1908.

Benson, Arthur C., *Walter Pater*, English Men of Letters series. New York: Macmillan, 1906.

Blake, Robert, *Disraeli*. 3rd printing, New York: St Martin's Press, 1967.

Blake, William, *The Prophetic Writings of William Blake*. 2 vols, ed. with a general index, glossarial index of symbols, commentary and appendixes, by D. J. Sloss and J. P. R. Wallis. Oxford: Clarendon Press, 1926.

Bradley, George Granville, D.D., *Recollections of Arthur Penrhyn Stanley*. New York: Scribner, 1883.

Briggs, Asa, *Victorian Cities*. London: Odhams, 1963.

Victorian People: A Reassessment of Persons and Themes. 2nd ed.: University of Chicago Press, 1955.

Brilioth, The Rev. Yngve, *Studies in the Oxford Movement*. London: Longmans, Green, 1933.

Brookfield, Frances M. (Mrs Charles), *The Cambridge 'Apostles'*. London: Pitman, 1906.

Buchan, John, *Pilgrim's Way*. Cambridge, Mass.: Houghton Mifflin, 1940.

University of Oxford College Histories: Brasenose College. London: F. E. Robinson, 1898.

Buckley, Jerome Hamilton, *The Triumph of Time: A Study of the Victorian Concepts of Time, History, Progress, and Decadence*. Cambridge, Mass.: Harvard University Press, 1966.

The Victorian Temper: A Study in Literary Culture. Cambridge, Mass.: Harvard University Press, 1951.

Burke, Edmund, *Reflections on the Revolution in France and Other Essays*, with an introduction by A. J. Grieve. London: J. M. Dent (Everyman's Library), 1910.

Burkitt, F[rancis] Crawford, *Jewish and Christian Apocalypses: The Schweich Lectures*. London: Humphrey Milford, 1914.

Carlyle, Thomas, 'Characteristics', *Critical and Miscellaneous Essays*, iii. Boston: Houghton Mifflin, n.d. [19??].

Latter-Day Pamphlets, in *The Works of Thomas Carlyle*, xx, Centenary Edition. New York: Scribner, n.d. [1898–1901?].
On Heroes, Hero-Worship and the Heroic in History. New York: A. L. Burt, n.d.
Past and Present. London: Chapman Hall, n.d. [18??].
'Shooting Niagara: and After?' *Macmillan's Magazine*, xvi (August 1867), 318–36.
Case, Shirley Jackson, *The Revelation of St. John: A Historical Interpretation*. University of Chicago Press, 1920.
Castiglione, Count Baldesar, *The Book of the Courtier*, translated from the Italian by Leonard Eckstein Opdyke. New York: Scribner, 1903.
Church, R. W., *The Oxford Movement: Twelve Years, 1833–1845*. London: Macmillan, 1922.
Clark, G. Kitson, *The Making of Victorian England*. Cambridge, Mass.: Harvard University Press, 1962.
Clark, Kenneth, *Ruskin Today*. New York: Holt, Rinehart & Winston, 1964.
Clarke, Charles P. S., *The Oxford Movement and After*. London: Mowbray, 1932.
Coleridge, Samuel Taylor, *A Lay Sermon Addressed to the Higher and Middle Classes on the Existing Distresses and Discontents, 1817*, vol. vi in *The Complete Works of Samuel Taylor Coleridge*, ed. W. G. T. Shedd. New York: Harper, 1856.
Collingwood, W. G., *The Life of John Ruskin*. Boston: Houghton Mifflin, 1902.
Cruse, Amy, *The Englishman and His Books in the Early Nineteenth Century*. London: Harrap, 1930.
The Victorians and Their Reading. Boston: Houghton Mifflin, 1935.
Culler, A. Dwight, *The Imperial Intellect: A Study of Newman's Educational Ideal*. New Haven, Conn.: Yale University Press, 1955.
Davis, H. W. C., *Oxford University College Histories: Balliol College*. London: F. E. Robinson, 1899.
Decker, Clarence Raymond, *The Victorian Conscience*. New York: Twayne, 1952.
Dilligan, Robert J., & Bender, Todd K., *A Concordance to the English Poetry of Gerard Manley Hopkins*. Madison, Wisconsin: University of Wisconsin Press, 1969.
Disraeli, Benjamin, the Earl of Beaconsfield, *Sybil, or The Two Nations*. London: Oxford University Press (World's Classics), 1950.
Dixon, Richard Watson, '*The Close of the Tenth Century of the Christian Era*', The Arnold Prize Essay for 1858. Oxford: Shrimpton, 1858.
Dolben, Digby, *The Poems of Digby Mackworth Dolben*, ed. with memoir by Robert Bridges. London: Oxford University Press, 1911.
Donaldson, Augustus B., *Five Great Oxford Leaders: Keble, Newman, Pusey, Liddon and Church*. 2nd ed., London: Rivington, 1900.

Downes, David Anthony, *Gerard Manley Hopkins: A Study of his Ignatian Spirit*. New York: Twayne, 1959.
   Victorian Portraits: Hopkins and Pater. New York: Bookman, 1965.
Drinkwater, John, *The Eighteen-Sixties: Essays by Fellows of the Royal Society of Literature*. Cambridge University Press, 1932.
Eliot, George, *The George Eliot Letters*, edited by Gordon Haight. 7 vols, New Haven: Yale University Press, 1955.
'The Ethics of Friendship', *Cornhill Magazine*, x (September 1864).
Faber, Sir Geoffrey, *Jowett, a Portrait with Background*. London: Faber, 1957.
   Oxford Apostles: A Character Study of the Oxford Movement. 2nd ed., London: Faber, 1933.
Fairwhether, Eugene R., *The Oxford Movement*. London: Oxford University Press, 1964.
Farrer, Austin, *The Rebirth of Images: The Making of St. John's Apocalypse*. Boston: Beacon Press, 1963.
Feiling, Sir Keith, *In Christ Church Hall*. London: Macmillan, 1960.
Finberg, Alexander, *The Life of J. M. W. Turner*. 2nd rev. ed., London: Oxford University Press, 1961.
Froude, James Anthony, *Thomas Carlyle: A History of the First Forty Years of his Life: 1795–1835*. 2 vols in one, New York: J. S. Ogilvie, n.d. [18??].
Frye, Northrop, *Anatomy of Criticism*. Princeton University Press, 1957.
   Fearful Symmetry: A Study of William Blake, with a new preface by the author. Boston: Beacon Press, 1947.
Frye, Northrop, ed., *Romanticism Reconsidered, Selected Papers from the English Institute*. New York: Columbia University Press, 1963.
Gardner, W. H., *Gerard Manley Hopkins (1844–1889): A Study of Poetic Idiosyncrasy in Relation to Poetic Tradition*. vol. I, London: Secker and Warburg, 1948; vol. II, New Haven, Conn.: Yale University Press, 1949.
Geldart, Edmund Martin, see Tradleg, Nitram, below.
Gerard Manley Hopkins by the Kenyon Critics. Norfolk, Conn.: New Directions Books, 1945.
The Germ: Thoughts Toward Nature in Poetry and Art. London: Aylott & Jones, 1850.
Gilchrist, Alexander, *The Life of William Blake*, with an introduction by W. Graham Robertson. London: John Lane (Bodley Head Edition), 1907.
Goodier, Alban, S. J., *The Jesuits*. New York: Macmillan, 1930.
Gosse, Edmund, *Father and Son, a Study of Two Temperaments*. 8th ed., New York: Scribner, 1918.
   The Life of Algernon Charles Swinburne. New York: Macmillan, 1917.
Gottfried, Leon, *Matthew Arnold and the Romantics*. Lincoln, Nebraska: University of Nebraska Press, 1963.
Halévy, Elie, *Victorian Years (1841–1895)*, vol. IV of Halévy's *History of*

233

the English People in the Nineteenth Century, transl. from the French by E. I. Watkins, with supplementary section by R. B. McCallum. New York: Barnes and Noble, 1961.

Hammond, J. L. & Barbara, *The Age of the Chartists: 1832–1854*. Hamden, Conn.: Archon, 1962.

Harrison, Frederic, *John Ruskin*, English Men of Letters series. New York: Macmillan, 1902.

Hart, Sister Mary Adorita, *The Christocentric Theme in Gerard Manley Hopkins' 'The Wreck of the Deutschland'*. Washington: Catholic University, 1952 (microfilm).

Hartman, Geoffrey H., *Hopkins: A Collection of Critical Essays* (Twentieth Century Views). Englewood Cliffs, N.J.: Prentice Hall, 1966.

Henson, Herbert Hensley, *A Memoir of the Right Honourable Sir William Anson*. Oxford: Clarendon Press, 1920.

Heuser, Alan, *The Shaping Vision of Gerard Manley Hopkins*. London: Oxford University Press, 1958.

Hobson, J. H., *John Ruskin, Social Reformer*. Boston: Dana Estes, 1898.

Holloway, John, *The Victorian Sage: Studies in Argument*. London: Macmillan, 1953.

Honig, Edwin, *Dark Conceit: The Making of Allegory*. New York: Oxford University Press, 1966.

Hopkins, Gerard Manley, *Poems of Gerard Manley Hopkins*, with preface and notes by Robert Bridges, ed. with additional poems, notes, and a biographical introduction by W. H. Gardner. 3rd ed., London: Oxford University Press, 1952.

Poems of Gerard Manley Hopkins, ed. with additional notes, a foreword on the revised text, and a new biographical and critical introduction by W. H. Gardner and N. H. MacKenzie. 4th ed., London: Oxford University Press, 1967.

The Letters of Gerard Manley Hopkins to Robert Bridges, ed. with notes and an introduction by Claude Colleer Abbott. London: Oxford University Press, 1955.

The Correspondence of Gerard Manley Hopkins and Richard Watson Dixon, ed. with notes and an introduction by Claude Colleer Abbott. London: Oxford University Press, 1955.

Further Letters of Gerard Manley Hopkins, including his Correspondence with Coventry Patmore, ed. with notes and an introduction by Claude Colleer Abott. 2nd ed., London: Oxford University Press, 1956.

The Journals and Papers of Gerard Manley Hopkins, ed. by Humphry House and completed by Graham Storey. London: Oxford University Press, 1959.

The Sermons and Devotional Writings of Gerard Manley Hopkins, ed. by Christopher Devlin, S.J. London: Oxford University Press, 1959.

Houghton, Walter, *The Victorian Frame of Mind: 1830–1870*. New Haven, Conn.: Yale University Press, 1957.

Hughes, Thomas, *Tom Brown at Oxford*, illustrated by S. P. Hall. New York: Macmillan, 1889.

[Hughes, Thomas], *Tom Brown's School Days*. Cambridge: Macmillan, 1857.

Hutton, Richard H., *Cardinal Newman*. 2nd ed., London: Methuen, 1891.

Huxley, Thomas Henry, *Evolution and Ethics and Other Essays*. New York: Appleton, 1896.

　　Life and Letters by His Son, Leonard Huxley, 2 vols, New York: Appleton, 1900.

Ideas and Beliefs of the Victorians: An Historic Revaluation of the Victorian Age, with a foreword by Harman Grisewood. New York: Dutton, 1966.

Irvine, George, *Apes, Angels and Victorians: The Story of Darwin, Huxley, and Evolution*. New York: McGraw Hill, 1955.

Johnson, E. D. H., *The Alien Vision of Victorian Poetry: Sources in the Poetic Imagination in Tennyson, Browning, and Arnold*. Princeton University Press, 1952.

Johnson, Wendell Stacy, *Gerard Manley Hopkins: The Poet as Victorian*. Ithaca, N.Y.: Cornell University Press, 1968.

Johnston, J. O., *Life and Letters of Henry Parry Liddon*. 2nd impr., London: Longmans, Green, 1904.

Jowett, Benjamin, *Pusey and Others v. Jowett: The Argument and Decisions as to the Jurisdiction of the Chancellor's Court at Oxford*. Oxford, 1893.

Jowett, Benjamin, *The Works of Plato*, transl. in English with analyses and introductions. 4 vols in one, New York: Tudor, n.d. [19??].

Keating, John E., '*The Wreck of the Deutschland:* An Essay and Commentary', *Kent State University Bulletin*, vol. li, no. 1, Kent, Ohio, 1963.

Kennedy, James M., *Henry Drummond: An Anthology*, with an introduction by Samuel Shoemaker. New York: Harper, 1953.

Keynes, John Maynard, *Memorial Essay on Alfred Marshall, Essays* in Biography. New York: Harcourt Brace, 1933.

Kersting, A. J., *Portrait of Oxford; a Selection of Photographs with Text by Edmund Vale*. London: Batsford, 1956.

Kingsley, Charles, *Hypatia: Or New Foes With Old Faces*. 13th ed., New York: Macmillan, 1885.

　　Sanitary and Social Lectures and Essays. London : Macmillan, 1902.

　　Scientific Lectures and Essays. London: Macmillan, 1885.

　　Yeast: A Problem. 4th ed., New York: Macmillan, 1893.

Kirk, G. S., & Raven, J. E., *The PreSocratic Philosophers: A Critical History, with a Selection of Texts*. Cambridge University Press, 1964.

Knickerbocker, William S., *Creative Oxford: Its Influence in Victorian Literature*. Syracuse, N.Y.: Syracuse University Press, 1925.

　　'Matthew Arnold at Oxford: The Natural History of a Father and Son', *Sewanee Review*, xxxv (1927), 399–418.

Kunitz, Stanley, & Haycroft, Howard, eds, *British Authors of the Nine-teenth Century*. New York: H. W. Wilson, 1936.

Lahey, G. F., S.J., *Gerard Manley Hopkins*. London: Oxford University Press, 1930.

Laver, James, *Manners and Morals in the Age of Optimism, 1848–1914*. New York: Harper and Row, 1966.

Lawrence, David Herbert, *Apocalypse*. New York: Viking Press, 1932.

Leavis, F. R., *New Bearings in English Poetry*. London: Chatto and Windus, 1932.

'Lectures Delivered Before the University of Oxford by Matthew Arnold, M.A., Professor of Poetry', *Westminster Review*, New Series, xxiv, art. vii, 4 (July, October 1863).

Levine, George, *The Emergence of the Victorian Consciousness: The Spirit of the Age*. New York: Free Press, 1967.

Liddon, Henry Parry, *Advent in St. Pauls: Sermons Bearing Chiefly on the Two Comings of Our Lord*. London: Longmans, Green, 1892.

> *Sermons on Old Testament Subjects*. 3rd ed., London: Longmans, Green, 1893.

> (Liddon, Henry Parry), *Henry Parry Liddon, A Centenary Memoir*, by various authors. London: Mowbray, 1929.

Loyola, St Ignatius, *Manresa: Or the Spiritual Exercises of St. Ignatius Loyola, for General Use*. Rome, New York: Frederick Pustet, n.d.

> *The Spiritual Exercises of St. Ignatius Loyola*, transl. by Thomas Corbishley, S.J. New York: P. J. Kenedy, 1963.

> *The Spiritual Exercises of St. Ignatius Loyola*, in Spanish and English, with a continuous commentary by Joseph Rickaby. London: Burns & Oates, 1915.

Mack, Edward Clarence, *Public Schools and British Opinion, 1780–1860: The Relationship Between Contemporary Ideas and the Evolution of an English Institution*. New York: Columbia University Press, 1939.

MacKail, J. W., *The Life of William Morris*. 2 vols, 2nd impr., London: Longmans, Green, 1922.

Massé, Henri Jean Louis Joseph, *Oxford*. New York: Scribner, 1906.

McChesney, Donald, *A Hopkins Commentary: An Explanatory Commentary on the Main Poems: 1876–1889*. New York University Press, 1968.

Meynell, Esther, *Portrait of William Morris*. London: Chapman & Hall, 1947.

Miller, Joseph Hillis. *The Disappearance of God: Five Nineteenth-Century Writers: Thomas De Quincey, Robert Browning, Emily Brontë, Matthew Arnold, Gerard Manley Hopkins*. Cambridge, Mass.: Harvard University Press, 1963.

Monypenny, William F., & Buckle, George E., *The Life of Benjamin Disraeli, Earl of Beaconsfield*. 6 vols, New York: Macmillan, 1912–20.

Moore, James J., *The Historical Handbook and Guide to Oxford*. Oxford: Shrimpton, 1897.

Morley, John, *On Compromise*. London: Macmillan, 1891.

Morrah, Herbert Arthur, *The Oxford Union: 1823–1923*. London: Cassell, 1923.

Morris, William, *Chants for Socialists*. London: Socialist League Office, 1855.
A Dream of John Ball, XVI, *The Collected Works of William Morris*, with introductions by his daughter, May Morris, 1910–15.
The Hollow Land: A Tale, I, *Collected Works*.
News from Nowhere, or an Epoch of Rest: Being Some Chapters of a Utopian Romance, XVI, *Collected Works*.
Signs of a Change, XXIII, *Collected Works*.

Müller, [Friedrich] Max, *My Autobiography: A Fragment*. New York: Scribner, 1901.

Nettleship, Richard L., *Memoir of Thomas Hill Green*. London: Longmans, Green, 1906.

Newman, John Henry Cardinal, *Apologia pro Vita Sua*. New York: Random House, 1950.
Catholic Sermons of Cardinal Newman, edited at the Birmingham Oratory. London: Burns & Oates, 1957.
The Idea of a University Defined and Illustrated: Nine Lectures Delivered to the Catholics of Dublin, edited with an introduction by Martin J. Svaglic. 3rd printing, New York: Holt, Rinehart & Winston, 1962.
Loss and Gain: The Story of a Convert. 6th ed., London: Burns & Oates, 1874.
Sermons Preached on Various Occasions. New ed., London: Longmans, Green, 1898.

Newsome, David, *The Wilberforces and Henry Manning: The Parting of Friends*. Cambridge, Mass.: Harvard University (Belknap Press), 1966.

O'Faolain, Sean, *Newman's Way*. New York: Devin-Adair, 1952.

Oxford and Cambridge Matriculations: 1544–1906, ed. by J. A. Venn. Cambridge, England: Heffer, 1908.

Paget, Stephen, *Henry Scott Holland: Memoirs and Letters*. London: John Murray, 1921.

Parkin, George R., *The Life, Diary and Letters of Edward Thring*. London: Macmillan, 1900.

Pater, Walter, *Miscellaneous Studies*. New York: Macmillan, 1900.

Pattison, Mark, *Memoirs*. London: Macmillan, 1885.

Pearson, Hesketh, *Disraeli: His Life and Personality*. New York: Grosset & Dunlap, University Library, 1951.

Pick, John, *Gerard Manley Hopkins: 'The Windhover'*. Columbus, Ohio: Merrill, 1969.
Gerard Manley Hopkins: 'The Windhover' (Charles E. Merrill Literary

Casebook Series). Edward P. J. Corbett, general ed. Columbus, Ohio: Merrill, 1969.

The Pictorial and Historical Gossiping Guide to Oxford. Oxford: Shrimpton, 1875.

Pope-Hennessey, Una. *Canon Charles Kingsley.* London: Chatto & Windus, 1948.

Porter, Noah, *The Educational Systems of the Puritans and the Jesuits Compared.* New York: M. W. Dodd, 1851.

Pusey, Edward Bouverie, *Nine Sermons Preached Before the University at Oxford and Printed Chiefly Between A.D. 1843–1855* (half-title: *University Sermons*). Oxford, England: John Henry and James Parker, 1866; repr. Rivington, London, 1879.

[Richardson, Coke], 'The Ethics of Friendship', *Cornhill Magazine* x (Sept. 1864). (Authorship given in *Wellesley Index to Victorian Periodicals* I, 1966.)

Ritz, Jean-Georges, *Robert Bridges and Gerard Manley Hopkins, a Literary Friendship.* London: Oxford University Press, 1960.

Romanes, George ('Physicus'), *A Candid Examination of Theism.* 3rd ed., London: Kegan Paul, Trench, Trübner, 1892.

Rosenberg, John D., *The Darkening Glass: A Portrait of Ruskin's Genius.* New York: Columbia University Press, 1961.

Roston, Murray, *Prophet and Poet: The Bible and the Growth of Romanticism.* Evanston, Illinois: Northwestern University Press, 1965.

Rothenstein, Will, *Oxford Characters: Twenty-four Lithographs.* London: R. H. Russell, 1896.

Ruskin, John, *The Works of John Ruskin,* ed. E. T. Cook and Alexander Wedderburn. 39 vols, library ed., London: George Allen, 1903–12.
    The Diaries of John Ruskin, ed. Joan Evans and J. H. Whitehouse. 3 vols, London: Oxford University Press, 1956–9.

Rutherford, Mark, see White, William Hale.

Saintsbury, George, *Corrected Impressions: Essays on Victorian Writers.* 2nd ed., London: Heinemann, 1895.

Sambrook, James, *A Poet Hidden: The Life of Richard Watson Dixon, 1833–1900.* London: Athlone Press, 1962.

Sanford, E. G., *Memoirs of Archbishop Temple, by Seven Friends.* London: Macmillan, 1906.

Schneider, Elisabeth, 'The Wreck of the *Deutschland:* A New Reading', *PMLA,* lxxxi, 1 (March 1966), 110–22.
    The Dragon at the Gate: Studies in the Poetry of Gerard Manley Hopkins. Berkeley: University of California Press, 1968.

Scott, E. F., *The Book of Revelation.* New York: Scribner, 1940.

Scudder, Vida, *An Introduction to the Writings of John Ruskin.* Boston: Leach, Shewell & Sanborn, 1890.

Simpson, William John Sparrow, *The Contribution of Cambridge to the*

Anglo-Catholic Revival, Oxford Movement Centenary Series. London: SPCK, 1933.

Smith, Goldwin, *A Plea for the Abolition of Tests in the University of Oxford*. Oxford: Wheeler & Day, 1864.

Spielman, M. H., *John Ruskin: A Sketch of His Work, His Opinions, with Personal Reminiscences*. Philadelphia: Lippincott, 1900.

Stanley, Arthur Penrhyn, *The Life and Correspondence of Thomas Arnold, D.D., Late Headmaster of Rugby School and Regius Professor of Modern History*. 3rd ed., 2 vols, London: Fellowes, 1844.

Staunton, Howard, *The Great Schools of England: An Account of the Foundations, Endowments, and Discipline of the Chief Seminaries of Learning in England, including Eton, Winchester, Westminster, St. Paul's, Charter-House, Merchant Taylor's, Harrow, Rugby, Shrewsbury, Etc., Etc.* London: Samson Low, Son, & Marston, 1865.

Stephen, Leslie, *Studies of a Biographer*. 4 vols, London: Duckworth, 1899–1902.

Templeman, William D., 'Ruskin's Ploughshare and Hopkins' "Windhover"', *English Studies*, xliii (April 1962), 103–6.

Tennyson, Alfred Lord, *The Poems of Tennyson*, ed. Christopher Ricks. London: Longman, 1969.

Tennyson, Hallam, *Alfred Lord Tennyson: A Memoir by his Son*. 2 vols, New York: Macmillan, 1899.

Thompson, E. P., *The Making of the English Working Class*. New York: Random House, 1964.

Thompson, The Rev. Henry L., *Christ Church: University of Oxford College Histories*, London: F. E. Robinson, 1900.
Henry George Liddell, D.D., Dean of Christ Church: A Memoir. London: John Murray, 1899.

Thorp, Margaret Farrand, *Charles Kingsley: 1819–1875*. Princeton University Press, 1937.

Thureau-Dangin, Paul, *The English Catholic Revival in the Nineteenth Century*. 2 vols, rev. and re-ed. from trans. by the late Wilfred Wilberforce. London: Simpkin, Marshall, Hamilton, Kent, 1914.

Tradleg, Nitram[Geldart, Edmund Martin], *A Son of Belial: Autobiographical Sketches*. London: Trübner, 1882 (Columbia University microfilm).

Trilling, Lionel, *Matthew Arnold*. New York: Norton, 1939.

Tuckwell, The Rev. W., *Reminiscences of Oxford*. London: Cassell, 1900.

Valency, Maurice, *In Praise of Love: An Introduction to the Love Poetry o, the Renaissance*. New York: Macmillan, 1958.

Van Dyke, Paul, *Ignatius Loyola, The Founder of the Jesuits*. New York: Scribner, 1927.

Wain, John, 'Gerard Manley Hopkins: An Idiom of Desperation', *Proceedings of the British Academy*, xlv (1959), 173–97 (Chatterton Lecture on an English Poet).

Ward, Mrs Humphrey, *A Writer's Recollections,* vol. i. New York: Harper, 1918.

    Robert Elsmere. London: Smith & Elder, 1905.

Ward, Wilfred, *The Life of John Henry Cardinal Newman, Based on his Private Life and Correspondence.* 2 vols, London: Longmans, Green, 1912.

Weinberg, Ian, *The English Public Schools: The Sociology of Elite Education.* New York: Atherton Press, 1967.

Wells, J., *Oxford and Its Colleges.* London: Methuen, 1899.

Weyand, Norman, S.J., *Immortal Diamond: Studies in Gerard Manley Hopkins,* with the assistance of Raymond V. Schoder, S.J. and an introduction by John Pick. New York: Sheed and Ward, 1949.

White, James F., *The Cambridge Movement: The Ecclesiologists and the Gothic Revival.* Cambridge University Press, 1962.

White, William Hale (Mark Rutherford), *Mark Rutherford's Deliverance,* edited by his Friend, Reuben Shapcott. 7th ed., London: Fisher and Unwin, n.d. [1904?].

Wilberforce, William, *A Practical View of Christianity: The Prevailing Religious System of Professed Christians in the Higher and Middle Classes in this Country, contrasted with Real Christianity.* Boston: Crocker & Brewster, 1829.

Wilkinson, Rupert, *Gentlemanly Power: British Leadership and the Public School Tradition; a Comparative Study in the Making of Rulers.* London: Oxford University Press, 1964.

Willey, Basil, *More Nineteenth-Century Studies: A Group of Honest Doubters.* New York: Columbia University Press, 1956.

    Nineteenth-Century Studies: Coleridge to Matthew Arnold. New York: Columbia University Press, 1949.

Wingfield-Stratford, Esmé, *Those Earnest Victorians.* New York: Morrow, 1930.

    The Victorian Tragedy. London: Routledge, 1930.

Wise, Thomas James, *The Brontës, Their Lives, Friendships and Correspondence.* 4 vols (The Shakespeare Head Brontë, Thomas James Wise and John Alexander Symington, eds.) Oxford: Shakespeare Head Press, 1933.

Wordsworth, William, *The Life of William Wordsworth,* vol. ii (vol. x in *Works of Wordsworth*), ed. by William Knight. Edinburgh: William Paterson, 1889.

Wright, Thomas, *The Life of Walter Pater.* 2 vols, London: Everett, 1907.

Young, George Malcolm, *Daylight and Champaign.* London: Cape, 1937.

    Victorian England, Portrait of an Age. Garden City, New York: Doubleday, 1954.

Index

Abbott, Claude Colleer, 116–17, 157
Addis, William, 18, 38, 40, 198, 220
Anglican Church, 10, 12, 17, 18, 19, 55, 56, 131
Annan, Noel, 23, 24, 163, 224
Apocalypse (Revelation) of St John of Patmos, 158, 159, 161, 164, 170–1, 223–4, 225, 226, 227, 228
Apocalyptic mood, 1, 9, 156, 158–95, 224–5, 228
　and Tarpeian imagery (the acrophobic metaphor),174–8 226
　and *The Wreck of the Deutschland*, 175, 182–95
　see also Carlyle; Hopkins; Morris; Newman; Ruskin; Tennyson
Aristotle, 15, 71
Arnold, Matthew, 1, 2, 3, 30–4, 41, 42, 111, 119, 137, 138, 139, 144, 156, 169
　and ambivalence about art, 137
　and battle of the self, 2–3
　and hierarchy of virtues, 138, 145
　and middle class, 213–15
　and new Victorian gentleman, 117, 126
　and Oxonian missionary zeal, 25, 36
　and Oxonian sweetness and charm, 25, 26, 30
　as Professor of Poetry at Oxford, 30–4
　and sense of gentle fellowship, 21
　and spirit of the whole, 1, 30, 32, 117, 126, 132, 138
　and Victorian spirit of doubt, 6, 46, 47
　Essays in Criticism, First Series, 29
　see also Appendix A
Arnold, Dr Thomas, 1, 136
　and ambivalence about art, 148
　and doctrine of work, 2, 123

　and hierarchy of virtues, 138, 218
　and middle class, 130, 132, 140, 213–15
　and new Victorian gentleman, 2, 117, 127, 138–40
　and Oxonian missionary zeal, 21, 23, 24, 25
　and Oxonian sweetness and charm, 24, 25
　and spirit of the whole, 138–40
　and Victorian spirit of doubt, 6
Art
　laudatory function of, 31, 64, 71, 72, 78, 93–9, 105, 108, 111, 209
　legitimate obscurity in, 100–1, 107
　mimetic function of, 65, 71, 72, 91, 93–4, 97–101, 108, 114, 209
　and Victorian ambivalence about, 2–3, 101, 105
　and Victorian spirit of doubt, 3
　see also Arnold, Matthew; Arnold, Dr Thomas; Carlyle; Corinthian and Doric principles in art; Hopkins; Innocence of the eye; Praise, objects and tools of; Ruskin; Truth, ideal truth and material truth in art or nature
August, Eugene, 221

Bagehot, Walter, 135
Baillie, Alexander, 25, 28, 40, 59, 68–9, 99
Balliol, 9, 10, 11, 15, 17, 39, 101, 119, 154
　and Broad Church party, 11–12, 37–8
　and its oarsmen, 40
　and missionary zeal, 23, 32, 34, 35, 36, 40
　see also Appendixes

Battle of the self, *see* Victorian temper
Blake, William, 163, 185, 223
Bridges, Robert, 1, 3, 50, 51, 54, 100,
    101, 102–3n, 117, 123, 131, 137, 181,
    183–4, 212, 213
Broad Churchmen and Broad Church
    beliefs, 10, 11, 12, 13, 14, 56, 57
    see also Appendixes; Jowett
Brontë, Charlotte, 66
Brotherhood of the Holy Trinity, 57
Browning, Elizabeth Barrett, 3
Buckley, Jerome H., 138, 160
Bulwer-Lytton, Edward, 133

Cambridge Apostles, 135, 211, 218
Cambridge University, 22–4, 26, 123,
    131, 201, 213
Campion, Edmund, S.J., 181
Carlyle, Thomas, 2, 3, 4, 65, 130, 133,
    139, 143, 153, 172–3
    and apocalyptic mood, 161, 162, 163,
        166, 171, 178, 223, 225, 228
    and battle of the self, 2
    and doctrine of work, 2, 84, 154
    and hierarchy of virtues, 138, 141–2
    and middle class, 130, 213–15
    and new Victorian gentleman, 2, 127,
        140–1, 172–3
    and rape of England, 2
    and Victorian spirit of doubt, 6
Castiglione, Baldesar, 124, 135
Christ Church, 40, 55, 205
    and missionary zeal, 34
    and Tractarian party, 11, 17
    see also Appendixes
Clough, Arthur Hugh, 2, 21, 203
Colenso, Bishop John, 13–14, 16, 17, 18,
    130
    see also Appendix A
Coleridge, Samuel Taylor, 158, 163, 223
Colour, *see* Nature, colour and sacrament
    of energy in
Corinthian and Doric principles in art,
    98–9, 110
Cult of friendship, the *see* Oxonian
    sweetness and charm, Arnold, Matthew;
    Arnold, Dr Thomas; Jowett; Hopkins

Dante, Alighieri, 159, 185
Darwin, Charles, 12, 121, 129, 144, 161,
    166, 167, 197
    see also Appendix A
Devlin, Christopher, S.J., 152–3, 222
Dickens, Charles, 3, 136, 171, 212

Disraeli, Benjamin, 133, 137
    and middle class, 130, 213–15
    and new Victorian gentleman, 126, 212
Diversity in excellence, *see* Victorian
    temper, and spirit of the whole
Dixon, Richard Watson, 3, 4, 51, 58, 67,
    102, 104, 112, 113, 117, 128, 133,
    164–6, 212
Doctrine of work, 2, 34–6, 106, 112,
    122–3, 125
    see also Arnold, Thomas; Carlyle;
        Hopkins; Ruskin; Tennyson
Dolben, Digby Mackworth, 50–5, 144
    and Robert Bridges, 208
Drinkwater, John, 203
Dualism, 209–10
    see also Nature, antitheses in; Nature,
        great chain of paradoxes in

Eliot, George, 2, 65, 66, 67
Essays and Reviews, 13–14, 16
    see also Appendixes
'Ethics of Friendship, The', and Oxford
    sweetness and charm, 28–9

Faber, Geoffrey, *Jowett: A Portrait with
    Background*, 10
    this author's debt to Faber, 204 (notes
        4, 6, 13, 14)
Fortunate fall, paradox of, 90, 91, 94
    see also Rosenberg
Frye, Northrop, 226

Geldart, Edmund Martin, 34, 206
Generic plenitude, *see* Nature, generic
    plenitude in
Genesis, 72, 122
Gentleman, new Victorian, *see* Victorian
    temper
Gentleman prophets, 132, 135, 215–16,
    218, 219–21
    see also Arnold, Matthew; Arnold,
        Dr Thomas; Carlyle; Disraeli;
        Hopkins; Ruskin; Tennyson;
        Victorian temper, and new
        Victorian gentleman
Gladstone, William E., 215, 218
Green, Thomas Hill, 25, 36

Halévy, Elie, 163
Hallam, Arthur Henry, 46, 47, 123, 135,
    205, 218
'Handsome heart, The', *see* Hopkins
Hazlitt, William, 203, 204

Hierarchy of virtues, *see* Victorian temper
Holland, Henry Scott, 25, 37
  and Oxonian sweetness and charm, 27–8
Holloway, John, 212
Honig, Edwin, 186
Hopkins, Gerard Manley
  and ambivalence about art, 2, 101–4,
    108, 111, 133, 148–50, 212
  and battle of the self, 3
  and celebration of nature, 6, 9–63
    passim
  and hierarchy of virtues, 120, 144–5,
    151, 156, 217
  and Highgate School, 9, 12, 31, 37,
    140, 215
  and 'inscape' and 'instress', 31, 46,
    71, 78, 79, 80, 108
  and middle class, 118–19, 213–15
  and new Victorian gentleman, 115–17,
    120, 126, 137–8, 145–57
  and poetical style, 4–5
  and 'Ruskinese point of view', 64, 65,
    68, 74–6, 105
  and spirit of the whole, 31, 71, 111,
    113–14, 117
  works discussed or quoted at length:
    (Poem 9), 47; (Poem 12, 'To
    Oxford'), 48–50; (Poem 13), 52;
    (Poem 28, *The Wreck of the
    Deutschland*), 182–95; (Poem 31,
    'God's Grandeur'), 85; (Poem 35,
    'The Sea and the Skylark'), 85–6;
    (Poem 36, 'The Windhover'),
    107–14; (Poem 37, 'Pied Beauty'),
    105–7; (Poem 38, 'Hurrahing in
    Harvest'), 82–3; (Poem 47, 'The
    Handsome Heart'), 146–7; (Poem
    54, 'The Brothers'), 147–50;
    (Poem 57, 'As Kingfishers Catch
    Fire'), 96–7; (Poem 65), 177–8;
    (Poem 73, 'St. Alphonsus
    Rodriguez'), 154–6; (Poem 74,
    'Thou Art Indeed, Just, Lord'),
    151–4; (Poem 75, 'The Shepherd's
    Brow'), 172, 175; (Poem 127), 53;
    (Poem 157, 'On the Portrait of
    Two Beautiful Young People'),
    150–1; (Essay, 'On the Origin of
    Beauty'), 74–6; (Sermons), 95–6,
    151, 161, 181–2
  see also Appendix A
Houghton, Walter, 31, 116, 139, 217
Huxley, Thomas Henry, 13, 14
  see Appendix A

Ignatius Loyola and Ignatian, *see* St
  Ignatius Loyola
Ilbert, Courtney Peregrin, 37–8, 198
Innocence of the eye, 67, 69, 71, 72,
  75, 79, 105, 109
Isaiah, 110, 210

Jesuits, *see* Society of Jesus
Johnson, E. D. H., 213, 216–17
Johnson, Wendell Stacy, 203
Jowett, Benjamin, 15, 26, 34–5, 42, 56,
  66, 119, 130, 164, 206–7
  and ambivalence about art, 102, 103,
    137
  and Broad Church movement, 11–20
  and doctrine of work, 34–6, 123, 154
  and *Essays and Reviews*, 13, 14, 16
  and hierarchy of virtues, 138
  and middle class, 130, 132, 213–5
  and new Victorian gentleman, 119,
    125, 131, 132, 136–7
  and Oxonian missionary zeal, 23, 24,
    35–7, 206
  and Oxonian sweetness and charm,
    24–6, 34
  and Tractarian wars, 11, 37–8
  and Victorian temper, 10
  see also Appendixes; Balliol

Keats, John, 14, 26
Keble, John, 10, 43, 57
  see also Appendixes
Kingsley, Charles, 43, 137, 158, 168,
  174, 215

Laudatory art, *see* Art, laudatory
  function of
Laver, James, and new Victorian
  gentleman, 123
Levine, George, 203–4 (notes 1, 3, 4 to
  Introduction)
Levitical sacrifice, 186
Liddon, Henry Parry, 19, 20, 21, 37,
  55, 56, 58–60, 61, 220
  and ambivalence towards art, 103
  and Apocalypse, 162, 164
  and Oxford Union, 39
  and Oxonian missionary zeal, 23, 25
  and Oxonian sweetness and charm,
    25–6, 34, 58–60
  see also Appendixes
Lucifer, 110, 210–11

Manichean mood, 95, 153

Middle ages and Victorian temper, 124, 135, 153
Middle-class gentleman, s.e Victorian temper, and new Victorian gentleman
Miles, Josephine, 26
Mill, John Stuart, 14, 142, 144, 203, 204, 213
  and spirit of the age, 3–4
  On Liberty, 6, 12, 197
Miller, Joseph Hillis, 217
Milton, John, 31, 159, 197
Mimetic function of art, see Art, mimetic function of
Morality and sensibility, Victorian, 142, 221, 222
Morley, John, 136, 158, 166–7
Morris, William, 66, 67–8, 159, 166, 194, 223
Müller, Max, and Matthew Arnold as Poetry Professor at Oxford, 33–4

Nature, antitheses in, 75, 77, 90–5, 99, 106
  bounty in, 1, 9–63 passim
  colour and sacrament of energy in, 79, 86–90
  Corinthian and Doric principles in, 98–9
  danger of, to Christians, 103–4
  generic plenitude in, 72–3, 74, 78, 95, 105–6, 108
  great chain of paradoxes in, 65, 76, 77–8, 92, 93, 97–8, 101, 209–10
  infinite variety in, 65, 68, 69, 72, 74, 75, 105–6
  mystery in, 76, 106
  sacrament of energy in, 78, 80–5, 96, 105–7, 109
  specific creation in, 65, 72–3, 74, 78, 95, 105–6, 109
  violence in, 92
  'Vital Beauty' in, 81, 92, 108, 112, 209
Nettleship, Richard, 11
Newman, John Henry, Cardinal, 6, 10, 18, 26, 42, 54, 56, 57–8, 61, 133, 164
  and ambivalence about art, 148
  and apocalyptic mood, 226
  and hierarchy of virtues, 138, 142–3
  and middle class, 130, 214
  and new Victorian gentleman, 122, 126, 140–4
  and Oxonian missionary zeal, 23, 25, 34

  and Oxonian sweetness and charm, 25, 30, 34
  and spirit of the whole, 127, 142
  Apologia pro Vita Sua, 18, 133, 197
  see also Appendixes

Obscurity in art, see Art, legitimate obscurity in
Oxford movement, 9, 21, 25
  see also Tractarian beliefs; Tractarian wars; Appendixes
Oxford University, 6, 21, 29–30, 37–41, 45, 102, 123, 131, 154
  and missionary zeal, 23, 25, 205, 221
  and sense of gentle fellowship, 21, 25
  and the Union, 38–9, 74
  see also Appendixes; Arnold, Matthew; Arnold, Dr Thomas; Balliol; Christ Church; Hopkins; Jowett; Liddon; Newman; Pusey
Oxonian cult of friendship, see Oxonian sweetness and charm
Oxonian sweetness and charm, 24–30
  see also Arnold, Matthew; Hopkins; Jowett; Liddon

Paradoxes, see Fortunate fall, paradox of; Nature, great chain of paradoxes in; Rosenberg
Pater, Walter, 33, 42–6, 197–8
  and Victorian spirit of doubt, 46
Plato, 2, 15, 20, 72, 90, 125, 184
Platonic pairs of opposites, 65
Poverty and the lower classes, some Victorian attitudes about, 3, 117, 121, 129–30, 135, 139, 218
Praise, objects and tools of, 78, 79, 80, 93
Pre-Raphaelites, 9, 66, 71, 76, 136, 146, 147, 200
Pusey, Edward Bouverie, 10, 11, 13, 15, 18, 19, 20, 25, 37, 55, 56–8, 60, 206
  and ambivalence about art, 103
  and Apocalypse, 164
  and missionary zeal, 34
  see also Appendixes; Tractarian wars

Rape of England, the, 1, 2, 72, 169
  see also Carlyle; Hopkins; Ruskin
Renaissance, 124, 135, 153
Romanes, George, 167–8
Romanticism and Romantic movement, 5, 48, 124, 212–13
Rosenberg, John, 66, 90, 94

Rossetti, Dante Gabriel, 31
Rugby School, 138–40, 217
see also Arnold, Dr Thomas
Ruskin, John, 1, 3, 26, 41–2, 62–3
and ambivalence about art, 100–4, 111
and apocalyptic mood, 161, 166, 176–8, 223
and doctrine of work, 2
and hierarchy of virtues, 120, 138
and middle class, 119, 121, 130, 212
and new Victorian gentleman, 2, 115–16, 123, 126, 132
and Oxonian missionary zeal, 23
and rape of England, 1, 72, 169
and spirit of the whole, 69–71
and Victorian spirit of doubt, 6
and 'Vital Beauty', 179, 185

St Ignatius Loyola, 43, 60, 64–5, 108, 113, 120, 153, 211
St Paul, 112
Schneider, Elisabeth, 182–5
Shakespeare, William, 5, 90–1
Smith, Adam, 122
Society of Jesus, 6, 35, 36, 41, 60, 62, 81, 102, 103, 120, 133, 134, 138, 146, 169, 210
Socrates, 20, 124
Spenser, Edmund, 116, 124, 156
Spirit of the whole, see Victorian temper
Sprung rhythm, 102
and great chain of paradoxes, 93
and sacrament of energy, 99
Stanley, Arthur Penrhyn, 23, 138, 140, 201
Stephen, Leslie, 23–4, 25, 27, 34, 35
Swinburne, Algernon, 137
Symonds, John Addington, 33

Templeman, William, 211
Tennyson, Alfred, Lord, 66, 123, 133, 135, 136, 212
and ambivalence about art, 128
and apocalyptic mood, 159, 166, 223
and battle of the self, 2
and middle class, 213–15

and new Victorian gentleman, 127, 132
and Victorian spirit of doubt, 6, 46, 48
Tractarian beliefs, 10, 56, 57
see also Appendix B
Tractarian wars, 9–30, 36, 46, 55, 204
see also Appendixes; Hopkins; Jowett; Liddon; Pusey
Truth, ideal truth and material truth in art or nature, 69, 70, 79, 108

Valency, Maurice, 118–19, 139
Victorian 'pathos' and new Victorian gentleman, 101, 117, 119
Victorian spirit of doubt, 1–7, 47–50, 143
Victorian temper, 1–7, 102, 111, 134–5
and ambivalence about art, 2, 102
and exuberance, 1, 6, 31
and hierarchy of virtues, 119–21, 138, 217
and new Victorian gentleman, 2, 9n, 101, 115–19, 123, 124, 125, 126, 128–37, 153, 213–16
and spirit of the whole, 142, 218, 220
see also Arnold, Matthew; Arnold, Dr Thomas; Carlisle; Disraeli; Hopkins; Jowett; Liddon; Middle ages; Newman; Pater; Pusey; Renaissance; Ruskin; Tennyson
'Vital Beauty', see Nature, 'Vital Beauty' in

Wilberforce, Samuel, Bishop, 13
Wilberforce, William, 163
Wilkinson, Rupert, and new Victorian gentleman, 130, 139, 217
'Windhover, The'
and sacrament of energy, 109
as symbol of nature, 110–12, 114
as symbol of Satan and Lucifer, son of the morning, 110, 210–11
wrong pronunciation of, 210
Wingfield-Stratford, Esmé, 212–13

Young, George Malcolm, 10, 12–13, 135–6, 215